CRICKET
AND
ALL THAT

CRICKET
AND
ALL THAT

Henry Blofeld

Illustrated by John Ireland

Hodder & Stoughton

For Bitten,
with much love, who as usual
has taken the writing of this one
on the chin.

Copyright © 2001 by Henry Blofeld

First published in Great Britain in 2001
by Hodder and Stoughton
A division of Hodder Headline

2 4 6 8 10 9 7 5 3 1

A CIP catalogue record for this title is available
from the British Library

ISBN 0 340 81973 1

Typeset in 10.75/13pt Rotis Serif by
Rowland Phototypesetting Ltd,
Bury St Edmunds, Suffolk
Printed and bound in Great Britain by
Clays Ltd, St Ives plc

Hodder and Stoughton
A division of Hodder Headline
338 Euston Road
London NW1 3BH

CONTENTS

FOREWORD

T he history of cricket is full of the great and the good, the clean shaven and the hirsute, the good eggs and the absolute stinkers. This book represents my personal family tree of the game's development over the centuries. The movers and shakers I have settled upon form, in my view, the main branches of this tree. I have given these branches a bit of a shake and one or two pretty diverting odds and ends have fallen out. This is by no means an exact record and I make no apology for choosing my own list of players or for leaving out names others may have wanted to put at the top of theirs. But, one way or another, those I have chosen, good or bad, were characters and have left their mark in whatever way in the tapestry of this remarkable game.

ACKNOWLEDGEMENTS

This is the sixth book I have written for Roddy Bloomfield whose accolade as Editor of the Year 2000, going from my own experience, was highly deserved. His patience would make the prophet Job spit on his hands. As always, it has been a joy to work with him. My thanks to him and to all his long-suffering colleagues at Hodder & Stoughton who managed to make the writing of the book such an exciting adventure. My special thanks also to Maggie Body who for the second time has used her exceptional copy editing skills to transform my loosely written manuscript into a coherent end product. Finally, I would like to thank John Ireland for his splendid caricatures.

PHOTOGRAPHIC ACKNOWLEDGEMENTS

The author and publisher would like to thank the following for permission to reproduce photographs:

Allsport, Bridgeman Art Library, British Library, Cliveden House, Patrick Eagar, Empics, Mary Evans Picture Library, Hulton Getty, Marylebone Cricket Club, Popperfoto.

CHAPTER 1

TURNIPS, TOFFS AND MR LORD

THE GAME OF CRICKET made an indecisive start to life, rather as if it had in its infancy fallen foul of the problems which, centuries later, came out in a rash all over Mr Geoffrey Boycott whenever he attempted to run between the wickets – which was not often. It couldn't make up its mind what to call itself. It was as if the noble pastime had arrived at the font only to find the parents had forgotten to dream up a name for the wretched infant.

In 1300 *creag*, which any fool can see was early Anglo-Saxon for cricket, appeared in the wardrobe accounts of King Edward I, but this was when the old boy was already sixty-one and could no longer turn an arm over. In those distant days the shepherds of the realm went about their duties with crooks, cricks or crooked sticks. After hooking a sheep by the back leg, for purposes we won't dilate upon, a shepherd would turn to his mate and say with verve and jocularity, 'Throw me a turnip, old thing.' With his crooked stick grasped in both hands, he would try and dispatch the turnip to cowshot corner. The first cricket bats were crooked and this is, of course, a word which is but a short step from cricket.

After that references that reached the scorecard tended to have a distinctly cautionary tone for a couple of centuries. In

1629 a hapless curate, who was only anticipating the John Player League, was hauled up before the Archdeacon's Court for playing at 'cricketts' with parishioners after divine service in Ruckinge near Maidstone. While under Cromwell 'krickett' was proscribed throughout Ireland and all 'sticks' and balls had to be burnt by the common hangman. The toffs didn't get properly involved until the eighteenth century, when a political pamphlet of 1712 reports the Duke of Marlborough, at a bit of a loose end after winning the War of the Spanish Succession, playing with Lord Townshend in Windsor Forest for a stake of £20.

In those eighteenth-century origins of the game gambling was never far from the heart of proceedings, so maybe the Bombay bookmaking fraternity have only been demonstrating the cyclic view of history. In 1730 it was reported that a game was played for a stake of a hundred guineas. This bet was made by the Dukes of Richmond and Devonshire, aided and abetted by the Earl of Albemarle and Lord James Cavendish. The eighth Earl of Winchilsea and the fourth Earl of Tankerville were both at it a bit later and there was Sir Horace Mann who may never have got a toehold in the House of Lords but he was very much one of the boys. The game was not without royal patronage either, for 'Butcher' Cumberland, a son of George II, who had earned his nickname from his ruthless treatment of the Highlanders at Culloden, played his cricket in the same style, along with his brother, Frederick Louis, Prince of Wales who tragically died from the effects of a blow on his chest from a cricket ball when practising on the lawns at Cliveden House a venue later to be made even more famous by a certain Miss Christine Keeler.

The team selection took place at the Star and Garter Tavern in Pall Mall. This splendid watering hole was a considerable sporting HQ. It was not only the centre of cricket in London, but also the headquarters of the Jockey Club. So, after a really heavy evening, you were probably just as likely to find yourself riding in the 3.30 on Epsom Downs the next day as you were to be opening the batting at the Artillery Ground in the City of London. It must have been very confusing. The Artillery Ground was enclosed and a fair number of big matches, which would otherwise have been played on the country estates of the noble patrons, found their way to the City Road. The chap who owned the pub in the corner had built a wall round the ground and in the 1740s began to charge spectators twopence (which he later raised to sixpence) to go in to watch. Being a main-chancer, I suppose he forced them to drink his booze as well.

In 1744 the 'noblemen and gentlemen' got together at the Star and Garter Tavern – in the saloon bar, I imagine – to thrash out what came to be called the laws of the game. With eminent good sense, cricket decided at an early stage that it would have laws and not rules. If anyone ever talks about the rules of cricket it has always caused the shock-horror we later saw when H.M. Bateman drew his famous cartoon of the guardsman who dropped his rifle on parade. Simply not done, old man.

You can picture how it all started. Half a dozen noblemen were being greased up to and given lunch by a number of social-climbing gentry in White's famous chocolate house in St James's. Many splendid bottles were drunk – if you slipped the waitress a couple of bob, and she knew you, she was prepared to come up with something a touch stronger than chocolate. The tenth bottle had just arrived when the second Duke of Richmond, who had been the life and soul of the party, suddenly smote his brow, drained his glass, banged his hands on the table and said, 'Chaps, I've had a brainwave. When we've polished off a few more bottles, we'll totter down the hill to the Star and Garter and see what we can do about the laws of cricket.' This was followed by loud and encouraging murmurs of approval and no little banging of glasses on the table which the second Duke rightly interpreted as meaning, 'Attaboy.' And so off they tottered.

This was familiar territory for the second Duke. Being very much on the ducal ball as far as sharp practice was concerned, he had insisted on drawing up strict Articles of Agreement for a match in 1727 between his own side and that of a distinctly plebeian-sounding Mr Alan Brodrick at Peper Harow in Sussex. (The Duke obviously knew something because one day Mr Alan Brodrick was promoted to Lord Middleton, which put things on a much more reasonable footing.) Among other things, the pitch that day was twenty-three yards long and to complete a run the batsmen had to touch the umpire's sticks.

By 1744 the second Duke had come strongly to the conclusion that the pitch should now be twenty-two yards long, for he had been bowling too many long hops for comfort and constantly found he was short of puff when batting. This was the first issue discussed in the Star and Garter and the second Duke had to be at his most eloquent to force the thing through. At the end of a lengthy debate, when feelings ran high, there was a show of hands and a narrow majority for twenty-two yards. Two stumps, one bail, a ball weighing between five and six ounces were waved through on the nod. So were the methods of dismissal. The game was taking shape.

After that, cricket in England for much of the second half of the eighteenth century was successfully hijacked by a tiny village in Hampshire called Hambledon. They played their first match in 1754. The Hambledon game could hardly have been more different from our own today. The bowling was underarm, no pads were worn, an over lasted four balls and 'if he runs out of his ground to hinder a catch, it's Out'. Thus spake the laws drawn up that pissy afternoon in 1744 by the Duke of Richmond and his chums in the Star and Garter. Obstructing the field was out, but was it? Read on. Under the heading of: *Batt, foot or hand over ye Crease*, the fifth paragraph reads: 'When ye ball is hit up, either of ye strikers may hinder ye catch in his running ground, or if she's hit directly

across ye wickets, ye other player may place his body anywhere within ye swing of his Batt, so as to hinder ye bowler
from catching her, but he must neither stroke at her nor touch
her with his hands.' Ye pays ye money and takes ye choice.
If this is not incitement to riot, I don't know what is. Try to
imagine what would have happened had that law still been
in place when Mr F.S. Trueman and Mr D.K. Lillee were plying
their trade, to say nothing of Mr F.R. Spofforth or Mr E.A.
McDonald. The Queensberry Rules would have been left
scratching their head.

Mind you, in those early days the ball was more often than
not bowled along the ground at the two stumps which were
then used with the single bail. The bats, as we have seen, were
curved in mild crook-like fashion, so the batsmen could cope
with this constant bowling of grubs. When Shepherd A rolled
a turnip along the wicket at a fearsome speed, Shepherd B
thanked the Lord that his crook was curved so that he could
cope with this unsporting behaviour. With a bit of luck, he
could scramble the vegetable matter towards silly point and
set off for a quick single, while Shepherd A let out all sorts
of oaths which may have been involuntary but were not at
all in keeping with the occasion.

The earliest players to achieve any real sort of lasting fame
were the members of the Hambledon side in the second half
of the century, arguably the most romantic side of all time.
Names like Lumpy Stevens and Silver Billy Beldham have a
ring to them which perhaps has never quite been matched.
Richard Nyren who lived in and ran the Bat and Ball Inn
overlooking Broad-Halfpenny Down – his bedroom window
looked down the wicket – had much to do with the rise of
Hambledon's cricket but it was Lumpy Stevens who was
responsible for the third stump being added in 1775. Two
years earlier he had played for five of Kent as a 'given man'
against five of Hambledon at the Artillery Ground in London.
John Small had come in last with 14 to win and Lumpy had

grabbed the ball. He repeatedly beat Small but the ball several times went between the two stumps, hitting neither and so not removing the bail. This will have infuriated Lumpy, a man of few words, but law-changing ones.

The most glamorous member of the side must have been Silver Billy Beldham. His dashing fair hair gave him his nickname. It was he who should have been the original Brylcreem Boy and not Denis Compton. Being generous spirits, they would have had a lot in common, although Silver Billy might not have been sure about Denis's methods of calling his partner for a single. Over many years he averaged 43 with the bat on pitches you would not believe and when he was approaching seventy he had to be 'barred' from playing in ordinary county matches. He was a magnificent striker of the ball and, with wrists of steel, the cut was a speciality. He set a new fashion, too, jumping out to drive and suddenly the underarm bowlers were under threat. The Reverend John Mitford stated that 'he took the ball, as Burke did the House of Commons, between wind and water.'

Another rich Hambledon character was David Harris who took underarm bowling to new levels which, like Beldham's driving, led to fundamental changes in batting techniques and helped prepare the way for the future development of the art. Harris let the ball go from almost under his armpit and was able to combine length and direction with pace and somehow he made the ball 'spit' at the batsman on pitching. He was crippled by gout, poor chap, and often had to sit on his stick between overs. That would have had Dickie Bird in a tizz. Then there was Tom Walker who batted for so long he was known as 'Old Everlasting'. He was the first bowler to experiment with round-arm and four years later he had turned to underarm lobs.

Having been the main attraction for twenty years, Hambledon went into decline at a time when the game was gravitating back more towards London. The Star and Garter Tavern had never been out of it. In 1774 there had been another migration from White's chocolate house at the top of St James's, presumably after the usual high-cholesterol lunch, to have a second crack at the laws of the game. They now decided after a tense debate that it was high time the batsman should be out Leg Before Wicket when he plonked his foot in front of the ball. But they decreed that he would only be out if he had deliberately put it in the way. If he was beaten by a humdinger which hit him on the leg plumb in front, he was not out, which was incontrovertible evidence that they were all plastered at the time.

A few years after this, the cricketing gentry who met there regularly, came to the conclusion they were barmy to travel to Kent and Hampshire and places like that to play when they could easily get a game at the White Conduit Fields up the road in Islington. As a result of this sensible decision, the White Conduit Club was formed and they played their first match in 1785. There was one fly in the ointment. The general public were admitted to the White Conduit Fields and the toffs didn't like it a bit. If they made a duck or dropped a sitter they didn't want to see the great unwashed laughing their heads off all round the boundary. If they were going to make fools of themselves, they wanted to do it in private. As a result, in 1786, the ninth Earl of Winchilsea, a stickler for privacy, and Colonel Charles Lennox, the nephew of the third Duke of Richmond, met with Thomas Lord, a ground bowler at White Conduit Fields. Lord was a good looking man who came from a Yorkshire farming family which had fallen on hard times and he would have been glad of any job he could get. These two asked him if he would try and find a suitable piece of land close to London where they could set up a private ground. The ninth Earl and the Colonel promised him full support and there was a smile on T. Lord's face when he left the meeting, for he realised he was on to a good thing. He was full of that gritty Yorkshire charm which has manifested

itself under those white rose caps in so many intriguing ways down the years. He was no fool either.

He scurried hither and thither about the surrounding countryside and it was not all that long before he had made contact with the Portman family. He found that he could rent from them a piece of land which has now become Dorset Square, just north of the Marylebone Road. The ninth Earl and the Colonel went with him to have a look. While T. Lord bowled an over or two to the Colonel in the nets, the ninth Earl searched the hedges to see if he could find any of the great unwashed lurking in the bushes or, indeed, hear them sniggering. As a precaution, he took his heavy stick with him. When he returned, having been unable to find or hear a single lurker or snigger, he and the Colonel agreed to sign on the dotted line. The first Lord's ground was therefore set up and cricket began to be played there in 1787, the same year as the members of the White Conduit Club decided to call themselves the Marylebone Cricket Club in recognition of their change of address.

Lord was a hard-headed business man and, when he learned in 1809 that the Portman family were going to raise the rent the following year, he decided to look elsewhere. He came up with a piece of land at what was known as North Bank, about half a mile south of the present Lord's, and moved his turf across. The second ground never really caught on. Maybe that was because the ninth Earl and the Colonel were not asked to run their eye over it first and this ground also turned out to be a lurker's paradise. MCC only played three games there. The problem was solved in 1813 when Parliament decided that the Regent Canal should run through the middle of the ground and so Lord was once more off on his travels. This time he found the ground that is still the headquarters of the game. The sacred turf made its second journey, no doubt picking up a ridge or two along the way. The first game was played in St John's Wood in 1814 when MCC took on

8

Hertfordshire, but that is not quite the end of this peripatetic story. In 1825 T. Lord was feeling the pinch and made up his mind to sell his ground for building purposes. When William Ward, the Governor of the Bank of England, came to hear of this, he paid Lord £5,000 for the lease and Lord swiftly high-tailed it back to rural Yorkshire. In 1820 Ward had made 278 for MCC against Norfolk which remained as the highest score made at Lord's for over a hundred years, and he did it with a bat weighing four pounds. Lord's was saved and Ward kept the lease until 1836, when he sold it on to J.H. Dark with the assurance that the ground was safe for cricket.

The MCC meanwhile was still based at the Star and Garter where in 1787 they took another look at the laws. They now decided, with the help of a glass or two of black velvet, that a batsman no longer had to be guilty of placing his leg deliber-ately in line with the ball for him to be lbw. They also removed the absurd 1744 law which allowed the batsman to do his best to prevent the bowler taking a return catch. Sanity was prevailing, although this last adjustment took away a good bit of fun for the spectators. Imagine the second Duke of Richmond and third Duke of Dorset beginning to dig their side out of a hole with a sturdy sixth wicket stand. Then Dorset pops back an easy return catch to the bowler. Richmond, who has been backing up rather dreamily, is suddenly put on red alert by a stricken yell from Dorset of 'Knock the bugger over!' A tremendous scuffle ensues as Richmond tries to block the bowler who doesn't think much of dukes anyway. From the other end Dorset is advancing at speed, uttering those blood-curdling yells more often heard on the hunting field. Rich-mond's reaction has been too late and when the bowler holds the catch, Dorset departs muttering audible threats to the bowler and his fellow Duke which involve both the rack and molten lead. It was a prospect which made the sixpenny entrance fee charged by the publican at the Artillery Ground look an absolute snip.

Two years after this the game received a whopping great blow in the solar plexus. Colonel Lennox, who must have had a shortish fuse, had been promoted in the Duke of York's regiment. The Duke himself, second in line to the throne, and one of the chaps who, from time to time, probably gathered in the Star and Garter and, I daresay, White's as well, opposed the promotion and insulted the Colonel in front of the regiment. He was immediately challenged to a duel. This was fought on Wimbledon Common on 26 April, 1789. The Colonel had ensnared the ninth Earl of Winchilsea as his second so, all in all, it was a pretty blue-blooded affair. The Colonel fired first and missed. No one seems to know what then got into the Duke of York, but he refused to return the fire. It must have made the Colonel feel an awful ass. Anyway, both were then able to eat a hearty breakfast at opposite ends of the Common and you could hardly blame them if they had a sharpener as well.

Charles Lennox who played most of his cricket as the Honourable Colonel Lennox, was a professional soldier, a considerable all-round athlete and a man of many parts, even if accurate pistol shooting in the early hours on Wimbledon Common was not one of them. He was passionate about cricket and did a great deal for the game, playing it with his soldiers all over the country. The Colonel succeeded to the dukedom of Richmond in 1806 and it was he who arranged the cricket match just before the Battle of Waterloo and his wife, the Duchess, who gave the famous ball at Quatre Bras the night before the battle. After Waterloo he became the Governor-General of Canada where he suffered a strange and unpleasant death. He had long had an obsession about hydrophobia and it was this that killed him after he had been bitten by his pet fox.

By now gambling was taking a different turn. Up to this point, led by the patrons, the players had bet big sums between themselves on the outcome of games and there were all types of side bets between individuals. Now the bookmakers, or 'blacklegs', took it over and an awful lot of what is happening at present in international cricket happened then to the game in England. Many well known bookies had their patch in front of the pavilion at Lord's. Mr Crockford and Mr Gully were both there and the Marylebone 'legs' were up to every trick in the business to make their money safe. When he was an old man, Silver Billy Beldham told the Reverend James Pycroft that the 'legs' would go down into Hampshire quite early in the season to 'buy us up'. He, needless to say, would have none of it. The bookies did their main business at the Green Man and Still in Oxford Street which was the professionals' answer to the gentlemen's Star and Garter. In June 1817, William Lambert, the Surrey allrounder who was a wonderful player, was banned for accepting money to throw a game when playing for England against Nottingham, and in the early 1820s the bookies themselves were banned from Lord's for having a corrupting influence on the game and its players.

The trouble was that those who sat in judgement on the game were not especially pure in heart either. One of them, the Reverend the Lord Frederick Beauclerk, the fourth son of the fifth Duke of St Albans, was a stinker. He was a pretty decent allrounder, for all that, who had been discovered while up at Cambridge by the good old ninth Earl of Winchilsea who was probably up for the spring meetings at Newmarket. The Reverend bit may suggest that the Lord Frederick was a pretty hot number on his knees. This was not the case, the Church being merely one of the accepted boltholes for younger sons whom the aristocracy tended to regard with a somewhat jaundiced eye. The Reverend the Lord Frederick was not one to allow any religious duties, real or imagined, to disturb his concentration and his parishioners had to get on the best they could without him. Dr W.G. Grace's patients were similarly short-changed if ever they wanted some medicine or an appointment between mid-April and mid-September.

With a name that was such a mouthful, it would have been nice to think that the reverend ducal owner was easy going and good natured, kind and generous to a fault, and over-flowing with enthusiasm. As it happened, he was as unscrupulous as he was talented. He admitted that cricket was worth at least six hundred smackers a year to him from gambling. This did not sit happily with a speech he made when President of MCC in which he said that cricket was a game 'unalloyed by love of lucre and mean jealousies'. When he was batting with a rival at the other end the Reverend the Lord Frederick would refuse to run the other bloke's notches. Whenever he was on the losing side or made a duck himself, he would try and bribe the scorer to suppress the scores. He was up to anything. He was made to look a fool one day by Silver Billy, who was then forty, when he bowled Lord Frederick a ball to which he had stuck wet dirt and sawdust, in the first year sawdust was allowed. Lord Frederick was not amused. He didn't half get his comeuppance one day at Nottingham though when, with a vengeance, he ticked off a professional called Stearman for slackness in the field. Stearman's response was to return the ball so fiercely to him that it broke a couple of fingers which almost gave him lockjaw and shortened his career by ten years.

Lord Frederick was a regular visitor to Lord's up until the moment when, to more than just the odd sigh of relief, he put his cue in the rack. On these visits he was invariably accompanied by an unpleasant dog which yapped all the time and was a perfect menace. The rule of the ground, proclaimed in large letters, was 'No Dogs Allowed'. It would not have been surprising if the Almighty had felt in need of a sharpener or two when he realised his representative from Lord's would be next through the door. He will have been relieved that his lordship was not accompanied by the dog.

While the characters were constantly changing, so too was the technical side of the game. It was in 1788 that Old Everlasting toyed with round-arm bowling. It lay dormant for almost twenty years after that until John Willes tried it again in 1807 in a game between twenty-three of Kent and thirteen of England – a perplexing configuration. Willes had had the idea from watching his sister bowl round-arm so as to avoid getting her hand entangled with her skirts. By then the batsmen had learned to cope successfully with lob bowling by using their feet and scores were getting bigger and bigger. At first round-arm made it much more difficult to score freely. It was an innovation which met with fierce opposition from a race of batsmen who had become spoiled and it was particularly denounced by William Ward who could make nothing of it. On 15 July, 1822, Willes opened the bowling for Kent against MCC at Lord's and was promptly no-balled by the umpire, Noah Mann. Willes threw down the ball in disgust, jumped on his horse and rode out of Lord's and out of cricket for good. You can see Lord Frederick's hand here.

In the first two decades of the nineteenth century the game was beginning to assume the shape of modern cricket. It was the men of Hambledon who were the real movers and shakers in all of this. They left an indelible mark.

CHAPTER 2

THE OLD FARTS
PAD UP

FOR MOST of the first half of the eighteenth century the issue of round-arm bowling had become a *cause célèbre*. The next forty years were taken up first with trying to repel it, then with reluctantly accepting it and finally with learning to play it, before the ultimate step to overarm was made in 1864. John Willes was the bowler who kept everyone on their toes as far as round-arm was concerned. But big issue though this was, it was rather overshadowed by another across the Channel in which the principal combatants were Arthur Wellesley, the first Duke of Wellington, and a French *arriviste* called Napoleon Bonaparte.

Although cricket had to take a back seat, there arrived on the scene at about this time one of the game's more splendid figures who was to have some memorable contests of his own, especially with the dreaded the Reverend the Lord Frederick Beauclerk. George Osbaldeston, always known in later life as the Squire, was the heir to an estate in Yorkshire. He had been born in London and sent to Eton where he had a brief and highly diverting stay. His strengths, which did not include the world of academics, lay in more extrovert and manly pursuits. He was not a modest lad but was probably speaking no more than the truth when he boasted that he could beat any boy

at single-handed cricket, or any boy of his age at fisticuffs. His other schoolboy activities included shooting, fishing and making fireworks which is not a hobby that many people admit to. He also enjoyed rowing and was particularly keen on hiring horses in Windsor and going to Ascot races. This latter activity has caused a number of Etonians over the years to be compelled to move on to the next stage in life sooner than they had planned. When he was shown the door, he legged it to a crammer's in Brighton. He then went up to Oxford – he surely cannot have been asked to pass a meaningful exam – where he kept a couple of hunters, irritated the hell out of the master of his college, and turned into a tearaway fast bowler. While at Oxford he also became a Master of Foxhounds who was not to be trifled with, a shot who could hold his own with the best and once killed ninety-eight partridges with a hundred shots, a fearless steeplechaser and a compulsive gambler. The Nigel Dempsters of the time must certainly have looked upon George Osbaldeston as one to follow in the unlikely event of their not having already made him their nap selection.

The Squire grew up to detest sporting parsons after a nasty experience with a neighbouring vicar in Yorkshire, and he was madly jealous of anyone with a title. So when he joined MCC and saw that dashing aristocratic man of the cloth, the reverend the Lord Frederick, walking into the committee room, he must have felt a bit like Cassius Clay when he stepped into the ring and sighted George Foreman in the opposite corner. In 1810, Osbaldeston challenged Beauclerk to a double wicket match for fifty guineas, each of them to play with a professional. Osbaldeston was ill and Lord Frederick, full of sympathy as usual, said simply, 'Play or pay.' The Squire scored one run and retired and William Lambert, his pro, did the business, winning by bowling wides at Lord Frederick which made him lose his temper and the match with it. His lordship promptly shuffled off to the committee room and had the law

changed. From then on the bowling of wides was prohibited.

Obsbaldeston was an extremely fast bowler and, as you would expect, a ferocious hitter. His forte was single wicket cricket and he was a hard man to beat. He met his match though in 1818 when he played George Brown, a professional from Brighton, said to be so fast that he bowled a ball which tore through a coat being held by an amateur long stop, and killed a dog on the other side who was presumably also an amateur. Osbaldeston was roundly beaten and in a fury he scratched his name off the membership list at Lord's. When he had second thoughts, his old adversary, who didn't forget much, put his foot down. Osbaldeston was one of the game's greatest characters and, after the Great War, the Honourable Lionel Tennyson was a worthy successor in the same line, as was Colin Ingleby-Mackenzie, in spirit at any rate, forty years after Tennyson. What fun the Squire must have been.

John Willes had made himself the principal martyr to the cause of round-arm by his theatrical over reaction that day at Lord's when Kent were playing MCC. The old farts were apparently led by William Ward, Thomas Lord, always a diehard reactionary, and John Nyren, son of Hambledon Richard. It was John who forcibly suggested in 1933 in the first edition of his famous book, *The Young Cricketer's Tutor and Cricketers of my Time*, that because of round-arm, 'the elegant and scientific game of cricket will degenerate into a mere exhibition of rough, coarse, horse-play!' But of course that aristocratic scallywag, Lord Frederick Beauclerk, whose word was absolute law at Lord's, was the man pulling the strings. Noah Mann may have no-balled Willes, but the decision to do so had been taken by Lord Frederick. He must that morning have gone into the sort of huddle in the umpires' room that some of the more modern-day administrative wizards indulged in during the one-day match at Lord's against Pakistan in 1992 when the seam appeared to all but those trying to hush it up to have been irrevocably picked. There

was nothing too complicated about Lord Frederick's views about Willes. They were spelt out some time later by Lord Harris who, being of the same calibre, will himself have admired much about Lord Frederick. Lord Harris said, 'When he [Willes] played on the same side as Lord Frederick his bowling was fair, when against him, the contrary.'

It was an extraordinary business because in some places round-arm was not only tolerated, it was actually encouraged. Two of the great exponents, William Lillywhite and James Broadbridge, were responsible for Sussex becoming the best side in the country in the 1820s. They may have jumped all over the place when round-arm was mentioned at Lord's, but down in Brighton they regarded it as an outward and visible sign of virility. Lillywhite, or Old Lilly, as he was known, was the master. He was thirty years old before he played his first recorded match, in 1822. If they had been playing 160 years later, these two might have been nicknamed Steptoe and Son. Old Lilly himself must have grown to look more and more like a wise old walnut which had been marinated in iodine for a very long time. He was only 5'4" tall, but he had great presence and dignity on the field. He wore a top hat and broad cotton braces with a high Gladstone collar and a black tie. He must have been a formidable sight, with a touch of the undertaker about him – which of course he was to so many batsmen.

Old Lilly and Broadbridge took the cricketing world by storm in 1827 in the three 'Experimental matches' Sussex played against All England. The establishment at Lord's, seeing Sussex's success, reluctantly decided they must have a careful look at this newfangled type of bowling. This first match was played at Sheffield and Sussex won by seven wickets. They won the second at Lord's, by three wickets. The talk at the time was that if William Ward, the Bank of England man, who had made 42 and 20 and had at last begun to master the art of playing the round-armers, had been able to

get a forthcoming Corn Law debate out of his mind, the second match would have been closer still. One can only conjecture at what, in 1962/63 in Australia, Mr F.S. Trueman might have said to the Reverend D. Sheppard if, after dropping yet another catch, he had told the sweating bowler that his mind had been on the affairs of the Lord's Day Observance Society. There is unlikely to have been anything too unctuously pious about Mr F.S. Trueman's reply. Happily for the establishment, All England won the third match by twenty-four wickets. It was felt that this was just as well, otherwise the old farts might well have taken terminal umbrage against round-arm, flexing their muscles and saying it was too dangerous. In 1828, MCC members went some of the way when they decided that the arm could be raised as high as the elbow. It was not for another seven years that they finally bit the bullet and accepted round-arm and allowing the hand to reach shoulder height. Old Lilly had won the day. But given a few inches, the bowlers took several more and the arm was lifted ever higher as the years went by.

Age did little to Old Lilly. He had reached fifty-two when he more or less turned his back on Brighton to take a permanent place on the ground staff at Lord's, a questionable career move for the old walnut at that age. In 1847, when he was fifty-five, he bowled unchanged in the Gents v Players match and he was picking up more than 200 wickets a year at a tiny cost. He didn't take much out of himself, for he bowled at a slow, precise and unsettling medium pace. His control of length and line was remarkable and it was this, combined with his tactical skills, which brought him the accolade of the Nonpareil. Modesty was not one of his faults and he once said of himself in all seriousness, 'I suppose that if I was to think every ball, they would never get a run.' He had a little bit of a temper too, and when Nicholas Felix, the Kent batsman, would suggest with a twinkle in his eye that the great Fuller Pilch was his master, Old Lilly would bridle with fierce indignation.

The next outstanding protagonist of round-arm was a Nottingham professional called Sam Redgate. He is said somehow to have combined fairness of delivery with great pace and spin and he had in his armoury a slower ball which was to be wondered at. He was probably the first to have dealt in this particular line of deception. In 1835 he played for the Gents at Lord's as a given man and clean bowled Fuller Pilch for a duck in each innings. It was in 1839, playing for All England against Kent at Town Malling, that he bowled the most famous over so far in the history of the game. The second ball bowled Pilch and the third bowled Alfred Mynn, which was a little bit like removing Beethoven and John the Baptist with successive deliveries. The fourth cleaned up Stearman, a worthy but bad-tempered pro whom we last heard of having a run in with Lord Frederick Beauclerk – but then who didn't? At the fall of each of these wickets the story has it that Redgate swallowed a large glass of brandy. Behaviour of this sort would surely have had the dreaded Lord Frederick Beauclerk, in the unlikely event of him having found the way to Town Malling in the first place, hastily putting in his eyeglass and staring vigorously out of the committee room window. But maybe as he was playing for the Gents, Redgate was allowed to indulge briefly in Gentish behaviour. He would have needed no encouragement, for it was not long before his thirst got the better of his talent and packed him off early to have a chat with his Maker.

By now Kent was the side that all the others wanted to beat and their three leading players have already crept into the story. Alfred Mynn, a fearsome fast bowling allrounder who became a national institution almost in the way which would have made W.G. Grace look to his laurels if he had been born a little earlier; Fuller Pilch, who had a mildly unfortunate Christian name for a man with a figure which would have been the envy of any aspiring guardsman, was the greatest batsman of his time; and Nicholas Wanostrocht, who called

himself Nicholas Felix when he played cricket, a most felicitous left-hander with a penchant for the cut. Wanostrocht changed his name for cricket because he had inherited a private school in Camberwell and felt that if he had played under his real name it may well have been at odds with the academic image he liked to create amongst his charges' parents. Also, of course, county scorers were not always the best of spellers.

They were a mildly incongruous three who set the standards in the years leading up to the middle of the century. Mynn came from yeoman stock well known for their size and for their athletic ability. In this respect Alfred did not let the side down for he stood 6'2" tall and weighed in at somewhere between eighteen and twenty stone. The trouble was that the good Lord, when putting Alfred Mynn together, had spread himself over the limbs, but had skimped a bit when it came to the grey matter. Mynn was also most emphatically not a business man and spent most of his life on his uppers. He never had what most mothers-in-law would call a proper job and cricket was his sole *raison d'être*. As he was an amateur, to start with at any rate, it did not give him the wherewithal to look after himself, let alone his wife and children. His father helped finance his cricket but when he kicked the bucket, the debt collectors began to knock at the door. A couple of benefit games were arranged for him over the years, although they barely stemmed the tide. Also, going professional like this cost him any amount of social kudos. In years to come his name would now have been written on the scorecard as Mynn, A. which would have been an inglorious fall from A. Mynn.

He made something of a habit of going bankrupt and grew to know his way blindfolded around the corridors of the local debtors prison. It argues a splendidly detached mind that he was able to go on playing cricket with an ever-increasing brilliance with all this hanging over him. He apparently had no fear that, the moment he stepped off the field at the luncheon

ALFRED MYNN

interval, the man in the bowler hat standing beside the sight-screen would step smartly forward and lay a hand on his shoulder. For a short time he made a supreme effort and joined his brother's hop business in Kent, but soon found that hops called for talents that were different from his own. He returned to cricket's fold an even deadlier bowler and off a shorter run too, suggesting that he had only been using the hop fields for bowling practice.

He had been taught to bowl round-arm by none other than John Willes. After a somewhat erratic start, he became extremely fast with an unerringly accurate length and line. He must have been a fearsome sight as he bore down on the wicket with huge, majestic strides looking for all the world like Gulliver setting off on his travels with a following wind at his back. His arm came round in a smooth swing with the ball almost invariably pitching on the leg stump before it whipped away to the off. He sometimes swung the ball as well, which will have made life even more complicated for the batsman. His hands were huge and he caught everything that moved at short slip and, as one would expect, he was the most ferocious hitter in the country. He was a brave man too, and after being hit on the leg in practice at Leicester before a match in 1836 between the North and South, he was unable to bowl, but made 146 not out which won the game for the South. At this point Lord Frederick Beauclerk broke the habit of a lifetime, almost certainly because he had put a lot of money on the South to win, and took pity on him, even helping him into the fly which started Mynn's journey home. The injury was so serious that he could only lie on the roof of the coach from Leicester to London and the doctors came close to cutting off his leg. Mynn refused to be beaten and was back at his best two years later in 1838. He was a man of great good humour and generosity and a vibrant extrovert whose sportsmanship was never in doubt. He was loved by everyone and caught the imagination of the public as few

manage to do. He died all too young in 1861 at the age of fifty-four.

Nicholas Felix could hardly have been a greater contrast to Mynn and they became the closest of friends, which was surely the attraction of opposites. The one thing they did have in common was an impressive inability to make ends meet. Felix was a man of many parts. He was a schoolmaster, an artist, a musician, an author, writing cricket books and school textbooks; he also invented the first bowling machine which was not round-arm but a catapult, as well as tubular batting gloves. Coming from a well-to-do family gave him a good start in life and really he should have achieved more than he did. He was a compact, stylish batsman and a lovely timer of the ball and, like everything else he did, he approached his cricket with boundless enthusiasm. Felix and Pilch batting together would have been heady stuff for the Kent crowd who, even in those days, were being trained on the best that Shepherd Neame could offer. Felix's under-achievement may have been a character defect in that he was probably one of those men with a short attention span who flitted from one thing to the next without ever fulfilling his natural talent at any of them – a sort of Jack-of-all-trades. He and the huge Mynn together would have been a cartoonist's delight.

Fuller Pilch was a native of Norwich where his descendants still run a sports business. He had migrated to Canterbury by way of Sheffield, Bury St Edmunds, back to Norwich where he kept a pub in Surrey Hill with the help of his sister, before being lured to Town Malling by the prospect of another pub as well as a ground-keeper's job, and then going on to Canterbury in 1842. Pilch was the greatest batsman of his era. He liked to play elegant strokes off the front foot and gave the ball a pretty good wallop. Fred Gale, the cricket writer, said, 'he had a terrific hit between middle-off and cover, which gained him many a four or five runs.' Maybe it was this which

enabled him to get on top of the round-arm bowlers. Pilch was a modest man who understood the order of the day in the countryside. 'Gentlemen were gentlemen, and players much in the same position as a nobleman and his head keeper maybe,' was how he liked to put it. He had a soft spot for country house cricket too, of which there was plenty in Kent. He told of how at the close of play he would take his supper in the butler's pantry (with a good drop of port if the butler was worth his salt) and the young master would come round later, after dinner with the family and their guests, to smoke a cigar, drink with him and talk cricket. Pilch's extraordinary talent was spotted early at a time when professional batsmen were a rarity. When Old Lilly had been taking all those wickets for Sussex, clubs in Kent were queuing up for Pilch, not least because of his ability to pull in the spectators. He was a fine upstanding man, almost as tall as Mynn but not so muscular or broad.

In the 1840s the move began to found county clubs. Sussex, inspired by Old Lilly and Broadbridge, had shown the way and now they were joined by Nottinghamshire, Surrey and Cambridgeshire, town as opposed to gown, who played on the public expanse of Parker's Piece. After a few successful years the county club dissolved, pushed out by the University who were playing on a neighbouring ground leased to them by a Mr Fenner. Kent was also one of the first counties although their side with Mynn, Pilch and Felix was brought together by the new generation of patrons, usually business men who had tried to turn themselves into country squires. The main innovation at this time came from Nottingham and the man behind it was a one-eyed brickie who turned himself into a pub keeper. William Clarke was an underarm bowler of the old school and a shrewd old devil he was too. It was Old Clarke who had set up an enclosed ground by the famous Trent Bridge Inn, of which he was the landlord, and which still stands proudly in the north-west corner of Trent Bridge.

It is one of cricket's pre-eminent watering holes. Of course, the old blighter charged admission to the ground. The people of Nottingham, bred on the tradition of Robin Hood who saved the populace from all sorts of unscrupulous profiteers, were highly miffed at having to leave the public ground on the old racecourse where they did not have to pay for the privilege of watching cricket. The worst they had to contend with there were the blandishments of the nineteenth-century equivalents of John McCrirrick instructing them how to waste their money on the horses. I am not sure what Robin Hood would have made of the idiosyncratic John McCrirrick, nor Maid Marion either.

Seeing that all roads most emphatically did not lead to Trent Bridge, Old Clarke, who had been playing cricket for thirty years, caught the coach to London and, at the age of forty-seven, joined the MCC staff as a ground bowler. Even in those days he was old to make the change although Old Lilly, who came to Lord's in the same capacity at the age of fifty-two, would probably have called him a whippersnapper. This may not today seem a natural progression for a chap who had come to London to make his fortune, as the pay was pretty ordinary. His agenda was to be in a position to make his mark in front of the selectors which he did with a vengeance because no one was able to play him. With round-arm all the rage, the batsmen had forgotten how to play the underarm stuff. Also, rather strangely considering it was the reason for the arrival of round-arm in the first place, it was considered to be not quite the done thing to go down the pitch to him, although batsmen knew this was the best way to cope. Like Old Lilly, his fellow brickie, Clarke had no small opinion of himself. 'If a man is fast-footed, he is ready money for me,' was how he put it. On one occasion Clarke asked a new batsmen if he was from Harrow. When this was confirmed, he immediately placed a fielder 'between point and middle wicket' for the 'Harrow drive' which comes from an involun-

tary edge and seems to be much favoured by the product of that educational establishment.

Clarke's entrepreneurial activities began in 1846 at the close of the MCC season which ended early so that the toffs could turn their attention to the grouse and be up on the moors for the Glorious Twelfth. The Government's business came to an end at this time of the year for the same reason. Clarke got together an All England XI, which was truly representative, to play three matches against twenty-two of Sheffield, eighteen of Manchester, and eighteen of Yorkshire. The clubs he visited were happy to pay for the privilege. In addition to their expenses, Clarke paid his players at the miserly rate of £4 to £6 a game, which matched the rates paid by MCC who had just reduced their tariff because the railways made travel so much faster, and he pocketed the rest himself. Clarke expanded the fixture list of his 'circus' each year and by 1854 they were playing thirty-four matches and this had become a serious nuisance to MCC because it so restricted the availability of players for their games. On the other hand, Clarke did a great deal for the popularity of cricket, taking the best players round the country with him to places where it scarcely had a toehold.

1850 had seen the death of that self-centred, arrogant and unfeeling autocrat, the Reverend the Lord Frederick Beauclerk. His self-indulgent approach to life had permeated through to MCC which had become a self-perpetuating and increasingly ineffective organisation, primarily concerned with looking after itself rather than the game. This meant that, if it had not been for people like Clarke, the game would only have shrunk and in time perhaps have disappeared. Although Lord Frederick was out of the way, the forces of reaction ruled supreme at Lord's for it was not a venue much given to radical thought. The presidency of MCC went round the House of Lords, although a couple baronets and, believe it or not, one commoner, Mr T. Chamberlayne of Sussex, slipped under the

rope in 1845, but he was a particularly well connected commoner. The Honourable Robert Grimston was a man of some influence at Lord's and he had about as much time for change as King Nebuchadnezzar, although, if anything, he was a little bit more outspoken. According to Fred Gale, Grimston's biographer, James Dark, who owned the lease of Lord's, once borrowed a mowing machine. It was at the height of its passion one day when Grimston went past. He walked on over to the top of the ground where there were some navvies at work. He offered them a pound if they would take their pick-axes and slip into it and smash up 'that infernal machine'. Good progressive thinking. I am sure Lord Frederick would have been egging him on.

Clarke may have been better known for his entrepreneurial activities, but he was no mean bowler. In seven seasons for his All England side between 1847 and 1853, he took 2,385 wickets at an average of 340 a season. His biggest haul was 476 in 1853. His side constantly played against inferior opposition and the opposing batsmen were, by and large, pretty moderate. As a result his opponents were allowed to field sometimes as many as 23 players which constantly increased Clarke's wicket-taking potential. Clarke also had a horror of ever taking himself off. For accuracy and cunning, he was on his own with his slow, almost round-arm delivery which he had assiduously copied from William Lambert of Surrey. He had a short run up, the ball was let go from the level of the hip, it had a curving flight and lifted awkwardly from the pitch. He also imparted spin from the legside. It was his meanness which let him down for he collected handsomely for himself while he paid his players a pittance. He was regarded by many as a jumped up northerner. Things came to a head in 1852 when there was a serious row over money between Clarke and some of his fellow professionals who thought they should be getting away with more of the swag. Those from the south were particularly put out and they let it be known

that after the treatment they had received they would not in the future be playing for or against Clarke's sides.

There is one charming link between Clarke's All England side in cricket's late middle ages and the start of the modern game. In 1854 Clarke took his eleven to Bristol where they played against twenty-two of West Gloucestershire. W.G. Grace later wrote in his book, *Cricket*, that this was the first important match he ever saw. Although he was only six, he remembered watching with his mother and how Clarke's figure still stood out for him. Clarke took eighteen wickets in the match. The following year Clarke did not play himself, but he was so impressed with E.M. Grace's display at long stop that he gave the boy a bat and later presented Mrs Grace with a book which he inscribed. WG had it in front of him when he was writing his own book.

By then Clarke had signed up a young Sussex bowler, John Wisden, who was not only a fine cricketer but was also as entrepreneurial and as competitive as Clarke himself. In that same year, Wisden and his Sussex colleague, Jemmy Dean, fed up with Clarke's meanness, formed a breakaway group calling themselves the United England XI and they set up a circuit of their own. Wisden was only 5'4" tall, weighing only just over seven stone at the start of his career and only careless spelling has concealed the fact that he was one of Norman Wisdom's forebears. He took over 220 wickets each season for the United England XI and in 1850 he clean bowled all ten wickets in the South's second innings against the North at Lord's. He was a capable batsman, too. When he had finished playing, he had a spell at selling cricketing goods before producing in 1864 the first issue of the almanack which still bears his name today. To swell the thin volume and make the reader feel that he had received value for money, many odds and ends were included which had nothing to do with cricket. The battles of the Wars of the Roses were there along with a piece about the trial and execution of Charles I. Just what keen young cricketers needed.

While Old Clarke was still alive wild horses couldn't have dragged him to compete with these traitors to his cause on the field of play. When he snuffed it in 1856 he was succeeded as captain of the All England XI by another Nottingham player, George Parr, who came to be as good a batsmen as any in the country and was known as the Lion of the North. He cut quite a figure. He wasn't very tall but he was thickset with blue eyes and a fine crop of auburn hair which was backed up by a heavy moustache and mutton chop whiskers. He was a commanding figure on the field. He had a bad temper and was not the easiest of men but an all-round sportsman who was as able with a gun or a rod in his hand as he was with a bat. He was a croucher at the wicket and up until that time there had been no finer player on the legside. At Trent Bridge there was a tree in the line of many of his leg hits which came to be known affectionately as Parr's tree and stood there until a gale tore it limb from limb in the 1980s. Under Parr's captaincy the two England XIs met first in 1857, and the bridges had been mended to the extent that the following year's game was played for George Parr's benefit. This became the most important fixture of the year. But perhaps the most important date in cricket's history lay just around the corner.

CHAPTER 3

SIXPENCE TO SEE THE DOCTOR

W.G. GRACE burst upon the scene in 1864 rather as the deafening roar of the first 16-pounder will have startled the seagulls one morning at Jutland the year after he died. A good number of bowlers put their heads down pretty quickly. The genius who was to stand the game on its head and became as well known to his fellow countrymen as Queen Victoria, Gladstone and Disraeli, appeared as if out of a puff of smoke. Contrary to rumour, he was born completely clean shaven, but in no time at all, the beard was up and running. In his mid-twenties he was already a cross between an Old Testament prophet, Alexander the Great, and Babe Ruth with more than a touch of King Kong thrown in. Over the next forty years he took cricket by the scruff of the neck and shook it many times while showing the world how the game should be played. When he had finished with it, we were left with the modern game of cricket more or less as it is now. No actor, be it, Garrick, Irving, Olivier or Gielgud, has ever set himself a part and played it half so well. There was drama and bathos, as well as romance and humour, on every page. All the time I rather fancy that WG was himself having the biggest laugh of all at the convolutions the country's establishment were going through to accommodate him, and at

times to stomach him. He knowingly tested them to the limit.

The joker had suddenly appeared. The self-serving, self-important oligarchy at Lord's had been in grave danger of disappearing up their own backsides. The private preserve of privilege and nobility was now invaded by a lower-middle-class boy with a squeaky voice and an unmistakeable West Country burr. A lot of awkward shuffling went on in the corridors of power, but they stood aside for him and watched as one cherished belief after another was kicked into touch. WG might have been the central figure in a masterful plot to discredit and disorientate the establishment. At its completion when all the no-go areas had been infiltrated, the revolution would begin and the tumbrils start to roll. The pompous rulers of the game were queuing up to take on board an upstart amateur who was paid more than any professional in the country. The paradox was complete.

WG had been decanted into this world, the product of his mother, Martha's, eighth pregnancy, on 18 July, 1848. They were already thick on the ground in Downend House with seven other little Graces raising Cain and Martha opted to produce number eight in Clematis Cottage, her midwife's home just round the corner. So WG put in an appearance smelling of flowers for the first and only time in his life. He was christened William Gilbert and, believe it or not, his mother actually called him Willie which can't have done his morale any good. As soon as he could toddle, he was out watching his father and brothers play cricket for this was the family obsession. It was clear before too long that he had a greater way with the implements of cricket than any of them, although his brother, EM, who was seven years older, was reluctant to agree. There was always a great rivalry between them which doesn't say as much for EM's judgement as it does for his jealous nature.

Only a few days before his sixteenth birthday in July, 1864, WG, still a beardless boy, went with the South Wales Club

on their tour to London and the Home Counties. I can't think why Gloucestershire was dragging its heels. The first game was against the Surrey Gentlemen at the Oval when he made 38 in the second innings and took four of the Gentlemen's first innings wickets. In the second match, against the Gentlemen of Sussex at Brighton, WG was under considerable pressure. Originally selected for two matches, his captain then decided to ask him to stand down for a better player for the game in Brighton. His brother, Henry, stamped his foot and refused to allow this to happen, although he himself was never playing in that game. WG was put in third and made his point with a grand innings of 170 to which he added 56 not out in the second innings. He was then asked to play against MCC at Lord's four days after his sixteenth birthday. Going in fourth this time, he made fifty on the usual atrocious Lord's pitch, after EM had been out for nought. Later that month he again played for South Wales at Lord's, against I Zingari, an exceedingly blue-blooded nomadic club, and he had a good all-round match. Neither WG nor EM, known as the Coroner, which he became, were ever invited to play for the IZ. There were many who regarded the Graces as country bumpkins – the Gloucestershire accent won't have helped – and rightly reckoned they had a highly dodgy amateur status. The next year WG played for the Gentlemen who were less selective, against the Players and helped them to a rare victory. If there were any remaining doubts as to not-so-little Willie's ability, they were dispelled once and for all in 1866 when he made his first first-class hundred which was a small matter of 224 not out, for an England side against Surrey.

WG lived up to this start to the tune of almost 55,000 first-class runs with 126 hundreds and just under 3,000 wickets. He was probably the greatest cricketer there has ever been, considering the appalling conditions in which the game was played at that time. WG was also a perverse chap in the sense that he gave not a fig for tradition; he loved to win at more or less any cost and would do almost anything to gain his ends if he felt he could get away with it. No other cricketer in the history of the game has attracted so many stories which come under the heading of sharp practice. No other cricketer in England has been so universally loved, except maybe Ian Botham – and he was no angel either. Such was WG's ability that there was no need for such extravagant behaviour, for he was so far ahead of his contemporaries. Being an intelligent chap, he will have known exactly what he was doing and why he was doing it. It is this side of him which makes him such a fascinating character and such an extraordinary contradiction.

The MCC knew they could not afford to let him go. They had effectively lost control of the game ever since William Clarke had come onto the scene with his professional All England XI. After his astonishing start as a player, MCC realised they had to get WG on board and in 1869, when he was only twenty-one, he was elected to the club which will have raised the odd eyebrow or two. He was proposed by the treasurer, one T. Burgoyne, who may have been more good honest plonk than the chateau-bottled institution his name might suggest, and seconded by R.A. Fitzgerald, the long-standing secretary, which shows how determined the club was to get him in. They probably thought they had him on an exclusive basis too, but it was the club and not the player who were overawed by this piece of legerdemain. There was not even a murmur when in the 1870s he began to organise games for the United South of England XI for which he was paid. So much for his amateur status and yet no one attempted to say boo to him, although old Grimston must have been sorely tempted to find a sovereign or two for the navvies. A young man of twenty-one from his background should by any normal standards have been overwhelmed by the thrill of being elected to cricket's premier club at such an early age and not have attempted to do anything but toe the line. Far

from it, and all it seemed to do was make WG even more aware of his worth. He may have been high-handed in his treatment of the club but, to give him his due, he was full of praise for the way in which they ran the game. Maybe even he knew that he could only push his luck so far.

He lived in a hirsute age and moustaches were all the vogue for the cricketing gentry. Yet WG went headlong for a huge beard which was almost overpoweringly free range. Sometimes beards hide more than the chins they cover. He confessed to being nervous before he made that 170 against the Gentlemen of Sussex at Brighton, but otherwise he never admitted a weakness and very seldom a mistake. His win at all costs approach produced plenty of embarrassing scenes and he was plainly contemptuous of convention. It is impossible to believe that a man who was as apparently controlled as WG, did not know exactly what he was about. The stories grew worse for, as the years went by, he became ruder and more convinced by his own invincibility. The umpires were in awe of him and so, too, were most of his fellow players, especially those who began in the game when he was already looking down from Mount Olympus. He was able to do what he wanted.

The stories about him are legion. In 1878, playing for the North against the South, Richard Barlow, the Lancashire professional, played defensively at a ball and stopped it in the crease beside him. WG was fielding at point and Barlow tapped the ball gently towards him so that he would not have to come in to pick it up. Having done this, it was Barlow's party trick to scamper two or three yards up the wicket as if starting a run before turning round and going back to his crease. It always got him a laugh from the crowd. On this occasion WG immediately appealed against Barlow for hitting the ball twice and the umpire had no alternative but to give him out. This was the letter of the law rather than the spirit, but WG was not interested in niceties of that sort. No one

W.G. GRACE

will have dared to have a go at him and the spirit of Lord Frederick Beauclerk would have been egging him on like nobody's business. Then, of course, Lord Frederick would have rolled over in his grave and vigorously ostracised WG for other aspects of his character.

When England were playing Australia in 1882, the Australian batsman, Sammy Jones, had completed a run and thinking that the ball was dead, set off up the pitch to do a bit of prodding with his bat. WG had encouraged Jones to think the ball was dead when he apparently took it back to the bowler. Then, seeing Jones stroll up the pitch, he walked quickly back to the wicket and broke the stumps. Again, the umpire had no option but to give the batsman out. It was cold-blooded and calculated. If, when he was bowling, WG saw a batsman trying to steal an advantage by backing up before the ball had been delivered, he would run him out in a flash without giving the time-honoured warning and something pertinent to the batsman as he stalked off. There was an occasion, too, when he had run three runs before the ball was returned and it then lodged in his clothing. In those days the ball was not automatically dead as it is today when this happens. WG and his partner proceeded to run another three and he then refused to give the ball back in case he himself was given out handling the ball.

WG's father had a great influence on him and was obviously a cricketer from a hard school, although it is difficult to imagine a kindly country doctor encouraging his children to piracy on the high seas in quite this way. It's a bit like the Mother Superior suggesting to a novice that the butcher's boy looks a nice hunk of meat. Of course, with WG there is a fine line between fact and fiction, but there was enough fact to induce the fiction. Of course, the old boy didn't always get it right. When he was batting and the ball flicked the outside of the leg stump and the bail hovered and fell, WG picked it up and put it back on the stumps, saying as he did so, 'It's a windy day umpire.' This time the reply was not encouraging.

'Ay, it is Mr Grace and mind it don't blow yer 'at off on way back to pavilion.' At least, that's how the story goes.

The best WG story of all was told by Neville Cardus. When reporting a match in the West Country he got into conversation with an old Gloucestershire player who had been in the side with him. It was sometimes said that WG cheated and Cardus put this to the old player.

'Nay,' he protested with pride in his voice, 'never. The Old Man cheat?' There was astonishment in his voice. ' 'e were too clever for that.'

This shows the respect and admiration in which WG was held by the other Gloucestershire players. They knew what a wonderful player he was and if he wanted to cut a few corners, well, that was up to him. He received great loyalty which shows how much the professionals admired him. The fact that he, as an amateur, was taking home more money than any of them had nothing to do with it. They will have felt it was his right. Another old pro once said of WG, 'There's lots can do it now and again, but the Doctor, he just keeps on doing it.' That will have had plenty to do with it too.

Matches were advertised as 'Admission threepence. If W.G. Grace plays admission sixpence.' Small wonder the umpires were ready to turn a blind eye when he was batting until they felt the spectators had had their money's worth. The three Graces always insisted on being paid for playing. WG was the captain of Gloucestershire at the age of twenty-one, EM was the secretary and in charge of expenses, which gave rise to much scandal, while GF was simply a player with an inordinate mileage allowance. Then there was a cousin Walter Gilbert who was not left out and seemed to collect on much the same grand scale. In the end, Walter Gilbert turned professional and was caught helping himself from the pockets of his colleagues' clothes which were hanging in the dressing room. After twenty-eight days hard labour, he found himself in receipt of a one-way ticket to Canada.

The Graces drove a coach and horses through conventional standards. WG was the worst offender and there was no one prepared to stand up to him, but far from being regarded as a somewhat dubious character, he was hero worshipped throughout the country. After the horrors of the Crimea and the disappearance of a much loved Queen from public view after the death of her adored Consort, Prince Albert, the public needed a hero on whom they could focus their attention. WG fitted the bill to perfection. I only hope that from time to time he allowed himself a high-pitched chuckle when he saw the establishment fawning on him after a particularly reprehensible piece of behaviour. The wish may be the father of the thought, but it would be dreadfully sad if, after all this masterful stage-management, he derived no pleasure from the tricks he got up to. If there was not a twinkle in his eye when, for example, he ran out Sammy Jones, there were no mitigating circumstances whatever.

In 1872, WG was exported for the first time. He went to Canada and the United States on a tour arranged and captained by R.A. Fitzgerald. Their hosts footed the bill for this all-amateur side and they were lucky to find that WG came just within budget. His reputation had preceded him and he was lionised wherever he went. He was very successful with both bat and ball and during the tour he struck up a great friendship with George Harris who became the fourth Baron soon after he returned to England, and went on to wield the sort of power at Lord's that dear old Lord Frederick once possessed. I daresay WG was looking to the future and there was an element of arse-licking in this. In the years ahead Harris supported him on a number of occasions when his behaviour was called into question. Even WG will have understood that having the odd friend at court was not a bad principle.

The Canadians took a more relaxed view about relations between the sexes than they did in England. Several of the team took full advantage of this, but not WG who was uneasy and shy in female company. This probably had much to do with his squeaky, high-pitched voice which seemed so absurd coming from such a huge man. Watching his team mates flirting with the local beauties may have been just the spur he needed. On his return to Gloucestershire, he stiffened the sinews, to say nothing of summoning up the blood, and proposed to the nineteen-year-old Agnes Day who was the daughter of a cousin, and he was accepted. It is uncertain whether this was one of the great love matches. Agnes Day lived in a smallish house with eight brothers and sisters, only one servant and a general shortage of cash. Whether WG was an irresistible attraction, or a convenient path to freedom and more spacious living, is a moot point. If she had known at the time that she would be spending her honeymoon in Australia, it would no doubt have acted as a strong magnet.

The Melbourne Cricket Club asked him to take a side to Australia in 1872/73 and WG demanded payment of £1,500 (about £50,000 today) and expenses, including first-class travel, which was beyond them. He wouldn't budge, but the following year negotiations were more successful and so his honeymoon was paid for. He insisted on taking along his brother, GF, as well. The professionals drew the short straw. They were paid £150 each and travelled steerage, with £20 for booze and incidental expenses. As a result WG was unable to get all the players he wanted. It will never have occurred to him to take a cut so that the others could have a bit more. There were any number of unpleasant incidents on the tour and all involving WG who seemed to take a healthy contempt for the colonials out to Australia with him. He was as intransigent as ever and it did not help the tour that the leading bookmaker in Melbourne was involved in the arrangements. The England players, including the captain, bet quite heavily on the outcome of matches and as a result were not trusted by the Australian public. (Copy to Lord Condon).

WG himself was considered to be a 'bumptious and over-bearing' captain and the Australians could not tolerate his patronising attitude towards them for they hated assumptions of superiority. Richie Benaud would have coped with him easily enough and may have tried to kid him which would have made for an interesting contest. Ian Chappell and WG would have understood each other, but they would have had their moments. It would have been nice to have had a ringside pew then. I can't see WG being much help at the press conferences which take place nowadays after each day's play. I don't think he would have much cared for being told what to do by all the smart young men in suits who give off an air of high octane industry as they bustle about behind the scenes these days.

On this tour, WG was disliked by his own professionals too and the main reasons were his undoubted snobbery and the superior financial arrangements he had worked out for himself. It was a most unhappy tour. When his team travelled to an up-country match, they were welcomed by the hotel proprietor of a quadrangle of iron shanties, who said, 'Pleased to meet you, Dr Grace, but we can't do you here like they do in the cities. Not much in the way of bloody bathrooms and such-like.' 'That don't matter,' squeaked WG. 'We Graces ain't no bloody water-spaniels.'

History doesn't relate what Mrs Grace's reaction was to all of this. Being married to WG must have had some compensations. They will not have been short of a bob or two, if ever he let her spend any of it. Against this, she must have felt that she was for ever in the midst of a rather unpleasant military campaign and she wouldn't have been human if she had not been embarrassed by her husband, not that that would have worried him. Maybe though, the doctor, in spite of his early shyness and hesitation, had hidden depths and she had the time of her life and was prepared to put up with anything. Perhaps, behind closed doors, they both had the most monumental chuckles. For all that, in Australia the legend of WG was severely bruised and it was his own fault.

With his hard outer shell, WG bumped and bustled his way along the late Victorian cricketing pathway, such as it was, with unrelieved success. His performances were better than ever. His fiftieth first-class hundred came at Clifton in 1875 and his hundredth at Bristol in 1895. He became increasingly cantankerous the older he got, and he thoroughly enjoyed a good row. Living life entirely on his own terms, he moved round England and the world like a headstrong Viceroy. His fame and seniority caused and perhaps entitled him to be indulged more and more. Gloucestershire were a formidable county side and they were the champions in the growing County competition in 1874, 1876 and 1877. The 1876 season was within a hair's breadth of being WG's last. He was shooting partridges in Northamptonshire early in September, having scored a hundred the day before against Lord Exeter's XI at Burghley. At one drive, thinking, as always, that he knew best, he moved out of the line of guns and climbed a high hedge. When the birds went over him he found he was in the middle of a hail of fire because the other guns couldn't see where he was. He was hit in the eye but, unlike Ranji who was to be blinded in one eye because of a shooting accident, his sight was not affected.

Visits to and from Australia were now happening with fair regularity and WG was always wanted as the major attraction. When he had taken that England side to Australia on his honeymoon in 1873/74, he first came across Fred Spofforth who was probably the fastest and best bowler in the world. Spofforth tended to have the better of Grace whom he detested, being a similar sort of chap himself. There is an extraordinary fictitious story of how, when WG was batting in the nets at Melbourne, this unknown bowler appeared and served up a couple of innocuous full tosses before coming in again and knocking over his stumps with the quickest ball

anyone had ever seen. WG was said to have been left spluttering, 'Where did that come from? Who did that?' At this point Spofforth disappeared but apparently there is incontrovertible evidence that he was in Tasmania at the time. It was, therefore, a good bit of old fashioned Australian propaganda, a tradition which they have maintained to this day. How often England have fallen for it.

WG was Spofforth's bunny, in England as well as Australia. In 1878, the touring Australians played MCC at Lord's. In MCC's first innings, Spofforth, the 'Demon', took six wickets for 4 runs, although WG had been out before he came on to bowl. He was fast, as his nickname suggests, but he realised the value of varying his pace and liked to have his wicket keeper standing close to the stumps. Two of his victims now at Lord's were stumped. More modern fast bowlers would have been hard pressed to think of a greater insult than having their keepers standing up close to the stumps. I can almost hear Mr F.S. Trueman spluttering. MCC were out for 33, Australia for 41 and when MCC batted again, the Demon opened the bowling. The first ball found the edge of WG's bat and was dropped behind the wicket; the second knocked his stumps over and MCC were all out for 19. *Punch* celebrated the occasion with the following:

> The Australians came down like a wolf on the fold,
> The Marylebone Club for a trifle were bowled,
> Our Grace before dinner was very soon done,
> And Grace after dinner did not get a run.

It was early on this tour that WG was so angry when William Midwinter, who had been born in Gloucestershire, preferred to play for the Australians against MCC at Lord's rather than for Gloucestershire against Surrey at the Oval. As a result WG and one or two others took a taxi to Lord's and kidnapped Midwinter whom they found sitting in the dressing room with his pads on ready to open the innings for Australia.

It obviously caused great ill-feeling and showed that WG would stop at nothing to achieve his ends. John Conway, the Australian manager, who had set off in another taxi in pursuit of Midwinter, had a blazing row with WG by the gates at the Oval and, as a result, the Australians refused to go down to Bristol and play Gloucestershire. WG wrote to the Australians regretting the incident, but they did not consider this enough. He then wrote a fulsome letter of apology to Conway, which was something he didn't make a habit of doing, and it had the desired effect.

WG's first child of four, a son, had been born in 1874 and was christened William Gilbert, which gave him quite a cross to bear. Soon afterwards the Graces moved to London so that WG could complete his medical studies at St Bartholomew's Hospital. His career had been put on almost permanent hold by the dictates of cricket. WG, the most famous sportsman the country had ever known, was now cooped up with the humblest of medical students. WG took it in his stride, neither expecting nor receiving any preferential treatment. This was another paradox. He strode through the cricket world as a modern Colossus. At Bart's he knew his place and was content with it. Even so, he still found the time to score almost 1,500 runs during the summer. But in his first game, against Surrey at the Oval, his surgeon boss, not a cricket afficionado, said he was going to come and watch him. WG won the toss but was so nervous about his surgeon's prying eye that he got out for next to nothing and the surgeon never came to see him again. It was not until 1879 that WG finally qualified for a white coat and stethoscope all of his own.

It was just before this that even MCC began to feel that maybe WG was too hot to handle. They decided to give him a National Testimonial in order to buy him a practice when he had passed his final medical exams. This was done in part because of his phenomenal achievements over the years and in part for all that he had done to help the club back to its

proper place at the head of the game in England. The hierarchy at Lord's were also becoming increasingly irritated and embarrassed by his blatant disregard of the rules which applied to all other amateurs. As we have seen, WG was up to everything. The hope was that, if he continued to play, he would not have to rely on match fees and outrageous expenses. The Duke of Beaufort and Lord Fitzhardinge were behind this initiative and they discussed it all with WG who came perilously close to falling in with their plans. That shooting accident had made him take a deep breath and consider, but in the end the imminent arrival of the Australians in 1878 kept him going. He longed more than anything to have another crack at them. Nonetheless, the Testimonial went ahead and it was an extraordinary coincidence that the final sum of nearly £1,500 was presented to him on the same day that he took his final *viva voce* at the Royal College of Surgeons. July 22, 1979 was the second day of his Testimonial match at Lord's and WG was content to face the examiners in the morning and the bowlers in the afternoon, which was typical of him. He had one piece of luck for the weather delayed the start until after lunch by which time he had returned from the Royal College. It was the kind of brinkmanship WG thrived upon.

His career went on and on. He was never far from controversy. He was always quick to defend the family honour, as he saw it, and he was never afraid to speak his mind. Still the runs kept coming as he strode round the cricket grounds of England, a figure so much larger than life. He went again to Australia as captain of Lord Sheffield's side in 1891/92 at the age of forty-three. He was past his best but his huge reputation was expected to do wonders for the gate receipts. The last time he had gone to Australia, it was on his honeymoon. Now he took Agnes for a second honeymoon and their two youngest children went with them. WG had warned Lord Sheffield that he would not be able to afford him, but his lordship wanted him at all costs. These turned out to be £3,000 (about £140,000 in today's money) and expenses for the whole family on top of that. There was a rumour that it was felt by some that WG's presence would be the perfect antidote to republican rumblings in certain Australian quarters. WG would have made one of the world's most unlikely diplomats, unless of course it was a question of gunboat diplomacy. Then, who better?

When WG was asked who was the next best batsman in England, he had famously replied, 'Give me Arthur.' Arthur Shrewsbury, the Nottinghamshire and England batsman WG so admired, who had become Lord Sheffield's cricketing adviser, was not entirely happy at Grace's selection. Not unreasonably, he felt that the expense would mean he would not be able to give the professionals a fair deal. He said to Lord Sheffield, 'I told you what wine would be drunk by the Amateurs. Grace himself would drink enough to swim a ship.' The early matches were all won and just before the First Test Match they played against twenty-four from Bowral and won by an innings. Among the twenty-four was a Richard Whatman whose sister Emily was to marry George Bradman and they went on to produce a son whose name was to keep Bowral on the map for evermore. It was a happy connection because if WG was the greatest cricketer of them all, Don Bradman was surely the next on the list – give or take Gary Sobers.

It was only when the Tests began that WG began to get up to his old tricks. John Blackham, the Australian captain, used an extremely worn old penny for the toss in Melbourne. After Blackham had won it for Australia, WG insisted on testing the coin by tossing it several times himself to see if it was 'loaded'. In the Second Test, John James Lyons drove a ball back to George Lohmann who, in trying to catch it on the half volley, scooped the ball up to WG at point. He threw it up triumphantly and the umpire, who was unsighted, agreed that Lyons was out. There was an unholy row with an umpire

about a caught behind decision against New South Wales. In the Third Test when WG went out to toss with Blackham, he insisted on tossing the coin because Blackham had won the last two tosses. Blackham didn't want a fight and acquiesced. By the end of the tour he had lost the affection and respect of the Australian public. Tom Horan, an Australian journalist who had supported WG until then, wrote that 'Grace developed a condition of captiousness, fussiness and nastiness strangely to be deprecated.'

Still the Old Man went on. He helped England win back the Ashes in 1893 and then two years later, in 1895 at the age of forty-seven, he had another *annus mirabilis*. He scored 2,346 runs while becoming the first batsman ever to score a thousand runs in May. Even better than that, his second hundred of the season, a trifling matter of 288 against Somerset, was his hundredth first-class hundred. At the end of the season three different testimonials added up to £9,073 (about half a million in today's language) which will not have been the least important part of it all for the old man. The only contradictory note was struck in Max Beerbohm's cartoon of an enormous WG with a tiny bat in his hand and in the distance behind him on one side a packed grandstand and on the other the funeral cortege of one of his neglected patients.

It was in 1896 that Ernest Jones, the Australian fast bowler, known to one and all as Jonah, bowled a ball which went through the famous beard. WG is supposed to have said, 'Steady, Jonah,' and Jonah to have replied, 'Sorry, Doctor, she slipped,' although there are other reported variations of the conversation. Even now he was unable to give the game up and it was not until 1908, when he was in his sixtieth year, that he played his last first-class innings, for the Gentlemen of England at the Oval. He lived his last few years at Eltham in south London, and was deeply disturbed by the war when it came. He briefly survived a stroke and then the Zeppelin raids came to depress him even further. One visitor, Lord Harris, asked him why they should worry him so after seeing off all those fast bowlers for so many years. 'I could see those beggars,' the old man replied, 'I can't see these.' A few days later, on 23 October, 1915, he died from a heart attack and for a day the greatest cricketer of them all stole the headlines from the Great War which, I suppose, was not the least of his achievements.

CHAPTER 4

THE GOLDEN BOYS

WG's very existence begs the question: what would have become of cricket if he had not put in such a timely appearance? He had arrived on the scene soon after those two veteran brickies, Old Lilly and Old Clarke, had left it. The former had perfected round-arm, while the latter was still cleaning up all round the country with a form of underarm which was decidedly prickly. WG stepped on the stage at the moment that overarm became legitimate and effectively steered the game from its rural beginnings to its modern manifestation. The old boy, as we have seen, was a mixture of Shakespeare's Falstaff and W.S. Gilbert's Robber Baron and as uninhibited as both. He trod a resolute path and set an example for the rest to wonder at and to emulate if they could.

When WG joined us in 1864, the game had already tiptoed over to America in 1859 for five matches on a tour which lasted for two months. Two years later, Spiers & Pond, theatre managers from Melbourne, had tried to lure Charles Dickens to Australia for a lecture tour, but he had had to pull the plug at the eleventh hour – perhaps he had felt *Great Expectations* coming on. Spiers and his friend Pond had clasped their brows at this devastating news and said in unison, 'Let's have cricket.' As a result, twelve intrepid spirits, ten from the south and only two from the north, where the insult was deeply felt, sailed to the Antipodes. By the time WG had called it a day, tours had become an accepted part of the game. Australia

and South Africa were up and running, the West Indies were flexing their muscles with a side from the Caribbean coming to England in 1890, the game was flourishing in India and the Parsees had sent over a side in 1886, New Zealand was learning, admittedly without much help from Australia, and the seeds were being sown elsewhere. WG had guided the game with sure hands into the Golden Age which produced the most exciting and idiosyncratic selection of cricketers the game has known.

It is impossible to put an exact date on the Golden Age. In the old days I suppose they would once again have shuffled down the hill from White's to the Star and Garter Inn. In the upper room, when the glasses had all been filled, the Duke of Richmond or may be the Duke of Dorset, would have stood up and said, 'Let there be a Golden Age,' or something like that, and sat down again to tumultuous applause. They would all then have put a note in their diaries on Tuesday 24th which said simply, 'Golden Age begins.' Although the Golden Age really embraced the reign of Edward VII, the starting point should be stretched back to the 1890s. Most of the principal participants in these hallowed years were playing by then. England's opponents were mostly Australia who played seven series against England in the nineties and another eight before the outbreak of the Great War in 1914, and there was not much between the two sides although Australia just had the better of things. South Africa appeared on the scene with increasing frequency as they improved, but the body politic of cricket at this level was not further enlarged until the West Indies toured England in 1928.

If the Golden Age began in 1890, it still does not allow us to include one famous character who had all the qualifications to be a part of this splendid era. He was no mean cricketer, although he did not quite sit at the top table of all. He had the extraordinary record of captaining England in the only Test Match in which he played, although it was on the silver

screen that he was really to make his name after a career on the boards in London. He moved to Hollywood in 1930 when he was within reach of seventy and it was the talking movies which turned him into a household name.

Charles Aubrey Smith, the only Test cricketer to hit the heights of Tinseltown, was born in 1863 of parents who both had strong family ties to the wine industry. His father did not inherit the family thirst and, having first qualified as a surgeon, in the days when they operated while wearing morning coats, became a GP in Chipping Campden. He sent Aubrey to Charterhouse and Cambridge, where he was extremely successful on the cricket field before turning out intermittently for Sussex, whom he captained between 1887 and 1889. He bowled off cutters at rather more than medium pace. To stop himself pushing the ball down the legside, he bowled round the wicket, beginning his run up almost in front of mid off. When C.I. (Buns) Thornton faced him for the first time, he did not take up his stance, thinking that Smith was loitering at mid off. Eventually he realised that this was where he was starting his run up from and said, 'Why, you are not coming round the corner, are you?' 'Round the Corner' Smith proved a nickname which stuck.

C. Aubrey Smith, as he was known later in the Hollywood-inspired lights, was asked to take the first ever England side to South Africa in 1888/89. They played all their matches against the odds until the two representative games at the end which were later to be given Test Match status. England won both with some ease and in the first Smith, who could bat when he put his mind to it, made only 3, but took seven wickets. It was his only Test Match because he became ill soon afterwards and could not therefore play in the second. He stayed in South Africa after the tour and founded a stock-broking firm in Johannesburg, making a bit out of the gold rush before it all went bottom up. He was lucky to get himself back to England without being in serious debt.

Smith was the most imposing of men. He was almost 6'3" tall with a chin which made its mark, a robust moustache below a patrician nose, and formidably bushy eyebrows above a pair of striking blue eyes. His accent was unmistakably aristocratic, his manners were impeccable and the ladies adored him. He should have been the eldest son of a duke rather than the son of a London doctor. He began acting when he was up at Cambridge and it became his life when he had finished playing for Sussex in 1896. After a long time on the stage in London, where he held his own but not much more, the movies came along and, fitting every American's idea of an English aristocrat to perfection, he wasted no time cashing in, even though he was getting on a bit. Smith was never a film star at the Clark Gable, Ronald Colman level of things, but there were those who said that this was because he was type cast into second-rate parts, and not because he was short of ability.

He was one of those rare actors who came to Hollywood because the film studios wanted him and not the other way round. For several years he was never out of work, in spite of the Wall Street crash which almost brought Hollywood to its knees, and he became a great favourite with everyone. He was the uncrowned king of the English community and the captain of the Hollywood Cricket Club – he was still playing well into his seventies. There is a lovely photograph of him, taken in his eighties, having a net wearing his whites and a homburg hat as he launches himself into a forward stroke with Boris Karloff keeping wicket in an amusingly predatory manner. He was still extremely elegant. It would have been lovely to think that Aubrey Smith had taken part in an important stand with Jessop in that famous match when England beat Australia by one wicket at the Oval in 1902. It was sad that the Golden Age and Aubrey Smith never quite met up because they deserved one another.

It was Neville Cardus at the height of his cricket-writing

passion who described Archie MacLaren as 'The noblest Roman of them all'. Old Trafford was Cardus's home every bit as much as it was MacLaren's and therefore unstinting devotion in his own inimitable prose style was hardly surprising. John Arlott, an eventual successor of Cardus's as cricket correspondent of the *Guardian*, wrote of the contradictions in MacLaren's character and called him 'disappointingly petty'. Even Jim Swanton, with a certain rolling of drums, went on record as saying, 'He was really an attractive rascal,' which was not quite the same thing. All were in agreement about his formidable ability as a batsman, but his character was as appealing to some as it was distasteful to others.

MacLaren was said to be a dreadful pessimist and he had the face to go with it. In the centre of team photographs, be it England, Lancashire or anyone else, he sat there stern and unwavering behind a severe black moustache and not even a suggestion of a sense of humour or the semblance of a smile. He might have been waiting for the bailiff to knock on the door. He was, nonetheless, very much the amateur, being all strung about with colourful blazers and caps or boaters and often with a tie as well. Yet in these photographs one can almost sense him fearing the worst. MacLaren was the man who succeeded another rascal, WG, to the captaincy when, at the age of fifty-one, Test Match cricket had become too much for the old man. But his captaincy like his character, was open to interpretation. All were in agreement that he was a magnificent batsman in the classical mould. The noble flourish of his off drive from the moment he picked up his bat when it curled round his head like a golfer at the top of his swing, to the long follow through which he would freeze momentarily, almost certainly in self-appreciation, was magnificent. MacLaren scored heavily for England in Australia where the pitches suited him. In 1895 after some time teaching at a preparatory school in the eternal search for cash, although at the age of twenty-three he was already the county captain,

he went down to Taunton to join the Lancashire side. Over the next two days he made no less than 424, which remained the highest first-class score in England until Brian Lara made 501 not out for Warwickshire against Durham in 1994.

MacLaren was permanently and embarrassingly short of cash all through his life and it gave him an inferiority complex. All came right in the end when his wife, Maud, was left a lot of money by her family in Australia, but this was only a few years before they both died and so it was a little too late. One day an elderly pavilion steward at Old Trafford was told many times by people he bumped into that MacLaren was looking for him. He ran him to ground in the ladies' pavilion with his wife and asked MacLaren why he needed him. 'I wanted to borrow five shillings to buy my wife some chocolates,' came the reply, 'but I found some money in your locker and so I took that.' No one came up with more harebrained schemes for righting his financial position and, needless to say, none of them worked. When playing against Northumberland in Newcastle, he received his salary cheque by post and it was only £200, much less than he had anticipated. He was not pleased and was complaining when he came across a friend, a Mr Stanger-Leathes, who had a horse running that day. Racing was MacLaren's other obsession. He followed his friend's advice to put it on the nose and won £1,000, but it had all gone within three days.

He had come from a reasonably well off family who had made their money in the cotton trade and lived in Manchester. Archie was the second of seven brothers and the first three went to school at Harrow, but when the money ran out, a humbler education had to be found for the other four. At Harrow, Winston Churchill was Archie's fag. When in later years he was asked what he was like, he would answer in an underlined upper-class accent, 'Snotty little so-and-so.' His family were perhaps not blue-blooded enough for Archie and how he would have loved to have been able to carry it off

like Aubrey Smith. The family money had obviously run out and he may have sailed pretty close to the wind in order to get by.

What a mixture he was. Often he would seem to be the eternal optimist, but then at other times, especially when captaining a side, he was the gloomiest of pessimists. Ranjitsinhji, who took the charitable view of everything, and was a great friend, said that MacLaren was 'Always cheerful and full of go. He imagines he is unlucky in everything, but Archie without his grumbling would be like curry without chutney.' At times he could be charming and great fun, but there were others when he was arrogant, dismissive and tiresomely grand. You never knew what you were going to get. He captained England twenty-two times against Australia which is more than anyone else has ever done, but never even managed to draw a series. He was in charge of Lancashire for twelve years and, although they had a fine side, they won the County Championship only once in this time. These are figures which speak for themselves. While one of his biographers goes so far as to say that MacLaren was 'possibly the greatest captain of all time', Alan Gibson in *The Cricket Captains of England* writes, 'It can hardly now be *lèse-majesté* to say he was a bad captain.' Together, they sum up the man.

Kumar Shri Ranjitsinhji was the most romantic player in the history of cricket. C.B. Fry recalls a fellow cricketer once saying of Ranji's batting, 'Come, Ranji, this isn't cricket, it's infernal juggling.' Those who watched him play will remember most of all his supple but powerful wrists which enabled him to turn the leg glance, which was probably the reason he was brought into this world in the first place, into a work of art. There was also the silk shirt buttoned, as often as not, to the neck as well as the wrists, and his charming and friendly ways. He was an original, just as WG had been, although it would not be easy to imagine two more different people. WG was good old roast beef while Ranji's batting, like his charac-

ter, was redolent of spices and curry with a fair amount of magic thrown in. It was as exciting as it was inexplicable in the way that an expert conjuror first arouses and then mystifies his audience. The sleight of hand is bewildering. This time Fry quotes maybe a despairing bowler: 'Yes, he can play, but he must have a lot of Satan in him.' Ted Wainwright, that pithy Yorkshire allrounder, underlined this last point when he gave it as his opinion that, 'Ranji, 'e never made a Christian stroke in his life.'

Ranji arrived in England in 1888 at the age of sixteen, after he had been disinherited as next in line to the throne of Nawanagar, with a considerable compensatory purse at his disposal. In the autumn of the following year he went up to Cambridge. There weren't many Indians about the place in those days and, although he was a prince, at first he was not easily accepted and nor was his cricket taken seriously. His colour counted against him. His extravagant lifestyle and his lavish hospitality may be seen as Ranji fighting for acceptance in what would otherwise have been a lonely world. Undergraduates in the 1890s would not have been that impressed by his social qualifications on the Subcontinent. Later on, he was not picked for the First Test in 1896 because Lord Harris, the President of MCC and a recently retired Governor of Bombay, had doubts about his qualifications and there were many who supported him. Sir Home Gordon said that during this debate a member of MCC threatened to have him expelled from the club 'For having the disgusting degeneracy to praise a dirty black'. By all accounts Ranji had a fierce temper and yet he somehow managed to control it which, in the face of this sort of provocation, must have been difficult.

If he had not been monstrously ditched as the heir to the throne of Nawanagar by a ringer, he might never have come to England to finish his education which would have meant that his genius for cricket might only have been revealed on the Subcontinent. It would then have been almost impossible

for him to have become the sublime and pivotal figure he did. India did not play Test cricket until 1932 and he would never have had the opposition or the pitches to develop his unique style of batting. In addition to the leg glance which he played with devastating certainty to anything on his stumps, Ranji also invented the art of both attacking and defending off the back foot. When he played for England for the first time in the Second Test, at Old Trafford, in 1896 he made 62 and 154 not out against Australia in a match which England lost by three wickets. These scores of Ranji's no doubt made Lord Harris and other racist members of MCC most unhappy, but they electrified the rest of the country. He only played in fifteen Tests between 1896 to 1902, and just failed to reach a thousand runs, and yet this extraordinary man completely changed the art of batting and captivated an entire generation and left an astonishing legacy.

More than a hundred years have gone by since he first played for England, but today he remains clouded in as much oriental mist and wonderment as he was then. He came to England and was quick to assume the style of a country gentleman at a time when another Indian, Mahatma Gandhi, was strutting about London in a morning coat. Ranji was wildly extravagant and got himself heavily into debt, although everything was paid back in the end. He owned the first motor car in Cambridge; he loved fine clothes and jewellery and never stinted himself. He walked round Cambridge with a bamboo cane on which his monogram was embossed in gold and which I was lucky enough to buy at an auction. It has turned Ranji into an even more romantic figure. He was the most genial of men and casual with it. It was said that no matter what he was doing you could tell him 'a mile off because of the elasticity of his walk'. His batting was his character: genial, casual and irresistible. In the end, he left serious cricket because the state of Nawanagar, so cruelly denied him fifteen years earlier, fell into his lap. The final postscript to his cricketing career comes

RANJITSINHJI

from Neville Cardus: 'When Ranji passed out of cricket, a wonder and a glory departed from the game for ever. It is not in nature that there should be another Ranji.' He was the Indian rope trick with pads on.

The Golden Age served up a rich fare and no one was more a part of it than Ranji's great friend and Sussex and England colleague, Charles Fry, once described as 'a ministry of all the talents'. He was a man of great and varied learning. As a scholar, he was at least comparable to his two great contemporaries at Oxford, who were also at Wadham, John Simon and F.E. Smith and he bettered them both in exams. He became a considerable journalist, first running and editing his own magazines and then writing pungent columns in the sporting pages of the London *Evening Standard.* Denzil Batchelor, whose own ouput as an author was enormous and whose rotund and rather thirsty sense of humour was always on parade, served for some while as CB's go-getting secretary. Batchelor once said, 'When Fry was in a mordant mood he became the incarnation of the ablative absolute.'

His athletic achievements were prodigious. At Oxford he won Blues for soccer and athletics in addition to cricket and, if it had not been for an injury shortly before the University match, he would have won another for rugger, a game he said he preferred to soccer. Even so, he turned out for Southampton in the FA Cup Final in 1802. While he was at Oxford he broke the world record in the long jump and would have gone to Athens for the Olympic Games in 1896, but he had forgotten to put the dates in his diary and apparently didn't know they were being held. He once scored six first-class centuries in successive innings, a feat which Bradman was later to equal but not beat. If this wasn't enough, he was a tall man with classical good looks and, all his life, was likened to a Greek god. The gods were indeed kind to him and, in view of this staggering start to life, it is not perhaps unreasonable to think that in some ways he failed to live up to it. When, much

later, he was in command of the Royal Navy training ship, HMS *Mercury* on the Hamble, he was visited by F.E. Smith who, although impressed, said to Fry afterwards, 'This is a fine show, CB, but, for you, a backwater.' Fry replied, 'That may be, but the question remains whether it is better to be successful or happy.' Which, more often than not, is an opt out. Fry's happiness may have been compromised by a strange and rather dreadful wife.

His cricketing skills were extraordinary. In his career he scored just under 31,000 runs averaging a little over 50, with ninety-four hundreds. He played twenty-six times for England in the days when Test Matches came along much less frequently than they do today and the opponents were mostly Australia and just occasionally South Africa. He was at his best in the years he and Ranji played together for Sussex, when even the Yorkshire bowlers feared to make the trip to Brighton. He and Ranji were not only the greatest of friends, they complemented one another on the field and off it. Although, with a bat in their hands, both were well nigh perfect, this perfection was many worlds apart. Fry had been a classical scholar at Oxford and he was no less classical at the wicket. On the other hand, Ranji conformed to no known discipline. His batting was a form of glorious oriental improvisation. It was not so much that he broke every rule in the book because there was no book and there were precious few rules. He made his own up as he went along. Fry's skill was to take batting as it was already known and to move it along a logical path to a higher platform than before. He did not invent new strokes: he took those that there were, dressed them up and streamlined them but their origins were still recognisable. Fry went on to the front foot in the classical manner, while Ranji twinkled away off the back foot and his bat was always chuckling at the bowler. As he grew older, Fry too was playing more off the back foot and the influence for this change was only twenty odd yards away at the other end of the pitch.

Fry and Ranji were great companions. When Fry captained England to victory in the 1912 Triangular Tournament, Ranji was in the dressing room at the Oval after England had beaten Australia. The crowd called for Fry, but earlier in the match they had heckled him because he refused to start after rain when it would have been to Australia's advantage. This had not pleased Fry and he now refused to grant them their wishes and go onto the balcony. Ranji gently chided him, 'Now, Carlos,' as he always called him, 'be your noble self.' Fry replied, 'This is not one of my noble days.' There was another occasion when, some years later, Gubby Allen, a pre-war England captain and post-war *eminence grise* at Lord's, remembered as a boy, being taken to tea with Ranji and Fry and being fascinated by the conversation. In a rare pause, Allen himself bravely asked, 'Who was the greatest batsman of all time?' There was a long pause which was eventually broken by Ranji who said rather formally, 'I think, Charles, that I was better than you on a soft wicket.'

Fry, who could never be silent for long, was upstaged by Neville Cardus when both were watching the 1936/37 tour of Australia from the press box. It was Remembrance Day, and as the assembled company arose at the appropriate moment to observe the two minutes silence, Cardus whispered to his neighbour, 'This'll irk you, Charles.' Cardus and Denzil Batchelor, his amanuensis, were both able to hold their own in conversation with Fry. Alan Gibson, who met him, found that he could occasionally get in a sentence which prompted a response, given three conditions: a) The sentence must be a question meriting an answer; b) Fry had just used the word 'however' with which he ended verbal paragraphs; c) He was taking off his naval cap which was where he kept his tobacco pouch, and was considering a pipe. Fry was appointed a captain in the Royal Navy because of his duties at HMS *Mercury*. He enjoyed striding about in his uniform looking, as Crusoe Robertson-Glasgow once said, 'Every inch like six admirals'.

How appropriate it was that Charles Fry was offered the throne of Albania. The probability is that the offer was made, although there was a school of thought which insisted it was a leg-pull by Ranji. If it was genuine, the surprise was that he refused it. He affected an eyeglass and had a Hollywood bearing which only Aubrey Smith could have bettered. He had a tendency to launch himself into impassioned monologues which were lent weight by his imperial and rather arrogant demeanour and it would have been hard to imagine a more suitable candidate for a kingdom. But I daresay the obituarists would have been in business pretty soon after his coronation. Years later, Fry's daughter, Faith, confirmed that it was a true story. A business partner of Fry's, Christopher Hollis, who I met in the 1960s when he was writing about cricket for the *Observer* and invariably making his notes in the press box on House of Commons writing paper, an institution he had briefly adorned, said of Fry that, 'He had a great capacity for living a fantasy life. It pleased him to tell the story, and by the end I fancy that he did not know himself whether to believe it or not.'

Fry and Ranji always made a great fuss of WG and it was ironical that Fry, without knowing it until it was too late, was responsible for WG's final departure from the England side at the age of fifty-one. Fry had become a selector in 1899 when, for the first time, the same selection committee chose the England side for all five Test Matches. Before this the authorities at each ground had chosen the side which was to represent England there. Fry had been a few minutes late for a luncheon meeting of the selection committee. 'The moment I entered the door, WG said, "Here's Charles. Now, Charles, before you sit down, we want you to answer this question, yes or no. Do you think that Archie MacLaren ought to play in the next Test match?"' Fry said yes and discovered that the committee had already decided that if MacLaren was to play, and Fry's was the casting vote, WG would be dropped.

His size and lack of mobility had finally counted against him. 'That settles it,' said WG, and MacLaren not only played but took on the captaincy as well.

In purely cricketing terms, the most dramatic of the principal performers in the Golden Age was Gilbert Jessop. There can never have been a more powerful, exciting or dramatic hitter of a cricket ball. His most famous innngs was against Australia at the Oval in 1902, coming in with England apparently doomed at 48/5 needing 263 to win. He proceeded to make 104 in an hour and a quarter and England won by one wicket after George Hirst and Wilfred Rhodes had famously not said, 'We'll get 'em in singles', before they set about their task of scoring the last 15 runs for victory. Perhaps the only truly comparable innings to Jessop's was Ian Botham's 149 not out against Australia at Headingley in 1981. If, in today's game, a batsman regularly scores his runs at anything over 40 an hour, his haste is considered to be almost indecent. Throughout his career, Jessop scored his runs at 80 an hour. Different times.

Those GPs in Gloucestershire were a restless lot. Jessop was the eleventh child of another doctor with cricketing genes to give away and who lived near Cheltenham. He was, of course, called Gilbert after WG. He was a bundle of energy who counted every moment as wasted when he was not playing cricket. He became a teacher at the age of fifteen and was twenty when he made his debut for Gloucestershire, against Lancashire at Old Trafford. His first job was to prevent Mold taking a hat-trick which he did by hitting his first ball for four. When he had hit his third four in that same over, WG was heard to say to his neighbour, 'Well, we've found something this time.' The alternative point of view was expressed by a typically one-eyed newspaper report in Lancashire the next day which said, 'If Mr Jessop's batting is no better than his bowling or fielding, he is scarcely likely to become an acquisition to the Western shire.'

Jessop was not a big man, standing 5'7" high and weighing eleven stone. Stocky, with unusually long arms and very strong hands, he used a bat which weighed three pounds. He was by no means a simple slogger and the late cut was his most productive stroke. He was called 'the Croucher' because of the way he crouched low over his bat, ready to pounce on the ball. He began life as a fast bowler when he batted in the lower middle order and was picked for his first Test Match as a bowler. He was also a brilliant cover point. His hands were almost infallible and the power and accuracy of his throwing was phenomenal.

He was anything but an academic and he went up to Cambridge in, curiously, the summer term of 1896 and immediately won a Blue. His college, Christ's, has always been sympathetic to University sport and maybe the fellows suddenly realised that, although the academic year was two-thirds over, desperate remedies were needed if Cambridge were to do any good against Oxford at Lord's. His athletic ability was enormous and his tutors at Christ's were obviously spellbound. Jessop played for Cambridge for four years, but he went down without a degree, having only completed seven of the ten terms since he first arrived. After Cambridge, he found a berth on the London Stock Exchange where he stayed until 1900 when he took over the Gloucestershire captaincy from WG.

Jessop met his wife, Millicent, who came from Hamilton in New South Wales, on the boat on the way home after the 1901/02 tour to Australia. He was playing a game of catch with two children on deck when two ladies walked past. The rubber pouch they were using hit one of them. She gave Jessop a withering look, the other smiled and they became engaged three weeks later. The memory of Jessop still lingers in Australia and in 1966 a Gilbert Jessop Society was founded by two chaps who worked at the Faculty of Law in Adelaide University. Cricket generally was at a low ebb and these two wanted to found a society which 'could represent the real

spirit of the game'. The University is close to the Torrens River and Jessop is the only batsman ever to have hit a ball from the Adelaide Oval into the river.

In his book about the history of Gloucestershire cricket, Grahame Parker tells the story of how Jessop wrote to Alf Dipper's father after Alf had scored more than a thousand runs in a season for the first time. Jessop was delighted and bet his father a brace of partridges he would make even more more runs the following year. The letter also told him that Alf's winter allowance had been cut to ten shillings a week. Jessop did not claim his brace of partridges for Alf missed most of the next season because of appendicitis. Although Jessop played as an amateur, he carried on in the tradition, established by the Graces, of making up for lost earnings through an excessive expenses allowance. He was as much of a shamateur as WG or any of the others.

But it was for that astonishing innings in the Fifth Test Match at the Oval in 1902 that Jessop will be longest remembered. The first 50 came in round about even time, but there are some who say the second arrived in only ten minutes and others who say it took twice that time. Whichever it was, it was incredibly fast and there is general agreement that the entire innings lasted for only seventy-five minutes. Small wonder that a parson dropped dead during the excitement when the Almighty must have taken his eye off the ball for just a moment. Jessop himself was supremely confident about that innings. The evening before, having dinner with the other amateurs, he offered odds of ten to one against him making 50 and of twenty to one against reaching a hundred. So he cleaned up all round. His other two most memorable innings were the 286 he made against Sussex at Hove in two and a quarter hours and the 157 he made in an hour against a West Indian side at Bristol in 1900. Even then, there were long delays because each time Jessop hit the ball out of the ground the West Indians lay on the grass convulsed with laughter.

The final place in the Golden Age's ultimate roll call must be kept for Stanley Jackson. He was a brilliant allrounder who played twenty Test Matches, all of them against Australia. He made five hundreds, averaging just under 50 and he took twenty-four wickets, swinging the ball away from the right-hander at just above medium pace. He captained England in 1905 and regained the Ashes when the Australians were beaten 2–0. Jackson headed both the batting and the bowling averages with 70 and fifteen respectively. He proved an extremely shrewd captain and kept a collection of rather tricky individuals happy and united. He got the best out of MacLaren by using him almost as his partner; C.B. Fry described this as his happiest season in Test cricket and he 'delighted in Jackson's captaincy', while Walter Brearley, a notoriously difficult character, took fourteen wickets for Jackson in the last two Tests.

Jackson and Archie MacLaren had been chums at Harrow and had captained the school at Lord's in successive years. They could hardly have been more different people though. While MacLaren was all up front and at you, Jackson was more thoughtful and reserved and, although he only had the job for one series, in 1905, he was maybe the best captain of them all. He was born into a good county family on 21 November, 1870, the same day as Joe Darling who captained Australia in that same series in 1905. He was already a keen competitor when he was at his preparatory school and when the headmaster, who was batting in the nets, promised any boy who bowled him out, a bottle of ginger beer, Jackson's final tally was eighteen bottles. He played for Harrow for three years and, in his second, his father who became Lord Allerton, offered him a sovereign for each wicket he took and a shilling for every run he made. He scored 21 and 59 and took eleven wickets. When he was congratulated on his performance, he replied, 'I don't care so much for myself, but it'll give the guv'nor such a lift!' He said some time later, 'I will give

him credit by saying that the money was promptly paid, but unfortunately his generosity ceased with that match.'

There was so much more to Jackson than just cricket which was to him nothing more than an interesting side-show to the real business of life. C.B. Fry reckoned he owed his success in cricket to 'the same sterling qualities of intellect and character which ensure success in any undertaking'. There was a shrewd level-headedness about Jackson and a complete absence of cunning which went to make him 'a fine man of business, a fine officer, and a fine cricketer'. Fry goes on to tell the story of Colonel Jackson doing his nightly round of sentries during the Boer War. Instead of the obligatory, 'Halt! Who goes there?' a Yorkshire voice asked, 'Beg pardon, sir, but it ain't true that Somerset have beaten Yorkshire, is it? I have betted 'arf a crown that it ain't true, and I know as you can tell me, sir.' Shocked as he was by the lack of discipline, Jackson said later, 'It went to my heart, as much that he should lose his " 'arf-crown" as that we should lose the match. But I happened to have seen the sad news in a cablegram from home, so I had to tell him the truth. Then I severely reprimanded him.'

While captain of Cambridge in 1893, Jackson presided over a strange incident in the University match. Cambridge had made 182 and Oxford were 95/9. In those days the follow-on was compulsory if a side was more than 80 runs behind on first innings. Oxford's last two batsmen were no-hopers and Cambridge did not want to bat last on a pitch which was getting worse. Jackson told C.M. Wells to bowl wides deliberately to prevent the follow-on. It was not long before the Law was changed to make the follow-on optional. Jackson's ploy shows that he was a man of strongly independent views, with more than a streak of ruthlessness in his nature, all hidden behind his cheerful easy-going appearance. In that same year Jackson was picked for all three Test Matches against Australia. He decided not to play in the last because he wanted

to turn out for Yorkshire who needed to win their match against Sussex to make sure of the Championship. They beat Sussex and won their first title, but Jackson's sense of values was not popular with everyone.

He finished playing Test cricket in 1905 and took up golf. For six months he practised in front of a mirror with a coaching manual at his side, without hitting a single ball. When he began to play in earnest, it took him only a year to become a scratch player. He was later to become a Member of Parliament for the Howdenshire division of Yorkshire for eleven years. One day in the House of Commons, Winston Churchill, who had been Jackson's fag as well as MacLaren's, introduced him to Lloyd George who immediately said, 'I have been looking all my life for the man who gave Winston Churchill a hiding at school.' He was not the figure in Parliament that his father, Lord Allerton, had been. Hubert Preston tells the story in Jackson's obituary in the 1948 *Wisden* that when he was waiting to make his maiden speech in the House, the debate took a difficult turn, and the Speaker passed him a note: 'I have dropped you in the batting order; it's a sticky wicket.' And another later: 'Get your pads on. You're next in.' In 1927 when he had finished with Parliament, he went to India as Governor of Bombay where he soon made a name for himself for behaving with admirable courage and self-control when someone tried to bump him off. Perhaps he was the most remarkable and impressive of all those who have captained England. Cricket's Golden Age would not have been complete without him.

CHAPTER 5

THE BODY WILL BE CREMATED

I**T IS NOT** surprising that cricket quickly became a focal point for Australian nationalism. The game which had been exported from England grew in the 1840s and 1850s and international cricket began in the following decade. Between 1870 and the end of the century scarcely a year went by without teams from England visiting Australia or Australian sides going to England. One of the main reasons cricket grabbed the public imagination in Australia was that it was played against England over whom Australians have always had a point to prove. They were heartily fed up – and quite rightly so – with Englishmen descending from afar and looking down their noses and patronising the colonials. This gave Australian cricket just the spur it needed and has been an encouragement which has never gone away. When Australia eventually becomes a republic, victory over England will still be the sweetest of all.

To start with, the visiting English sides played their games against the odds taking on sometimes as many as twenty-two opponents. The Australians showed themselves to be quick learners, however, and this did not last for long. When the first ever Test Match – it acquired that status afterwards – was played in Melbourne in March 1877, it was

Australia who won by 45 runs. No matter that Charles Bannerman who made 165 not out when no other Australian scored more than 20, had been born a Kentish Man, in Woolwich, before his family emigrated, or that he had been coached by William Caffyn who had played alongside Julius Caesar for Surrey. This was first blood to Australia who had rather the better of the early exchanges between the two sides. This had much to do with the furious fast bowling of Fred Spofforth who had been selected for that first Test Match, but had refused to play because Billy Murdoch had not been chosen as his wicket keeper. Spofforth and Murdoch both played in the second which England won by four wickets, although Blackham continued to keep wicket, and so it was not long before Spofforth's point of principle had evaporated. He and Blackham soon developed a method of signalling so that his keeper knew exactly what was coming next and I suppose this weakened the case for Murdoch.

We have already seen that England and WG had made contact with Spofforth on earlier tours. He was tall and slim with dark hair and a clipped moustache, giving him a distinctly sinister appearance which will have done nothing for the batsman's sense of well being. If it had not been for Spofforth, the Ashes may never have come into existence. In 1882, the Australians played one Test in England, at the Oval, which they won by 7 runs in the tensest of finishes. One spectator died of a heart attack while another bit through his umbrella handle, although I am glad to say that the catering at the Oval is nowadays a little more palatable. Spofforth took seven wickets in each innings and England were bowled out for 77 in the second. It was after this match that the famous obituary notice appeared in *The Sporting Times* which led to the founding of the Ashes.

In Affectionate Remembrance
of
ENGLISH CRICKET
which died at the Oval
on
29th August, 1882.
Deeply lamented by a large circle
Of sorrowing Friends and Acquaintances
RIP
N.B. The body will be cremated and the Ashes
taken to Australia.

By taking fourteen wickets for 90, Spofforth must be held largely responsible for a joke which may have given a certain romance to series between the two countries, but has also been responsible for some excruciatingly boring cricket down the years. It was after the Third Test in Australia the following winter, when England were 2–1 up, that the famous urn materialised. In Melbourne a group of ladies burned a stump and put the Ashes in the small urn which now lives its life in perpetuity in the museum at Lord's. The urn was presented to the Honourable Ivo Bligh, England's captain. It was then that the sides decided to play a fourth Test which Australia won, levelling the series at 2–2. The young ladies had jumped the gun, but Ivo Bligh hung onto the urn and brought the Ashes home and for years the urn stood on a mantelpiece at Cobham Hall, the Bligh family home in Kent. Some time, soon after its arrival, a housemaid knocked the urn down onto the floor when dusting and it opened. The ashes came out and the butler, whom the housemaid had summoned and was very much on his toes, apparently scooped in some more from the fireplace before putting the two halves back together. When the Honourable Ivo, by then Lord Darnley, died the urn was given to Lord's. The urn has never been opened since coming to Lord's and nobody knows for certain what is inside.

In spite of the efforts of Charles Turner who was inevitably nicknamed 'The Terror' and took 101 wickets in seventeen Tests, Australia had a lean time of it in the eighties. It really needed the arrival of their first icon, Victor Trumper, just before the turn of the century, to put them firmly back on the winning track and also to give the game there an important boost. Trumper took the art of batting to new levels, as Ranji had done in England. He played in forty-eight Tests, scoring just over 3,000 runs with an average of less than 40: figures which do not begin to tell the whole story.

Trumper, whose father was born in England, was a remarkable mixture. He did not have the oriental wizardry of Ranji and yet he was equally bewildering. Bowl him six identical good length balls and each one would hit the boundary in a different place. No two strokes would be the same and yet neither the bowler, the fielders, nor the spectators would have had any idea where the ball was going. He concealed his intentions even more than Ranji. While those watching at close quarters could not tell where the ball was going, even at the moment of impact, Trumper knew exactly. The straight good length ball was the one which asked for it the most when Trumper was batting and he dispatched it according to his whim for he had all the strokes. He was at his best batting on a pitch which the rain had turned into a real old fashioned 'sticky', where the ball leapt at the batsman's face from a good length. It was as though he knew that these conditions called for an extra special effort. Maybe there were other times when there was nothing much in it, and he was not too bothered. How else can you reconcile a Test average of only 39 with the genius which belonged to Trumper?

He was an unusual human being, too. Completely without side or arrogance and modest to a fault, his approach to life never changed. He was an extremely generous and kind-hearted man. If a fellow player took a particular liking to a bat he was using, he would give it to him. If there was a bad seat in a train, he would always take it and, on long journeys,

if there was a compartment over the wheels, Trumper would make sure he had it. He never stopped helping other people and nothing was too much for him. It is rare to find someone like this in any walk of life, let alone in the cricketing world where so many spend their lives looking after no one but themselves. His father was unlikely to have been born in Yorkshire. He was especially loved by children and they found him so easy to approach. It was during his Testimonial match in Sydney that he left the pavilion, went out of the entrance gate at the Paddington end of the ground and walked a fair way round to the entrance at the back of the Hill. He had a pocketful of threepenny pieces, the entrance fee for children, and handed them out one by one to the crowd of urchins. They were waiting there for him because he had done this so many times before.

Often when Trumper returned home to Paddington after making a big score at the Sydney Cricket Ground, he would have a hit with the lads in the lane behind their houses. They didn't think much of him because he let them bowl him out. When he ran a sports shop, a boy would come in to buy a composition ball and would go out with a couple of bats, stumps and bails, pads and gloves all for the price of the sixpence which was the cost of the composition ball. Yet there was a seam of iron in his soul. When a cocky young bowler told everyone he could get Trumper out, it got back to the Great Man. When their teams met in a grade match at Hampden Oval (now called the Trumper Oval), the young spinner was brought on to bowl at him. Trumper faced ten balls and in five minutes had scored 50 off nine of them.

In another grade match he played against the young Arthur Mailey who could hardly believe his luck. Mailey bowled leg breaks and googlies and spun the ball a mile. He was another of the great characters of Australian cricket, an extremely funny man and a brilliant cartoonist. It was as if his role in life, besides taking English wickets, was to try and stop the world taking itself too seriously. When he came on to bowl at Trumper that day, his second ball – Mailey claims not to be able to remember the first – a perfect leg break, was driven to the offside boundary with the best shot he had ever seen. Later in the over, which he feared might be the only one he would get, he decided to try his googly. The spin made the ball curve in the air away from the right-hander, and it pitched in the right place. Mailey himself goes on:

> As at the beginning of my over, he sprang into attack but did not realise that the ball, being an off-break, was floating away from him and dropping a little quicker. In a split second Vic grasped this and tried to make up the deficiency with a wider swing of the bat. It was then that I could see a passage-way to the stumps with our keeper, Con Hayes, ready to claim his victim. Vic's bat came through like a flash but the ball passed between his bat and legs, missed the stumps by a fraction, and the bails were whipped off with the great batsman at least two yards out of his ground ... As he walked past me he smiled, patted the back of his bat and said: It was too good for me.' There was no triumph in me as I watched the receding figure. I felt like a boy who had killed a dove.

When Charlie Macartney made 345 against Nottingham-shire, he said to his fellow players while reading the paper the next morning: 'It says here that my innings was reminiscent of Trumper. What rot! I wasn't fit to tie up Vic's laces as a batsman.' Trumper once lifted George Hirst over the square leg boundary. His captain went up to Hirst who could only say, 'But look at his legs. Look at his legs, right in front of wicket.'

'Never mind his legs,' came back the reply, 'look at where the ruddy ball is.'

On a 'sticky' in Melbourne in 1904, he faced Hirst and Rhodes on the pitch of their dreams and yet both ended up bowling wide of the off stump in defence, while Trumper made

74 of Australia's 122. Statistics tell so little of the story of Trumper, the man, and how cruel it was that in 1915 he should have died from Bright's disease at the age of thirty-seven.

There were so many wonderful characters who played such an important part in the Golden Age and it is a crime that I have got this far without mentioning either of those two canny Yorkshiremen who have just crept into the last paragraph on the receiving end of Victor Trumper, George Hirst and Wilfred Rhodes. They posed the amusing question. Who, apart from WG, was the greatest allrounder? The only possible answer: 'He batted right-handed and bowled left; and he came from Kirkheaton as they both did.' They played for thirty-eight and thirty-three years respectively with all-round figures to match. They were doughty, streetwise and pitchwise Yorkshiremen who kept both their county and their country at the centre of cricketing affairs. The stories of both are legion.

When Yorkshire played Gloucestershire, Jessop made stirring hundreds in both innings. Rhodes took a pounding from the Croucher, but still took 14/192 in the match. Hirst just failed to equal Jessop's feat, making 111 and 92.

'Why, George,' said an admirer, 'you did nearly as well as Mr Jessop.'

'No,' replied Hirst weighing it up briefly, 'his was against good bowling.'

Years later, Rhodes talked to the author and journalist, A.A. Thomson, about this match. 'Jessop was a terror, and he'd tanned us so hard in the match before we reckoned in this game we'd make him go and fetch 'em. So we bowled wide on the offside. He fetched 'em all right. He went off like a spring-trap and, before you'd seen his feet move, he was standing on the offside of his stumps, pulling 'em over the square leg boundary. After the tanning he gave us that day, we made up our minds we'd never let him fetch 'em again, it was too expensive. Ever afterwards we bowled so tight he never put a big score up against us again. No. I'm wrong.

There was one. But I hardly like to tell you about that one.' (In 1901, Jessop made 233 for the Rest against the Champion county.) On another occasion Rhodes was asked to reveal the secret of his brilliant running between the wickets with Jack Hobbs. 'I'll tell you,' he said, 'when I'm coming, I say *Yes*, and when I'm not, I say *No.*'

These stories encapsulate Hirst and Rhodes as they were. Jessop's reputation isn't damaged either.

I have still left out the best bowler of them all who had a strange career and was never the easiest of men. Sydney Barnes played in twenty-seven Test Matches between 1901 and 1914 in which he took 189 wickets, including 14/144 in his last against South Africa in Durban. If it had not been for his sheer bloody-mindedness, he would have been a permanent member of the England side at this time because he was a genius with a cricket ball in his hand. He had a colossal chip on his shoulder about almost everything, especially about those in authority and what he saw as his rights. He was also after every penny he could get which was why he spent almost his entire career, apart from two full seasons for Lancashire in 1901 and 1902, playing in the Leagues. He was better paid there than he would have been by Lancashire or Warwickshire, the two first-class counties for whom he turned out. He reckoned he was always undervalued and underpaid, that he never got the recognition he deserved and was constantly overworked. He downed tools at the slightest provocation and throughout his career none of the sides he played for could be sure of his loyalty. If he felt he had suffered an injustice, he withdrew his labour and sulked. He worked as a civil servant and had the most impeccable copperplate hand writing, but overall he must have been a grumpy old sod.

It is no exaggeration to say that he was the best bowler there has ever been. He advanced the art of bowling just as WG, Ranji and Trumper had taken forward the art of batting.

The only difference was that in Barnes's case there was no one able to take it on from him. He bowled at more than medium pace and was able to spin from leg and from off with equal facility and without any change of action. He ran in for twelve paces, moving effortlessly up to the crease before a final, smooth upward leap. His leg break was his most devastating weapon and it was delivered with the palm of his hand and his wrist facing the batsman without any rotation of the wrist. He spun the ball with his immensely strong fingers. Because he imparted a considerable amount of spin, the leg break first swerved in towards the batsman's pads before turning back the other way, and the off break swerved to the off before breaking back into the batsman. His tally of 6,229 wickets in all matches, at a cost of 8.33 each, is ample evidence of his many skills.

Barnes's inscrutability was never more apparent than when he was asked to try and explain how he managed to bowl as he did. As an old man he was interviewed by John Arlott:

'Now, the legend is that even on perfect wickets you bowled a leg break. What about this particular ball?'

'Well, I don't know; it came along with the others,' was the unhelpful reply.

'How did you bowl it?'

'For a fast ball, a fast leg break was exactly the same as bowling an off break.'

'Did you spin it off the third finger?'

'Yes, every ball I bowled I had to spin – fast, slow or medium.'

Maybe Barnes wanted the secret to die with him, for he was decisive enough in all the other aspects of his life. He was bowling at J.T. Tyldesley who, after his retirement, was captaining the Lancashire Second XI against Staffordshire. Tyldesley was dropped at slip off the last ball of an over and Barnes didn't move.

'What's the matter?' his captain asked him.

'Why,' said Barnes, 'did so-and-so miss that catch?'

'Well – I suppose he just missed it.'

Again Barnes asked, 'Why did he miss that catch?'

'Oh, Barnes, how should I know? Anyhow, he missed it.'

'I'll tell you why he missed it,' Barnes went on. 'He wasn't ready. What's more, Tyldesley won't play forward again all day.'

Barnes was taken to Australia by Archie MacLaren in 1901/02 on the basis of one game for Lancashire which caused a fair number of eyebrows to be raised. Barnes played in the first two Tests in which he took nineteen wickets. A knee injury then put him out of the rest of the tour and long before the end he had succeeded in alienating just about everyone, including MacLaren. They were crossing the Tasman Sea to New Zealand after the Australian leg of the tour when a ferocious storm blew up and they feared for their lives. When it was at its fiercest, MacLaren was heard to say, 'Well, there's one consolation. If we go down that bugger Barnes will go down with us.' Barnes was chosen for the Third Test in England the following year and after taking six Australian wickets for 49, was dropped for the Fourth which suggested that he had had another inconvenient attack of principle along the way. He was never happy to comply with the demands of the feudal system which were still very much in operation. He came up against MacLaren again when he refused to sign a contract for Lancashire for the following season. MacLaren dropped him for the last county match, but Barnes turned up, changed and went out onto the field. He had to be ordered back into the pavilion. He was never one for tugging his forelock in the prescribed manner. He is more likely to have pioneered a rudimentary gesture involving two fingers.

His purple period came right at the end of his Test career – just before the outbreak of the Great War. At the age of thirty-eight he was taken to Australia in 1911/12, the first time he had been picked as of right rather than as a replacement. The Second Test was played at Melbourne and Australia

won the toss and batted. In no time at all, they were 11/4 with Bardsley, Kelleway, Hill, and Armstrong back in the pavilion and Barnes had taken all four for the single which Hill had taken off the first ball he faced. Barnes went on to take thirty-four wickets in the series and England won 4-1. The 1912 summer in England, which was dreadfully wet, saw the Triangular Tournament between England, Australia and South Africa. In five Tests Barnes picked up thirty-nine wickets and took England to victory in the competition. In the First Test against Australia, at Lord's, he went wicketless and Charlie Macartney, known because of his manner and his style as the Governor-General, made 99.

Some years later at a dinner in Oxford, Ian Peebles, who himself bowled leg breaks for England, asked Macartney just how good Barnes was. The Governor-General wrinkled his brow and paused in careful thought before replying without trace of affectation.

'I'll tell you how good he was. In 1912 as I went out to bat I told the chaps I was going to hit this Barnes for six.'

He paused again to give full weight to the point before adding, 'I had to wait until I had scored 68 before I did.'

The following winter Barnes was off again, this time to see what he could make of the matting wickets in South Africa. He never found another surface which suited him so well and he was virtually unplayable taking forty-nine wickets in the first four Test Matches. This meant that he had taken 122 wickets in fifteen Test Matches, in one of which he didn't bowl because of rain at Manchester. In spite of his success in South Africa Barnes was still not at peace with his fellow human beings. Having taken all those wickets, he flatly refused to play in the last Test as another point of principle jumped up and smacked him behind the ear. The South African cricket authorities had promised Barnes they would do something to help him financially because he had taken his wife and son out with him for health reasons. They didn't do what they said they would and so, inevitably, he dug in his toes. If Barnes had been able to fit in and to toe the line through his career, he would surely have broken all the records in the book. In 1938, at the age of sixty-five, he was still playing for Bridgnorth in Shropshire and that year he took 126 wickets at an average of 6.94. What an extraordinary contradiction he was.

Another figure who was important at this time was the enigmatic Pelham (Plum) Warner, a good but by no means great batsman who captained England against Australia and South Africa. All his cricketing life he had effectively been a lackey of Lord Harris, the ruler of Lord's, whom he revered and, like Lord Harris, he was a passionate imperialist. It was C.B. Fry who talked of Pelham Warner 'being groomed for the role of pavilion magnate' and who called him, a trifle patronisingly, 'an imperturbably accomplished school bats-man.' In his recent excellent book, *A Social History of English Cricket*, Derek Birley goes so far as to describe Warner as 'The ultimate establishment man, equally facile with bat, pen and political manoeuvre and a travelling salesman for cricket.' In spite of a hundred in his first Test Match, against South Africa, Warner, a small and rather mouse-like figure, was one who, whenever in doubt, used his pads as a first rather than a second line of defence. He was, not surprisingly, therefore, strongly opposed to any change in the lbw law. He was a man who, through most of the eighty-nine years of his life, and in any eventuality, seemed to use his pads rather than his bat if he thought he could get away with it. Warner was born in Trinidad and was perhaps never able to forget his colonial past.

He captained England in ten of the fifteen Test matches he played, but was never the first choice for the job. When Mac-Laren was not made captain for the 1903/04 tour of Australia because of his journalistic activities, Warner was offered the job, although he was even more involved with Fleet Street.

This never counted against him and in 1926, when he was the chairman of the selectors, he was also the cricket correspondent of the *Morning Post*. Those in charge at Lord's must have been pretty sure that he would give unwavering support. Warner was not a strong man in any sense of the word. Once, when he was getting runs for Middlesex against Yorkshire, George Hirst said of him, 'If God had given him "a proper stummick" he would have had all the bowlers looking both ways for Sunday.' Harry Altham, himself a great establishment man and also at least a minor saint, said in his *History of Cricket* that of all the important figures in the game, there was 'none better loved than that of Plum Warner, the Happy Warrior, in his Harlequin cap.' Maybe the wish was the father of the thought. Soon after the Boer War Warner was in Cape Town where he met Rudyard Kipling who had just written those disparaging lines, 'With the flannelled fools at the wicket or the muddied oafs at the goals.' Warner was with a soldier who had been a notable rugger player and now asked Kipling if he might not have been rather too hard on sportsmen. I wonder what Warner made of the Great Man's reply which was, 'You have to hit an Englishman more than once on the jaw before he will take a thing seriously.'

Warner's journalism was prolific, but it was almost as if he did not want to admit to it. When he reported matches in which he was playing for *The Times* where all writers were anonymous, he would refer to himself in the text as 'Mr Warner', presumably to try and further the process of mystification.

Nothing has been more enigmatic in the entire history of cricket than Warner's role as manager of the Bodyline tour to Australia in 1932/33. He seemed to spend those few months leaping first one way over the fence and then other, in addition to spending an uncomfortably long time perched precariously on the top of it. We will come to that more fully in another chapter. Meanwhile, although his presence was almost guaranteed in the committee room at Lord's, where the movers and shakers will, no doubt, have been more than grateful for his support, his main role seems to have been in agreeing with other people's initiatives rather than pushing forward with his own. He was extremely good at coming out with such things as, 'The very word cricket has become a synonym for all that is true and honest.' The irony of this particular sentence is that it is taken from a speech he made soon after arriving in Australia at the start of the Bodyline series in which he cut such a curiously fragile figure.

Like many weak men it appeared that he used his power to frustrate those who couldn't easily fight back . . .: or so he thought. On the 19th February 1926 he was asked as the principal guest to the annual dinner of the Gloucestershire County Cricket Club at the Grand Hotel in Bristol. One of the players there was Charlie Parker, the left-arm spinner, who played in 602 games for Gloucestershire and took a total of 3,278 first-class wickets. Yet he only played in one Test Match and was convinced that the man who had stood in his way was Warner. When the dinner ended, Parker and his chum, Reg Sinfield, decided to go up in the lift to the balcony at the top of the hotel for some fresh air. The lift was full when suddenly the attendant shouted, 'Make way, make way. This is Mr Pelham Warner', who was on his way up to bed. Parker's eyes blazed and in a flash he had grabbed Warner by the coat's lapels, if not the throat, and gave speech:

'I'll never in my life make way for that bugger. He never once had a good word to say for me. The so-and-so has blocked my Test career . . . . Make way for him . . . . ? Mr Bloody Warner will go to bed when I've finished with him.'

For a moment the grip tightened before Sinfield said to him, 'Come on, Charlie. T'isn't worth it.' The grip slackened and Warner scurried up the stairs to his room. What is more, he never once mentioned the incident to any of his friends.

The Golden Age produced the googly. B.J.T. Bosanquet, who began life as a fastish bowler and no mean batsman, found the pitches pretty unhelpful and, right at the end of his four years at Oxford, hit upon the googly. He found while playing 'twisty-grab' on the billiard table, that he could produce an off break with a leg break action. He had then practised this playing stump cricket and bowling to his friends in the nets. He bowled it for the first time in the University match at Lord's in 1900. The first wicket he took with it was that of an earnest left-handed batsman from Leicestershire called Sam Coe who suffered the indignity of being stumped after the ball had bounced four times, when he had made 98. Bosanquet was never able to control his 'bosie', as it is still called in Australia, as well as later exponents of the art managed to do, but nonetheless it helped him win two Test Matches for England. In March 1903, returning from New Zealand, the first bosie he bowled in Australia hit Victor Trumper's middle stump which was not a bad way to start.

Bosanquet played his first Test for England at Sydney in 1903/4 and took three pretty expensive wickets. This was a match made more memorable for the first appearance of Reggie Foster, the oldest of the three Worcestershire brothers. He made 287 in his first innings for England, which remained a record for Ashes matches until Don Bradman made 334 at Leeds in 1930. Foster, who took the late cut to new levels, only played eight Tests and was never available to play against Australia in England. He was free to captain England against South Africa in 1907, when England won, but died of diabetes at the age of thirty-six.

On the tour in 1903/04, Bosanquet took 6/51 in Australia's second innings in the fourth Test at Sydney and made sure England regained the Ashes. In 1905, at Trent Bridge, he took 8/107 against Australia in the First Test, ensuring another England victory. He had been dropped from the side by the Fourth Test of that series, and at the end of the year gave up regular cricket after taking twenty-five wickets in his seven Test Matches. His son, Reggie, became the past master of the art of reading the news on Independent Television until a colourful lifestyle kyboshed him at a relatively early age.

Bosanquet may only have appeared briefly in the footlights, but he was another innovator who imposed himself on his art and gave it a new weapon. England were themselves soon to fall foul of his invention. The South African, Reggie Schwarz, had been present at the birth of Bosanquet's googly and also played for Middlesex. He was now to use it to good effect against the Englishmen when they visited the Cape in 1905/06 under Plum Warner and lost 4–1. Not content with Schwarz who, in practising the googly, had lost the ability to bowl the leg break and as a result bowled a non-stop diet of bosies, the South Africans had Vogler, White and Faulkner in their side who could also bowl googlies. This in addition to one of the most curiously named of all Test cricketers, 'Tip' Snooke, an opening bowler rather than a googly merchant, who took twelve wickets in the Third Test of that series. Three years before South Africa had called upon the services of one Percy Twentyman-Jones for one Test against Australia. With a name like that, his natural habitat should surely have been

a saloon bar with pistols on each hip, eager to become Percy Twentyoneman-Jones. In his only Test he made nought in each innings, but it is a name which trips off the tongue and lingers most satisfyingly on although he later, and rather faint-heartedly, called himself simply, P.S.T. Jones. It was not long after England's trial by googly in South Africa, that Australia had Dr H.V. Hordern to bowl leg breaks and googlies against England in 1911/12. After that, along came Arthur Mailey, Clarrie Grimmett, and Bill O'Reilly and many more in the long line of Australian googly bowlers stretching down to Shane Warne. Then, there were all those wrist spinners from the Subcontinent and elsewhere. Bosanquet was on to something and did not want for disciples.

CHAPTER 6

A HERO OF
THE PEOPLE

JACK HOBBS is one of the most important figures in the history of cricket. His genius enabled the art of batting to develop further from the point at which it had been left by WG. As we have seen, it had already been embellished by the lovely lingering touches applied so delightfully by Ranji and Fry, and by Trumper and Jessop. Hobbs was now to take the essence of all these influences and blend them into a composite whole, just as WG had assembled under one roof all the many threads of batting which had been the brainchildren of all those splendid characters from the game's middle ages. Don Bradman was to be the next master figure to take this act of consolidation further still. Hobbs's first game for Surrey was in 1905 against the Gentlemen of England, captained by WG. His last Test Matches were played against Australia in 1930 when the young Bradman broke all records by scoring 974 runs in the series. Hobbs's first-class career came to an end four years later, when he had score 61,237 runs and made 197 hundreds. His had been an overwhelming mastery which had begun at the Oval on a bitterly cold Easter Monday twenty-nine years earlier and had got better and better.

There will be those reading this book who will complain that the arrival of Hobbs has been left much too late. Of

course, he was another figure from the Golden Age and was at his first pinnacle in the last three years of peace. Yet, like so many others, the Great War split his career in half and the second half of Hobbs transcended all that he had achieved in the first. To have included him earlier would have meant mixing up pre-war and post-war and would have got us all into a muddle.

Hobbs's records speak for themselves. What made him such a remarkable figure was the commonplace nature of his background – in Cambridge his father had been a net bowler at Fenner's – and this made him the game's first genuine folk hero. In their own ways Hirst and Rhodes had, by the time they had become famous, turned into Yorkshire figures who were cunning and larger than life. They became the epitome of Yorkshiredom and Yorkshireness and cricket was their stage. Hobbs never allowed himself to poke his nose in front of the rest of the pack; he never knowingly hogged the stage. There remained within him all his career the humble, nervous country boy who first came to the Oval for a trial, pointed in the right direction by Cambridgeshire's other famous cricketing son, Tom Hayward, who had also made his home at the Oval.

Hobbs was almost invariably in the limelight because of the runs he scored but, far from ever consciously seeking the limelight, he did his utmost to avoid it. There was no swank or side about Hobbs who took nothing for granted. He was unassuming and unobtrusive and his nature was retiring and temperate. He merged into the crowd, whether coming out of the pavilion with the fielding side or leaving the ground at the end of the day. In private, he had a delightfully impish sense of humour but never would have allowed himself to be seen as a wag by the crowd. He wanted to be as inconspicuous as possible. It was his very ordinariness which was responsible for his immense popularity because it was so easy for the public to identify with him. Hobbs was truly representative

'Squire' Osbaldeston was a fearless striker of the ball and from his appearance, not a man with whom to pick an argument.

Frederick, Prince of Wales, hits the right note at Cliveden House with his sisters, the eighteenth-century equivalent of the Brontë sisters. It was at Cliveden that he was hit on the head by a cricket ball, a blow that led to his death in 1751.

John Nyren was a distinguished chronicler, of the broadsheet rather than the tabloid variety. His father presided and resided at the Bat and Ball Inn at Hambledon.

The Bat and Ball Inn at Hambledon is the most famous of all cricket's many watering holes.

The great, the good and the hirsute with WG in charge – the England team in 1887, the centenary year of the MCC.
Top row R.G. Barlow, W. Scotton, W. Barnes, A.N. Hornby
Middle row Hon. A. Lyttleton, W.G. Grace, A.G. Steel, Lord Harris
Bottom row G.Ulyett, W.W. Read, A. Shrewsbury.

A galaxy of all the leading cricketers, Gents and Players, in English cricket in 1880, show how dress had evolved since the Hambledon days. It is not difficult to spot W.G. Grace.

Although not his normal stock-in-trade, Gilbert Jessop, 'The Croucher', shows that legside subtleties can be the order of the day, if need be.

WG with his merry Gentlemen in their annual joust with the Players at Lord's in 1898, WG's last season in Test cricket.

George Hirst, Wilfred Rhodes and Schofield Haig in 1905. Lord Hawke's shock troops for Yorkshire look distinctly benign, benevolent and battle-hardened.

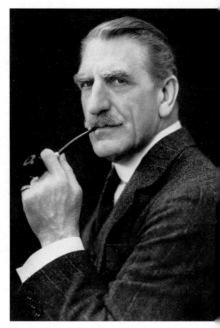

'The Demon', the darkly sinister F.R. Spofforth, whose fast bowling played such a part in Australia's early successes over England.

Sir Charles Aubrey Smith with a Hollywood villain in his sights rather than a recalcitrant umpire.

Below A boyish Victor Trumper models a turn-of-the-century and not particularly fetching long-sleeved sweater.

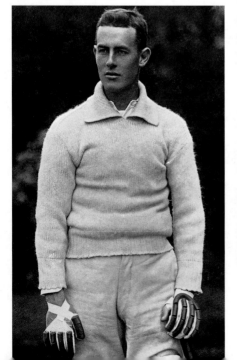

Above The famous photograph of Trumper closing in for the kill. The bowler and umpire, if they had any sense, will have already gone to ground.

Above 'The Ministry of all the talents'. C.B.
Fry in 1903 is about to destroy yet another
bowling attack, and maybe to tick off the
dressing-room attendant for not making
much of a job of his pads.

Below Learie Constantine, later Lord
Constantine, announced the arrival of a
whole generation of dashing West Indian
cricketers.

Above 'Plum' Warner, not perhaps the
figure of schoolboy innocence the
photographs so often portray.

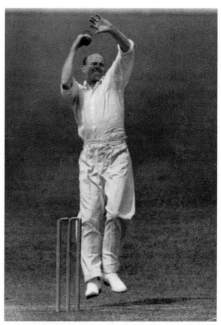

Above 'Tiger' Bill O'Reilly, maybe the best
leg spinner of them all, possessed a tongue
and a pen which both imparted at least as
much spin as his right hand.

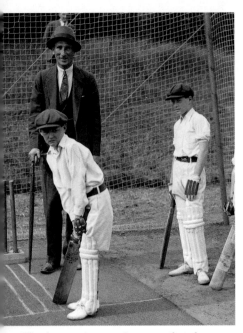

The dapper city gent is none other than Douglas Jardine at his most avuncular, judging young hopefuls in a net at a garden party in Regent's Park in June 1934.

Jack Hobbs, balanced and imperious, dismisses one from his presence – watched from behind the stumps by the Ancient Mariner.

With a distinctly unfriendly bodyline field of six short legs, Harold Larwood whistles one past Bill Woodfull.

Walter Hammond tosses at The Oval in 1938 as a smiling Don
Bradman prepares to guess wrong. Watching is the legendary and
jovial groundsman 'Bosser Martin', on whose pitch England made
903/7 declared.

ord Hawke turns in his grave. Len Hutton leads out England against India at Old Trafford
the first series in which England are captained by a professional.

Poetry in motion – one of the great actions of all time. Ray Lindwall bowls against England at The Oval in 1953.

Keith Miller in the paddock at Epsom in 1956 with the Duke of Norfolk (*centre*) and the Earl of Roseberry who played for Surrey as Lord Dalmeny.

Jim Laker (*left*) celebrates his tally of a mere 9/37 in the first innings against Australia at Old Trafford in 1956. He went one better in the second with 10/53. Fred Trueman doesn't quite know what to make of it.

of anyone and everyone who came through the turnstiles at the Oval or wherever. He was a heavy smoker in an age when there was thought to be nothing wrong with that and it was perhaps one more way in which people could identify with him. He was hero-worshipped to such an extent by one admirer who faithfully dogged his footsteps and picked up all the fag ends the great Man dispatched into the gutter. This chap kept this celebrated and concentrated mass of nicotine in a tin box, although history does not reveal what became of it. It was impossible for schoolboys to identify in the same way with WG or Ranji or Fry. They were giants who could be admired and cheered to the echo but they came from faraway. Hobbs was always the man from next door whose problems seemed to be as if they were one's own. It was as though Hobbs's skills were owned by the people. He made everyone feel that it was they who were out there scoring all those runs and not him.

In that first match, for Surrey against the Gentlemen of England, Hobbs made 88 in the second innings before he hooked, a trifle rashly, at Walter Brearley and was caught at square leg. As he walked out the bowler said to him, 'I should drop that stroke if I were you.' 'I didn't drop it,' Hobbs said looking back on the moment. 'I learned how to do it properly.' The twenty-two-year-old Hobbs knew where he was going. Earlier in his innings he had faced WG himself and it was not long before he had experienced the old man's craftiness. He was about to embark upon a quick single when he was stopped by the urgent request from WG to tap the ball back to save him from having to retrieve it himself. Hobbs's first county match came next, against Essex, and in the second innings he made 155. He finished the match by holding a catch in the outfield and the crowd followed him to the gates of the pavilion. His captain, Lord Dalmeny, awarded him his county cap there and then as he came off the ground and I wonder how many cricketers have been awarded their county

cap after only two games. Even this heady start made not the slightest difference to Hobbs's demeanour. He never let his hair down lower than that shy grin and his greatest excess will have been to light another cigarette. He was always a most amusing companion with a happy sense of humour and impeccable manners.

He went to Australia in 1907/08 under Arthur Jones and, after being chosen for the Second Test Match in which he made 83 in the first innings, he was never dropped by England for loss of form throughout the rest of his career. In South Africa, two years later, he and Wilfred Rhodes, who had come together as openers for the first time, laid the bogey of the quartet of South African googly bowlers, although England lost the series by three matches to two. The 1911/12 tour of Australia saw the high point of Hobbs's pre-war batting style when, given the chance, he was down the pitch and at the bowlers. While Barnes and Frank Foster bowled out the Australians, Hobbs and Rhodes made sure that England were not short of runs. Captained by J.W.H.T. Douglas when Pelham Warner, the official captain, had been taken ill soon after arriving in Australia, England won the series 4–1. Then came the Triangular Tournament in 1912, and the tour to South Africa in 1913/14. Hobbs and Barnes were mainly responsible for winning both.

One of Hobbs's regular colleagues at this time was Frank Woolley who many have thought, especially those living in Kent where they treat their own almost as seriously as they do in Yorkshire, was the most gloriously elegant batsman ever to have struck a cricket ball. In a career which lasted for thirty-two years, he made almost 59,000 runs and took just over 2,000 wickets and hung onto a small matter of 1,018 catches in an almost matter-of-fact cack-handed way. Artistically, left-handers are born with an advantage over right-handers in that there is a natural beauty about their stroke making which does not belong to those who bat the right

way round. No one can surely ever have hit a cricket ball with a gentler, more unhurried touch and with a greater timing and felicity than Woolley. The fastest bowling was dispatched with time to spare and after the two overs he always needed to acclimatise himself, there was nowhere safe to bowl at him. All his strokes came from a great lazy arc of the bat and it was Robertson-Glasgow who wrote of Woolley: 'There was all summer in a stroke by Woolley, and he batted as it is sometimes shown in dreams.' Not to be outdone, Cardus put it another way: 'An innings by Woolley begins from the raw material of cricket and goes far beyond.' Those who saw them both say that Graeme Pollock has been the nearest equivalent which gives a strong clue as to what we missed. Woolley was perhaps the closest cricket has ever come to producing a Rudolf Nureyev.

The only blemish on Hobbs's record in this period was a slightly inconsistent record for Surrey, although he had much to do with their winning of the Championship in 1914. One of his rare failures came against Middlesex at the Oval when he made only 4, although Surrey still went on to reach more than 500. The following July morning, one Gavrilo Prinzip shot and killed the Archduke Franz Ferdinand at Sarajevo which set in motion a series of Test Matches played mostly in France which were to change things for ever. There was just time for Hobbs and Hayward to hit 122 each against Kent, and Hobbs then made 226 against Nottinghamshire at the Oval and another hundred against Worcester. His benefit match against Kent had to be transferred to Lord's because the Oval had been requisitioned by the army, and it was over in two days. After that Hobbs and Hayward were still able to put on 290 for the first wicket against Yorkshire, their last century partnership, but, by then, Kaiser Bill had already handed his sweater to the umpire and was marking out his long run. Eventually the season was closed down by the strength of public opinion reinforced by a letter to *The Times*

by WG. The Germans had invaded Belgium and the Battle of the Marne was the next engagement on the fixture list.

Jack Hobbs spent the first two years of the war working in a munitions factory before joining the RAF. He got the all clear early in 1919 and returned to the Oval to try and carry on as if nothing had happened. Inevitably, the game was in a turmoil and the huge casualty lists of the five years had made as big an impact on cricket as they had on all other walks of life. Hobbs's return to the Oval was one of the few reassuring indications that some things remained the same.

The first barmy post-war decision was that County Championship matches were to be played over two days instead of three in order to take advantage of the long light evenings. By playing until half past seven it was hoped that it would tempt a lot of people to come along after work. All it did was to make the players extremely tired and produce an inordinate number of drawn matches. After one year they went back to three-day games. Cricket's administrators have seldom been touched by common sense.

Just as the Second World War was to do twenty-five years later, the Great War had a much worse effect on English than it did on Australian cricket. Considering the proximity of England to much of the action, and the country's inevitably greater involvement, Gallipoli notwithstanding, this was not surprising. The immediate and profound legacy of the massive slaughter which took place just across the road, as it were, is impossible to understand. England went to Australia in 1920/21 under the worthy and persevering Johnny Douglas and lost all five Test Matches. In addition to Hobbs and Douglas, Wilfred Rhodes, Patsy Hendren, Frank Woolley and Herbert Strudwick had all survived the hostilities and claimed back their places. Injury prevented Hobbs from playing in the series in England in 1921 which was dominated by Australia's formidable pair of opening bowlers, Jack Gregory and Ted McDonald. He only played one innings against them, early in

the tour, when he turned out for Lionel Robinson, a rich philanthropist whose money was never able to buy him the social success he craved, on his delightful ground at Old Buckenham near Attleborough. It was there that Hobbs took on the full might of Gregory and McDonald in difficult conditions and made 85 before he again pulled a muscle he had first injured in Australia the winter before. Hobbs, when pressed, reckoned this was probably the best innings he played in his life.

When it came to the Test series that year, England, without Hobbs, found that time had taken its toll and there was no Sydney Barnes or Frank Foster. The younger Australians under Warwick Armstrong, who was bigger than ever, giving the impression of a ship of the line under full sail and making two centuries in the series, were a formidable side. It was Armstrong, fielding in the deep on a windy day at the Oval in the Fifth Test in 1921, who picked up a sheet of a newspaper which was blowing past and appeared studiously to read it. When asked what he was doing, he said he wanted to find out who they were playing. He contracted malaria while serving in New Guinea during the war. He felt a bout coming on while waiting with his pads on to go out and bat during a Test against England in 1920/21. He immediately sent to the bar for two stiff whiskies, drank them both without water and went out and made a hundred. He was gallant enough. Once, in a Test Match at Old Trafford he bowled consecutive overs from different ends on either side of a hold up after Lionel Tennyson had illegally declared the England innings. Armstrong knew exactly what he was doing and no one enjoyed the joke more. This begs the question of whether the umpires were too frightened of this enormous and hugely dictatorial man, or whether they were not attending. I suspect the latter, but at least they were not able to be caught out by the dreaded television replays.

In 1921, the still broke Archie MacLaren, who was then forty-nine, boasted that he could pick a side which would

beat Armstrong's invincible Australians. At the end of their tour he was given the chance to prove his point when his eleven played the Australians at the Saffrons at Eastbourne. He picked six of the Cambridge side whom he had watched lose to the Australians by an innings earlier in the summer. There were the three Ashton brothers, Gilbert, Hubert and Claude, C.S. Marriott, Percy Chapman and Clem Gibson. He also enlisted the services of Aubrey Faulkner, the South African googly merchant who was now thirty-eight, G.N. Foster, one of the famous brothers, Mike Falcon who captained Norfolk, a Minor County, from 1911 to 1946, and whom MacLaren had proposed as a seam bowler for the Test series. The wicket keeper was George Wood. Marriott was ill and so, in the end, MacLaren plumped for his old Lancashire colleague and friend, Walter Brearley, who was forty-seven. MacLaren won the toss and batted first and his side were bowled out most ignominiously for 43. Brearley, one of only four bowlers, pulled a muscle while batting and took no further effective part in the match. The Australians were then out for 174, but Faulkner now made 153 and Gilbert Ashton 75 and the Australians were left to score 196 to win. When Gibson defeated Arthur Mailey at the end, the Australians were out for 168 and MacLaren had made his point. After the match, he went up to Walter Brearley and thanked him warmly for contributing to the victory. Brearley reminded him that he had not bowled a single ball. MacLaren was quick with his reply: 'Exactly, Walter, that's why we won.' The Fates had been kind because Neville Cardus had defied his sports editor's wishes at the *Manchester Guardian* and travelled down to Eastbourne to write about the match so it is has been well preserved for posterity.

The Test Matches in Australia in 1920/21 had seen the introduction to Test cricket of their idiosyncratic, articulate and highly amusing leg spinner, Arthur Mailey, whom, as a small boy, I was lucky enough to meet towards the end of his

life when he stayed each year with some great friends of my mother and father in west Norfolk, Archie and Ruth Scott. Archie, enormously tall, was the first gentleman bookmaker – and an enormous success he made of it too. Mailey used to come to our boys' cricket matches and we could hardly wait for him to turn up, not because of his fame, although that probably helped, but because he was such fun and loved to take his coat off and bowl us a few leg breaks and googlies. He seemed to enjoy it as much as we did, even though his arthritis must have made it hard work.

Over the years he brought a good many of the former Australian players to Hillington, and then Runcton when the Scotts had moved, including Don Bradman. Nicholas, the youngest of the Scotts, who would not have been out of shorts at the time, well remembers being bowled at on the lawn by Mailey with Bradman keeping wicket. After that, he almost certainly will have felt there was nothing more that life had to offer. Mailey, a prodigious talker, told the story that he once pointed out to Bert Oldfield, his wicket keeper, that Hobbs could not spot his googly. Hobbs himself was inclined to disagree and said that Oldfield had almost certainly agreed with Mailey just to stop him talking. Mailey came from a working-class background from Surry Hills in Sydney, and when he first played for Australia in 1920/21, he went to a reception at Government House. The Governor's wife said to him a trifle patronisingly, 'I expect this is your first visit to Government House.' To which Mailey replied, 'No, I was here a year ago to help fix the gas.' His humour never left him. When, later in life, he kept a butcher's shop in Sydney he sold tripe. Above the tripe on the counter hung a notice which said: 'I bowled tripe, then I wrote tripe and now I sell tripe.'

One of those who was killed in the war was Warwickshire's extremely promising allrounder, Percy Jeeves, who was unwittingly to leave behind him a vastly bigger legacy than anything he can have dreamt about. When he was playing

against Gloucestershire at Cheltenham in 1913, one of the spectators was P.G. Wodehouse. In 1967, PGW replied to a letter from Roland Ryder who had been secretary of Warwickshire and had written asking him if it was Percy Jeeves's name PGW had pinched for his famous manservant. This was PGW's reply:

Dear Mr Ryder,

Yes, you are quite right. It must have been in 1913 that I paid a visit to my parents in Cheltenham and went to see Warwickshire play Glos on the Cheltenham College ground. I suppose Jeeves's bowling must have impressed me, for I remembered him in 1916, when I was in New York and starting the Jeeves and Bertie saga, and it was just the name I wanted. I have always thought till lately that he was playing for Gloucestershire that day. I remember admiring his action very much.

Yours sincerely

P.G. Wodehouse

'Indubitably, Sir,' in other words.

At the end of the war the British public were so involved in rejoicing in their freedom that the results against Australia in 1920/21, when England lost all five Test matches, hardly seemed to matter. While Mailey had a highly successful series, taking thirty-six wickets in the four matches in which he bowled, England had their own idiosyncratic debutant, Rockley Wilson, who professed to bowl leg breaks which tended to roll rather than break. After four years as a Blue at Cambridge, he made his life teaching at Winchester and played for Yorkshire during the school holidays. After heading the national bowling averages in 1921, he was chosen for the tour of Australia, although he was then forty-one. He only played in the Fifth Test in which he took three wickets, but as a conversationalist he was every bit Mailey's equal. During the tour, Wilson upset both the Australians and the MCC by

writing a piece for the *Daily Express* in London in which he was critical of the umpires. The following summer he was in good voice as usual in the Long Room at Lord's when he spotted the advancing Lord Harris and broke off in mid-sentence to greet him and shake him by the hand. No one had been more miffed at Wilson's contribution to the columns of Fleet Street than Lord Harris who now, in a decidedly unfriendly manner, only just broke his stride in acknowledge-ment of Wilson's outstretched hand. After his lordship had swept by, Wilson turned back to his friends and almost cer-tainly while fiddling with his Adam's apple, said to them, 'Lucky to get a touch, really, lucky to get a touch.'

Lord Harris was a martinet and the hardest of nuts to crack. He was obsessed by the need for proper residential qualifica-tions before a player could turn out for a county. No less a person than Walter Hammond had been born in Kent when his father was stationed there as a serving soldier, but had gone to school in Gloucestershire who wanted to claim him. Lord Harris, by his rigid application of the rules, delayed his appearance for Gloucestershire by a year. His justification appeared in *The Cricketer* under the extraordinary heading, 'Effects of Bolshevism'. In it, he had written that, 'Bolshevism is rampant and seeks to abolish all rules and this year cricket has not escaped its attack.' A fellow peer, Lord Deerhurst, who was President of Worcestershire, bumped into Lord Harris in the Long Room where he remarked with considerable feeling, 'May I congratulate your lordship on having buggered the career of another young cricketer.' That other famous cricket-ing peer, Lord Hawke, who had been the top, bottom and sides of Yorkshire cricket for so long, had his say at Yorkshire's county dinner in answer to the suggestion by Cecil Parkin of Lancashire, who had already been labelled a Bolshevik by Pelham Warner, that Hobbs should captain England. 'Pray Heaven no professional may ever captain England.' A touch of social unrest was beginning to creep in, but the old guard,

fearing the worst, were quick to form squares. The Bolshevik Revolution was keeping a lot of people on their toes.

After Douglas had lost the first two Tests against Australia in 1921, the selectors turned to one of the greatest characters ever to have played for, let alone captained, England. The Honourable Lionel Tennyson, the fearless grandson of the Poet Laureate, Alfred, Lord Tennyson, played cricket as he lived life which was with a certain swashbuckle. Looking back to 1914, he said he packed 'in feverish haste, so anxious was I not to run any chance of missing the war'. He was a hard-hitting batsman who was an inspiration but, when it came to trying to stop the Australians, found that he had much in common with King Canute that day when he went for a paddle. He will always be remembered for his heroic batting in the Test at Leeds when he had made 63 and 36 against the fearsome pace of Gregory and McDonald, using only his right hand, having injured the other in the field. He was not a poet himself, although when he was serving in Mesopotamia during the war, he was said to have perpetrated the following:

> I love you, Sue, I love you true,
> I love you in your nightie.
> When the moonlight flits across your tits,
> Oh, Jesus Christ Almighty.

In which case, he should have stuck to it. I have these few lines on the word of the Yorkshire journalist and author, A.A. Thomson, and a more runaway, hirsute character, Buns Cartwright, who was patron saint and governing body of the Eton Ramblers for longer than anyone could remember.

While Jack Hobbs went on piling up the hundreds for Surrey, and against England's opponents too, the Test side did its confidence no harm against a weak South African XI. They then lost in Australia in 1924/25 after putting up much more of a fight than they had four years earlier. The side was

captained by the debonair Arthur Gilligan and during the
series Hobbs and Sutcliffe put on four opening partnerships
of over a hundred. It was Crusoe Robertson-Glasgow's view
that, 'Arthur Gilligan ran up to bowl like the winner from
scratch covering the last twenty yards in the Powderhall
Handicap. He ran nearly as fast as he bowled . . .' which for
a time was very fast indeed. For a year or two he and Maurice
Tate made Sussex's attack the most formidable in the country.
Then Gilligan received a nasty blow over the heart when
batting and his cricket never recovered. He was the truest of
amateurs and played the game without cunning or deception.
There will have been plenty of laughter too, which will have
been presided over by that splendidly impish character from
Middlesex, Patsy Hendren, who scored over 3,500 runs for
England and a great many of them with the hook which was
his *pièce de resistance.* Then came 1926 when the Australians
were again the visitors to England and, after four drawn Tests
played over three days, the final match at the Oval was a
timeless affair. England recalled Wifred Rhodes at the age of
forty-eight and they won in four days by 289 runs with
Rhodes taking six wickets in the match, and four in the second
innings. Hobbs and Herbert Sutcliffe both made hundreds in
the second innings when they put on 172 on a 'sticky' wicket
with one of the great exhibitions of bad wicket batsmanship.

Sutcliffe was Hobbs's fourth and greatest partner. He was
twelve years younger than Hobbs who, when he scored his
hundredth hundred in 1925, had only batted once with Sutcliffe and was rising forty-one. Sutcliffe himself had not
begun his first-class career until he was twenty-four because
of the war. They came together for England in 1924 against
that poor South African side and in the first Test at Edgbaston
they put on 136 for the first wicket. Arthur Gilligan and
Maurice Tate then bundled out South Africa in three-quarters
of an hour for 30. In the Second Test at Lord's their opening
partnership was worth 268 and they never looked back.

Sutcliffe was born in Pudsey but his batting was not of Pudsey. To start with he played the hook and scored many runs from his flowing drives which will have caused a sharp intake of breath among his next door neighbours. He drove and cut with a freedom Pudsey might not have approved of either. He also had a strange hybrid defensive stroke which he played to short-lifting balls on the off stump. He came half forward and twiddled his bat by rolling his wrists and killed the ball stone dead a yard or two up the wicket. This stroke did not come from any known coaching book and old Ted Wainwright would surely have questioned its Christian origins. Wainwright would not have known what to make either of his habit of using eau de Cologne in the dressing room. Sutcliffe talked like an amateur rather than a Yorkshireman, came out of the army with a commission and had his suits made in Savile Row. In spite of all these handicaps, he managed to score more than 50,000 first-class runs and against Australia he made 2,741 at nearly 67 an innings which is a much higher average than any other English batsman has ever managed.

He was a curious mixture. It would have been no surprise if he had played as an amateur, as his own son Billy was to do. When Arthur Carr was sacked from the England captaincy in 1926 and replaced by the young Percy Chapman, Sutcliffe felt strongly that it should have been given to Hobbs. He himself had no wish for the job. Perhaps he felt it would have got in the way of his business interests which of course included serious occupation of the crease. He was not interested in the Yorkshire captaincy either, for in 1928 when he was in South Africa, he received the following letter from the Yorkshire secretary, Mr F.C. Toone:

Dear Herbert,
At the committee meeting yesterday you were appointed Captain without your status being altered. It is hoped that this will be agreeable to you and that you will accept the

same and will be happy and successful in your new and honoured position.

Sutcliffe cabled his reply, not to Toone, but to Lord Hawke.

Official invitation received yesterday. Great honour. Regret to decline. Willing to play under any captain elected.

Presumably he had had no advance indication that he was considered the likely replacement for Major Lupton, but then in those days professional cricketers did what they were told. Sutcliffe's refusal allowed William Worsley, the father of the Duchess of Kent, to take over instead.

Sutcliffe played cricket without any visible emotion. He was neat and precise in appearance with never a hair out of place and his face gave about as much away as a well-made blancmange. Hobbs seemed positively skittish in comparison and he had never found it difficult to smile in that shy way of his. For all their differences, they developed arguably the greatest opening partnership of all time. No two batsmen in history could ever have run better between the wickets and they stole the most extraordinary singles. The basis of their running was that they both implicitly trusted the judgement of the other. You never found Jack Hobbs coming down the wicket at the end of the over and ticking off Sutcliffe for not backing up either. How appropriate it was that the two of them should have played such a big part with that stand of 172 on a rain-affected pitch at the Oval when England won back the Ashes. The other attribute they both possessed *in excelsis*, and which is so important for batting on difficult pitches, was their extraordinary judgement of the ball to leave alone.

By the time England returned to Australia in 1928/29, the face of cricket was beginning to change, even though Hobbs and Sutcliffe were still in place. The West Indies had, in 1928, made their first tour to England, losing all three Tests by an innings; in 1929/30, England were to play a Test series for

the first time in New Zealand and they were to visit India on a similar mission in 1933/34. The body politic of cricket was expanding. The biggest influence of all for change was to lift his head above the parapet for the first time in that series in Australia when for the first ever Test match in Brisbane, one Donald George Bradman, a young man of twenty, was included in the Australian side. It is a matter of history that he failed in this match, making 18 and 1, and was made twelfth man for the Second Test in Sydney. He was reinstated in Melbourne for the Third, where he scored 79 and 112, and was never again dropped from the side. This series in 1928/29 belonged to Walter Hammond who had come into Test cricket the year before in South Africa and whose record suffered only in comparison with Bradman's. He now made 905 runs in the five Test Matches and the only man ever to beat this total had had to settle for those two small scores for Australia in that First Test Match.

CHAPTER 7

LARWOOD'S LEG THEORY

For THE NEXT TWENTY YEARS Don Bradman took over the world of cricket in a way that only one man has done before or since, and that was WG. The shy but self-possessed and articulate country boy from Bowral found himself playing for New South Wales against South Australia in Adelaide in 1927 when he was nineteen. He had taken the place of the injured Archie Jackson, another remarkable young batsman who was to die of tuberculosis at the age of twenty-three. On 16th December, Bradman walked out to bat at the Adelaide Oval and promptly hit the famous leg spinner, Clarrie Grimmett, for two fours in the first over he faced. He reached his 50 in sixty-seven minutes and when he was out for 118, he had become the twentieth Australian to make a hundred on his debut in first-class cricket. In early November the next year he made 87 and 132 not out for New South Wales against MCC, and on 30th November played for Australia in the First Test in Brisbane. When he retired, in 1948/49, he had scored 28,067 first-class runs and hit 117 centuries, one every third time he went out to bat, with an average of 95.14. In fifty-two Test Matches he made 6,996 runs and averaged 99.94. Figures often do not tell the full story. With Don Bradman they most certainly do and, for the English bowlers of the time, it was not a particularly funny one.

Bradman's grandfather had migrated to Australia from a village on the borders of Suffolk and Cambridgeshire and the family had changed their name from Bradsen to Bradman on reaching Australia. His father was a successful farmer, but because of his wife's poor health, the family – Don was the youngest of five children – moved to Bowral from the village of Yeo Yeo. His father, George, turned his attentions to carpentry, while Don was educated at the Bowral Intermediate High School where the facilities for sport were pretty slender. After school each day he amused himself by throwing a golf ball at the brick base of a huge water tank and hitting the rebound with a small stump which did wonders for his reflexes. This was to form the basis for his astonishing cricketing skills. There were no other small boys in the area for him to play with and so he honed his formidable competitive skills by taking on himself and the water tank on a daily basis. It was rather as if Beethoven's introduction to music had come from a comb and piece of loo paper.

Soon after the Great War had ended, his father took him to Sydney to watch one day of a match New South Wales played against Victoria when Charlie Macartney made 87. Many years afterwards, a fellow NSW player, Tim Caldwell, who was also to become President of the Australian Board, was making a speech at the same dinner as Bradman. He let Bradman, a great friend, know what he was going to say. It included a reference to this earlier game as the point at which Caldwell had become hooked on cricket. Caldwell said on the telephone, 'Macartney made 80-odd.'

'What do you mean, 80-odd?' came Bradman's reply. 'It was 87.'

'How do you know that?' Caldwell asked.

'I was there, too,' came the answer.

It was not long before Bradman began to pile up prodigious scores on matting wickets in local country cricket and word soon reached Sydney. He was summoned for a trial by the

New South Wales cricket authorities and then brought down to Sydney to play for the St George club. Grass surfaces were no problem for him either and before long he had made 320 not out in a final against Moss Vale. The following season, 1927/28, he made his way into the New South Wales side.

It is difficult to comprehend the impact Bradman made on Australia with the depression looming and a national hero urgently needed. This perhaps also helps explain the ferocity the public showed when in 1932/33 Douglas Jardine was to try and take him away from them. What type of young man was it who was able to pursue such a relentless path from the very start? Was Bradman a natural loner or was his isolation the result of his phenomenal sporting success in a jealous, greedy and unsympathetic world? Was he in it for the money, for the pursuit of fame or the craving for perfection? He made enemies along the way, but it requires a certain character to be able to accept that without concern and never to feel the need to try and make amends. He was unashamed of his eagerness to make money and saw it as a sort of divine right. It did not worry him either that his colleagues were unable to compete in the same way or indeed that there should be one rule for him and another for everyone else, although he will not have seen it quite like this. The jingle of the till was for ever playing a tune in Bradman's ears.

In 1930, he swept through England scoring 1,000 runs before the end of May, almost 3,000 runs in the season and a record 974 in the five Test Matches. He was not twenty-two until the end of that summer. Yet by then he had settled on the path he was to continue along throughout his career. When WG had kicked over the traces, none of his colleagues seemed to mind too much, for they were prepared to accept that he was in a class of his own and an impressively idiosyncratic character with it – which may have counted for quite a bit. They had shrugged their shoulders and left WG to it. As a man, Bradman was far less conspicuous and suffered as

a consequence. In a world which, even in the 1930s, was becoming increasingly commercial, Bradman's colleagues resented the way in which he would suit himself. Take a cricket bat out of his hand and, unlike WG, they felt he was no different from them. They also resented his superiority as a player and were, not surprisingly, extremely jealous of him. There were some pretty querulous chaps in that Australian side. Bradman was an unrepentant Anglican imperialist, while throughout the thirties there were a number of players like O'Reilly and Fingleton, both doughty and unforgiving opponents, who were staunch Roman Catholics of Irish origin and fiercely nationalistic to boot. There was never much chance of them liking Bradman. Yet he never let any of this get him down, outwardly at any rate, and he continued to amass runs in the same relentless manner throughout his career and twice managed to get over illnesses which came close to killing him.

Bradman's remarkable success from the moment he arrived in England made him enormously popular with the public. But his colleagues who, on previous visits, had rated pretty high in the way of these things, now found they were ignored, while Bradman was being showered with presents and was always the centre of attention. They did not like it. Agents devoted their lives to finding ways to exploit his success. He was offered appearance fees, he was asked to endorse sports goods and a production company made a record of him playing the piano, which he did more than adequately – it is impossible to imagine him doing anything badly. With help from a journalist he was also writing *Don Bradman's Book*. His appetite for money was as insatiable as his appetite for runs and his pursuit of the former did not affect his formidable accrual of the latter. When he made 334 in the Third Test at Headingley, a supporter gave him £1,000, a considerable sum in those days which he did not share with his colleagues and it made him an even greater figure of envy. Australia won

the series 2–1 and all the credit went to Bradman, although there were one or two other useful players in the side like Bill Woodfull, Herbert Ponsford, Clarrie Grimmett, Bert Oldfield and Stan McCabe.

There were those in the team who took the regrettable but all too predictable sour grapes attitude to his success, but there were others who recognised his genius and were happy he should prosper because of it. What his fellow cricketers could not stomach was that Bradman made little or no attempt to bridge the ever-widening gap between himself and his fellow players. They hardly ever saw him off the field. His life was one of non-stop appointments and engagements and just about the only time they caught a glimpse of him was in the pavilion. 'Who's the stranger?' they would ask each other on their occasional sightings of him. Bradman was abstemious and did not smoke and was seldom to be found in a bar. They felt he was not playing a team game and it was here, maybe because of his shyness, that he was particularly insensitive. But then he was a man whose own privacy was always important to him and he did not find it easy to make friends in a hail-fellow-well-met sort of way. It may have been an inbred instinct which made him suspicious of others and as a result he grew further and further apart from his fellow players.

He had a sarcastic sense of humour which was often used to pierce the armoury of a perceived opponent. In the late thirties, Jack Fingleton was going through a stage of being unable to get a run. Before a Test Match in Melbourne, word got around that he took his bat along to the Roman Catholic Archbishop, to have it blessed and sprinkled with Holy Water. Fingleton opened the innings and was out for not very many. Bradman, whose usual habit was to pass the incoming batsman on the grass, delayed his exit from the dressing room until Fingleton had come through the door. Then he picked up his bat and said in his high-pitched voice, 'Well, boys, I'll go and see what I can do with a dry one.' He made a double

century and will not exactly have endeared himself to Fingleton. This incident may have helped acccount for that unfortunate laughter at the Oval in 1948. After the war Bradman took a heavy toll of the Indian bowlers when they toured Australia. He was asked many years later how good a left-arm spinner he thought Vinoo Mankad had been. It took him a moment or two to work out which one he was. 'Oh, yes, I remember,' in the same squeaky voice, 'he was the one who put all the jokers on the offside and I hit him through the legside.' Point made.

His opponents saw little of him too, except when he was batting. As captain he saw no need to respect the tradition of going along to the other dressing room to be introduced to the newcomers in the side. In one game at the Adelaide Oval when South Australia were playing New South Wales, he even used the tannoy to let the fielding side know he had declared. Later in the same match he sent a message to the NSW dressing room inviting them to follow-on. While normal mortals felt the need for net practice in between matches, Bradman did not. He had not picked up a bat for nine days before coming to Headingley for the Third Test in 1930. Australia batted first and he made 105 before lunch, 220 before tea and was 309 not out at the end of the day, which will have turned those of an envious disposition into new shades of greenness. The arrival of that cheque for £1,000 which was more than double a player's tour allowance, will have done nothing to mend relations.

The Great Man was still furious when the Australian Board fined him £50 because part of his book had been serialised in a newspaper. The Board also refused him permission to stay in England at the end of the tour, but then allowed him to leave the ship in Adelaide on the return journey to take part in a project the Board itself had sanctioned. He was flown on ahead of the team to Sydney. Bradman and the rest of the side had been given a tumultuous welcome when the ship

docked in Adelaide and a motor car company used the arrival as a publicity stunt. As a result, Bradman was given a new Chevrolet, the others got nothing. This hardly helped his relations with the rest of the side who did not like being used in a walk-on role to glamorise his fame. More recently, Richard Hadlee was in similar trouble with his New Zealand side on a tour of Australia when he won a car and drove it off over the horizon. It requires unusual generosity to solve these problems to everyone's satisfaction. By then, this self-possessed loner was just twenty-two and he was acting as if this was a preordained course for him to follow. He strode on looking neither to the right nor the left. The tone was set for everything which was to come and he only got away with it because, like WG, he was in a class of his own.

Bradman's phenomenal progress round England in 1930 set in motion a sequence of events which was to have such far-reaching effects that relations between England and Australia were almost terminally damaged. If it had not been so serious, it would have been hysterically funny and goodness knows what a skillful dramatist would have made of it all. The only thing missing would have been the female lead, but I am sure that would have caused an imaginative script writer no problem. Almost seventy years on, most of the principals seem, by the end of it, to be little more than caricatures of themselves. Perhaps the main lesson from the Bodyline story was that the glorious days of empire were crumbling at a fearsome speed. It is frightening that so many important people could have behaved as stupidly as they did without ever coming to their senses.

In 1932/33 in Australia, England were to have another crack at the Ashes and you did not have to be a genius to work out that if England were to have a chance, they had somehow to curb Bradman. In the meantime he had gorged himself for two seasons on the state bowlers at home and the West Indian bowlers on their first official visit to the

Antipodes. The do-down Bradman campaign gained weight and became sharply focused when Douglas Jardine agreed to captain the England party. Rockley Wilson, who had taught him as a boy at Winchester, had said when hearing the news, 'I think we will win the Ashes, but we may lose a Dominion.' How nearly right he was.

At that time of his life Jardine did not like Australians very much. He had played for Oxford against Warwick Armstrong's side in 1921 and the match had been reduced from three to two days to give the Australians a day off before a Test Match. When the end came, Jardine who had played beautifully in his assured upright way, was 94 not out and not the slightest attempt was made to try and quicken things up at the end so that he would have had the chance to reach his hundred. Instead, there was talk of a train to catch rather than of bowling a couple more overs and this may have bred a resentment in Jardine which came to flower so dramatically more than eleven years later.

He had toured Australia in 1928/29 with Percy Chapman's side and his haughty, unsmiling bearing together with his upright, stiff-legged walk, the knotted silk handkerchief round his neck, topped off by the highly colourful Harlequin cap, made him a prime object for the barrackers. 'Eh, eh, Mr Jardine,' shouted one of them when he came out to bat, 'where's the butler to carry your bat for you.' There was another time when he was fielding near the boundary on a baking hot day. The flies were worrying him and when he tried to swot them away with his hands, a voice rang out, 'Jardine, leave our flies alone.' They would have been at his throat whenever they had the chance. Being the man he was, he made no attempt to acknowledge the barrackers or to jolly them along and every movement he made seemed full of disdain, if not contempt. Jardine and Australia were not on speaking terms long before the Bodyline tour. It is interesting that in later years, Bill O'Reilly, who played in all the five Test matches

and was the fiercest of opponents of England's tactics, was to become good friends with Jardine and they clearly had a respect for one another. Many Australians will have had a sneaking regard for him because he was transparently as brave as a lion. They would have admired that.

There are all sorts of theories and stories about the origins of Bodyline – Harold Larwood always called it 'my leg theory'. It has been said that late in the 1930 tour of England, Bradman had shown unease against genuine fast bowling. Before the side was picked for Australia, there was a dinner at the Piccadilly Hotel in London where one of the diners was Arthur Carr who captained Larwood and Voce at Nottingham. He had experimented with a form of Bodyline in England and it has been said that at any rate the germs of the plot were planted that evening, even if the details of the campaign itself had not been worked out. If that dinner party had taken place in modern times, the tabloids would have set a couple of waiters up for life in payment for their eavesdroppings.

Perhaps Bodyline was not the brainchild of Jardine who was not himself a member of the selection committee which picked four fast bowlers. In the entire history of the planet though, there cannot have been a man who, once the idea had been suggested, would have embraced it more warmly or have been better qualified to put it into action. If Jardine hadn't existed, Hollywood would have been hard pressed to invent him because both Aubrey Smith and David Niven were much too nice. It would be surprising if a large part of the Bodyline plot had not been hatched on the voyage to Australia which took three weeks, however much talking had gone into the build up to the tour. Even so, Bodyline was not launched immediately on the unsuspecting Australians. When I was in Sydney in the 1970s, I had a long conversation with Larwood in his house at Randwick, and he still insisted there was nothing wrong with his bowling except that the Australians couldn't play it. He was also the staunchest supporter of his

captain whom he still referred to as 'Mr Jardine', while bemoaning the passing of the amateur captain and the damage it had done to the game.

The mechanics of Bodyline are simple. The requirement is for short-pitched fast bowling aimed at the batsman's body at shoulder height with seven or eight men on the legside. There would be two forward short legs, three behind square and often two men covering them, at fine leg and at deep backward square leg where the eighth man would have been used. There was also a wide mid on. I spoke at some length about Bodyline to Bill O'Reilly, the tall Australian leg spinner who played in all five Test Matches. O'Reilly, the most outspoken of men, always had plenty to say, even if you met him in the lift on the way down to breakfast and ventured a speculative 'good morning'. When the subject was Bodyline he was vituperative in the extreme and, in his own mind, very clear. What had made it such an appalling and unacceptable form of attack, he assured me, was the field placing with seven or eight on the legside and as many as the captain wanted behind square. Nowadays it would be impossible to recreate the exact circumstances of Bodyline with not more than two fielders allowed behind square on the legside. O'Reilly gave the impression that an hour or two in the stocks would have been an infinitely preferable way of passing the time, even if the mob had had a healthy supply of rotten eggs at their disposal.

At the time, it was thought, rather piously perhaps, that the great batsmen of the Golden Age would have coped: Ranjitsinhji, Fry, Trumper and the rest. But it would have been as new to them as it was to Bradman and company in 1932/33. Modern batsmen have had to cope with the West Indies attack of four, sometimes five, fast bowlers for nearly thirty years since the late sixties. Their output of bouncers or short-pitched balls must at times have been comparable to the amount the Australians received under the auspices of Jardine and

Larwood. With five men behind square on the legside, scoring runs would always have been extremely difficult, but for contemporary batsmen survival on its own might not have been as tricky as the Australians found it then. Modern batsmen have learned an awful lot about the art of playing the short-pitched ball, of getting out of the way, of ducking and moving inside the line when it comes at your body. If they had been successful it would have produced a form of stalemate which would have been a less dramatic problem. In those days most batsmen did their best to score off every ball bowled to them and in this, no one was more successful than Bradman. This contemporary mindset played into the hands of Jardine and his bowlers and made Bodyline so dangerous. Bowling of this type was new, unexpected and unthinkable. If it had not been outlawed, the batsmen of that time would eventually have come up with a way of combating it more effectively – just as they have done at every other stage of the game's evolution when something new has come along. But with both sides constantly pitching the ball halfway down the pitch, it would have been desperately boring for the spectators.

When discussing Bodyline, there is still so much that is not known that one can only guess at the finer details, egged on by the circumstantial evidence. It was not used until the two games before the First Test and Bob Wyatt, the vice-captain, was in charge when the wraps were first taken off. This late arrival argues either that it was not agreed upon until well after the side had arrived in Australia, or that it was part of a plot not to give the Aussies and Bradman enough time to come up with an answer. Bradman was unfit to play in the First Test at Sydney where England won by ten wickets after Stan McCabe had shown that, given a bit of luck, it was possible to deal with Bodyline when, hooking brilliantly, he made 187 not out. Larwood took five wickets in each innings of this match. In the second match Bradman was back in the side and was bowled off the edge trying to hook his first ball

from way outside the off stump against Bill Bowes, giving the Yorkshireman his only wicket in the series. After Bradman had taken guard, Bowes had spent a long time arranging and rearranging his legside field, making Bradman certain that he was going to get a bouncer. He was moving into a position to hook even before the ball was out of Bowes's hand and he got the shock of a lifetime when he found that it was pitched up. He then made 103 in the second innings and Australia went on to win a match played on a posthumously slow pitch.

It all came to a head in Adelaide during the Third Test when Larwood felled Bill Woodfull, the Australian captain, whom he hit over the heart. Then he broke Bert Oldfield's skull as he tried to hook and the ball flew off the edge into his head. Both balls had been on or outside the off stump and had not been bowled at the body. The ground was packed and for a time it seemed that the crowd, most of whom were dressed in three-piece suits, would come over the fence. For the rest of the match a considerable posse of policemen were stationed behind the main stand just in case. It was now that the Australian Board sent an angrily worded cable to MCC at Lord's complaining that England had not been playing in accordance with the spirit of the game. The reply inevitably supported the captain and management and ended by saying that if Australia wanted to end the tour, MCC would agree but with the utmost reluctance. Of course, no one in England knew exactly what had been going on. After Woodfull had been hit, Warner went to the Australian dressing room to see how he was. He was greeted by an angry Woodfull who made his famous riposte, 'I don't want to see you, Mr Warner. There are two teams out there. One is trying to play cricket, the other is not.' This story was leaked to the press by none other than Don Bradman, and Warner, who thought Jack Fingleton had been the guilty party, put it about that he had had an apology from Woodfull who was swift to deny it. Jardine was furious and the England team issued a statement in full sup-

port of their captain. The day after Woodfull had been hit –
his widow attributed his death in 1965 to that blow – Oldfield
was injured which again brought the huge crowd to boiling
point. Later, in a rare show of compassion, Jardine cabled
Oldfield's wife, Ruth, saying that his side hoped her husband
would make a quick recovery. He later arranged through a
friend in Sydney for two dolls to be sent to their two young
daughters.

Cables flew backwards and forwards while relations
between the two sides grew worse. England won in Adelaide
where no one had been more disorientated at the crease than
Bradman, and both the two remaining Test matches after that
which gave them the series 4–1. Bradman's average had been
kept to 56 in the four Tests he played which most people
would have been happy about, but for Bradman it was nothing
short of failure. In the last Test Larwood, who took thirty-three
wickets in the series but was never again to play for England,
broke a bone in his left foot. Perhaps the only man to come
out of it wondering what all the fuss had been about was
Jardine himself. England's victory meant that he had accomplished his mission and he was as unbending and haughty
when it was all over as he had been at the beginning. He
hadn't quite lost a Dominion, but he had done his best. He
will have felt a certain quiet satisfaction at the way it had all
worked out. It will not have been in his make up to feel
exhilarated.

His cold, calculating approach to it all is well illustrated
by the story of his exchange with the Nawab of Pataudi in
the First Test. Pataudi became the third Indian prince to play
cricket for England and, like the other two, Ranji and Duleep,
made a hundred in his first Test. Later on in that match at
Sydney, one of the Australian batsmen was hit on the body.
Pataudi then ignored Jardine's call for him to move across
from the gully to make another backward short leg. 'I see,'
Jardine said in his most acidulated tones, 'I see that His High-

ness has conscientious objections. You go across, then, Hedley,' he said to Verity. In spite of his hundred, Pataudi was given only one more Test.

It is impossible to say at what precise point Bodyline was devised, but it is clear enough that it was brought about by the determination of the English to stifle Bradman. Whether Jardine was in on its inception or not, he needed no persuading of its potential. Arthur Carr and Percy Fender, another who was at that dinner at the Piccadilly Hotel, were likely and unashamed protagonists, just as Gubby Allen, one of Jardine's four fast bowlers, would never have any part of it, seeing Bodyline as a gross infringement of the spirit of the game. Allen took twenty-one wickets in the series, bowling in the normal way, although the sheer relief of the Australian batsmen no longer to be facing Larwood may have been worth a few wickets to him. This leaves the one enigmatic figure I have touched upon earlier in the book, Pelham Warner, who was the manager of the tour. He undoubtedly had a high opinion of himself and, like many people who want to be liked, Warner's views vacillated, depending, presumably, on who he had last been talking to. We have already seen that he was sycophantic in his approach to Lord's, MCC, and Lord Harris, in particular. He was summed up to perfection by Crusoe Robertson-Glasgow's description of him when they first met: 'Here he was in the flesh, bald as an ostrich egg under his Harlequin cap, slight, pale of face, and with nothing but cricket in his conversation.'

As manager in Australia neither Warner nor his assistant, Lionel Palairet, both of whom were Oxford Blues and, like Jardine, entitled to wear a Harlequin cap, said anything in public which was in condemnation of Jardine's tactics. For all that, his comments on Bodyline both before and after the tour make curious reading, to say the least, when put alongside his deafening silence when he was in Australia. Warner was also chairman of the selection committee which chose

four fast bowlers. When Surrey played Yorkshire at the Oval in 1932, Bill Bowes bowled Bodyline at Jack Hobbs who was at the end of his career. Hobbs made clear and strong protests against this form of attack. He even walked down the pitch and remonstrated with the bowler. Warner was on his high horse in condemnation of the tactics in the *Morning Post* the next day: 'I am a great admirer of Yorkshire cricket . . . but they will find themselves a very unpopular side if there is a repetition of Saturday's play. Moreover, these things lead to reprisals, and when they begin goodness knows where they will end . . . On Saturday Yorkshire fell from her pedestal and her great reputation was tarnished.'

When he wrote that he can surely have had no idea of what was being planned for Australia. He continued his attack in *The Cricketer*. 'Bowes . . . sent down several short-pitched balls which frequently bounced head high and more. That is not bowling. Indeed it is not cricket, and if all fast bowlers were to adopt his methods there would be trouble and plenty of it.' It was curious too that Bowes was only picked for the Australian tour five days before the party sailed, with Warner writing that it came about as the result of a last minute hunch. As chairman of the selectors, Warner appeared to approve of the decision and when it was suggested that they had left it a bit late, his enigmatic reply was, 'Lord Roberts got ready for South Africa in three days.' On his arrival at Fremantle, he launched into his speech about cricket being synonymous for all that is true and honest. Was Warner being an innocent abroad or mightily apprehensive of what the future might hold? He never said in his subsequent book whose idea it was that England should bowl in this way. He never mentions any disagreements within the side and, most damningly, he remained, in public, the unquestioning manager until the tour was over.

Jack Fingleton in *Cricket Crisis* quotes an unnamed impeccable source who told him: 'I really think Warner did all he

could to stop it . . . but I know that he could make no impression on Jardine and was a most unhappy man.' I wonder if Gubby Allen who hated Bodyline and was a protégé of Warner's, was Fingleton's source. Allen himself had written a very revealing letter from Australia to his father in which he said, 'Douglas Jardine is loathed . . . he is a perfect swine and I can think of no words fit for Mummy to see when I describe him.' He went on to portray Larwood and Voce as 'swollen-headed, gutless, uneducated miners'. Warner would still not go the whole hog when he later wrote of Jardine: 'Here was a great captain who had, in my view, encroached on the ethics of the game.'

Warner was a weak man, unable to face up to his responsibilities and in no way did he have the measure of Jardine who walked all over him. The tour was barely halfway through when he was warding off accusations by saying, 'The tactics of the captain on the field have nothing to do with me as manager,' which was bunkum. He and Palairet were unable to say boo to a goose unless, perhaps, Lord Harris had been sitting between them. If they had faced up to what was plainly their duty, Jardine could have been dropped from the captaincy and from the team, and even sent back to England, or the managers themselves could have resigned. But the haughty Wykehamist had both his managers in the palm of his hand and I doubt he had any problem nodding off at night. When Warner was one day wringing his hands at a party in Adelaide, he was asked why he had not done something about Bodyline. His answer was, 'What can I do? What can I do?' Clem Hill, the famous Australian left-hander and a contemporary of Warner's, came back with, 'You can come down off the fence for a start, Plum.' A strong manager would certainly have sparked off an unholy row within the touring party, but it would have been small price to pay when compared to the unpleasantness that unfolded throughout the tour.

Pelham Warner was the one man in a position to do something about Jardine and Bodyline, but in the end was not man enough to do it. He has to bear an awful responsibility for what happened. Later, in his book, *Cricket Between Two Wars*, Warner wrote: 'one of the strongest arguments against this bowling is that it breeds anger, hatred and malice, with consequent reprisals. The courtesy of combat goes out of the game.' What a pity it was that he forgot all about this sentiment for those few months while he was in Australia – or at least to do anything about it.

Once the initial flames had died down, Bodyline smouldered on like a huge damp bonfire for longer than anyone wanted. The immediate concern for MCC was Australia's planned visit to England in 1934. A considerable inquest began. At first, those in charge at Lord's were reluctant to understand the enormity of what had happened. The President of MCC, Lord Hailsham, who was, appropriately enough, the Secretary for War, felt that Jardine had 'worthily upheld England's reputation'. Walter Hammond and George Duckworth, who had both supported Jardine in Australia, now jumped over the fence and attacked what had gone on. But Jardine was asked to captain England against the West Indies in 1933 when Martindale and Constantine subjected England to Bodyline tactics in the Second Test at Old Trafford. The England batsmen did not enjoy it, but Jardine never flinched and made 127. There was something admirable about the man. By the time the touring party for England's first ever tour of India was chosen, Warner had still not been able to drum up enough support to have Jardine sacked. In January 1934, the issue was still in the balance and Warner, writing to Sir Alexander Hore-Ruthven, the Governor of South Australia, said of Jardine, 'I am not sure I would trust him. He is a queer fellow. When he sees a cricket ground with an Australian on it he goes mad! He rose to his present position on my shoulders, and of his attitude to me I do not care to speak.'

The situation was saved by Jardine himself who had stayed on in India after the tour for a holiday, and in April 1934 sent a telegram published in the *Evening Standard* in which he said that he had 'neither the intention nor the desire to play cricket against Australia this summer'. Larwood still remained and the powers at Lord's sent Sir Julian Cahn, a former President of Nottinghamshire who Derek Birley in *A Social History of English Cricket* describes as 'an absurdly pretentious fellow', to try and extract an apology from the bowler who had had some pretty nasty things to say about the Australians. Larwood famously dug in his heels. 'I'm an Englishman – I will never apologise.' He said he was unfit for the First Test and then refused to play in the second because Woodfull had not withdrawn the 'not cricket' remarks he made to Warner at the Adelaide Oval. So, in the nick of time, the series was able to go ahead without fear of repetition or reprisals. The Australians won 2–1 and in the first three Tests Bradman failed to reach 50, but he made his point in the last two with innings of 304 at Leeds and 244 and 77 at the Oval which gave him an aggregate of a mere 758 in the series. In 1935, on the principle, I suppose, of better late than never, legislation was introduced to stop short-pitched fast bowling at the batsman's body. Even then, one was left feeling that Lord's had been reluctant to grasp this particular nettle, as if they could still not really bring themselves to believe the stories they had heard from Australia in 1932/33. The blood may have stopped flowing, but the pain still lingers, almost seventy years on.

The root of this whole problem was beautifully and inadvertently summed up by Bill Voce. He was asked by Neville Cardus which was the best ball to bowl at Bradman, and he answered. 'There's no ruddy best ball to bowl at the Don.'

CHAPTER 8

A CRICKETING COMMONWEALTH

MOST OF THE LAST DECADE had revolved around Bradman, and Jardine too, in so far as the two of them had interacted upon each other. It is easy to forget that there were other important historical figures playing in these years. Walter Hammond, one of use great England batsmen of all time, was shaded only by the prodigious feats of Bradman. The two Bills, Woodfull and Ponsford, formed as successful an opening partnership as Australia have ever had. The line of Australian leg spinners was continued by Clarrie Grimmett, the diminutive New Zealander who had played alongside Arthur Mailey for two or three years, and was a fascinating figure who did not play Test cricket until he was thirty-three. Hedley Verity was the next in the long list of England left-arm spinners, while the likeable Percy Chapman's happy encounter with the captaincy cannot be ignored. Herbert Sutcliffe soldiered on until 1935 and there was the all-too-brief appearance of Ranji's nephew, Duleepsinhji, as an England batsman. It was in 1928 that the West Indies came to England for their initial Test series and spectators were able to enjoy the spectacular and definitive performances of Learie Constantine and, two years after that, George Headley came on the scene. The game was being given its first West Indian slant.

Percy Chapman, the very epitome of the amateur, took over the captaincy for the last Test of the series against Australia in 1926 when Hobbs and Sutcliffe, on a drying pitch, and the forty-eight-year-old Rhodes with the ball, won the match and the Ashes for England. Chapman was a most charismatic character. He was tall, debonair and full of charm and boyish enthusiasm. He captained by nature in a carefree manner rather than by deep design, which will not have suited everyone. He was a fearless left-handed strokemaker who, at his best, drew comparisons with Woolley. It was a daunting prospect taking over from Arthur Carr for that one Test match in 1926 with such experienced old campaigners as Hobbs and Rhodes in the side, but he did the job well. Rhodes not only bowled magnificently but also will have done much of the thinking for Chapman who, in Rhodes's words, 'did as he wor told'. Chapman's unique cricketing record was to have scored hundreds at Lord's for Oxford against Cambridge, for the Gentlemen against the Players and for England against Australia. Martin Donnelly, another left-hander of whom we will hear later, did much the same, although his third hundred was for New Zealand against England.

Chapman's greatest innings was at Maidstone for Kent against Lancashire. He came to the wicket when Kent were 15/3 and the Australian fast bowler, Ted McDonald, was in full flow. In little more than three hours he made 260 in yet another innings immortalised from the press box by Neville Cardus. It was his fielding, for which averages don't exist, which picked Chapman out from the others. His catching at slip and gully where he made full use of his long reach – he was a couple of inches over six foot – was at times difficult to believe. If there was one catch more than any other, it came in Larwood's first over of the 1928/29 series in Australia. Woodfull edged the ball between third slip and gully and, according to E.W. Swanton; 'it was next seen in the out-stretched left hand of Chapman whose leap had taken him from the gully almost into Hendren's lap (at third slip).' When he caught Bradman at Lord's in 1930 in the same position, Neville Cardus was watching with Sir James Barrie.

'But why is he going away?' asked Barrie as Bradman walked off.

'Surely, Sir James, you saw that marvellous catch?' Cardus replied.

'Yes,' said Barrie, 'but what evidence have we that the ball which Chapman threw up in the air is the same ball that left Bradman's bat?'

He went on playing for Kent until 1939 and was to die all too young at the age of sixty-one. He became lonely and tried to find solace in the bottle in the way that middle-aged loneliness so often does. Chapman was, of course, Walter Hammond's captain in his defining series, against the Australians in 1928/29. Hammond was not the only cricketer to suffer from the misfortune of being compared to Bradman. At that time he was probably a finer sight at the crease than Bradman ever became. In a sense Hammond was the more complete cricketer. He made 50,551 runs, he took 732 reluctant wickets for he was never an enthusiastic bowler and held onto 819 catches, most of them seemingly by sleight of hand in the slips. Yet perhaps these figures do not tell quite the story of the classical mastery of his batting in his early days, or the poise he was to acquire as time went on. But throughout his career the shadow of Bradman loomed large beside him. Hammond felt beholden to do better than the Australian and at times was guilty of attempting too much simply to try and outdo Bradman, and paid the penalty. Against Bodyline in 1932/33, Bradman had a poor series by his standards and averaged 56 which was still more than Hammond who also fared badly in comparison in England in 1930 and 1934. After winning the first two Tests in Australia in 1936/37, with Hammond scoring a double century in Sydney in the second, England lost the series 3–2. In the Fourth Test England needed

392 to win and they were 148/3 overnight with Hammond 39 not out. He was bowled by Fleetwood-Smith with the third ball the next morning. George Duckworth pertinently said later, 'You wouldn't get Don out in first over with Ashes at stake.'

Hammond, who was championed by Pelham Warner, was a curious mixture. He was ruled by strange moods. He was a loner at the same time as being a compulsive womaniser, he was an ardent social climber for whom appearances were desperately important and he was not always sensible with the little money he had. His marriages, undertaken because of his insecurity, were not a roaring success, he had a con-siderable thirst and an obstinacy to go with it and was not always an especially nice man. There was a kind side to him though. In 1932/33 he had been sent out at Melbourne against Victoria with instructions to hit Fleetwood-Smith, a left-aim googly bowler, out of the series. He made 203 and Fleetwood-Smith took 2/124 and did not play in any of the Tests. After the match Hammond sought out the bowler who was then twenty-two, and spent time giving him encouragement and advice. Fleetwood-Smith never forgot this and so there was an irony about that match-winning ball four years later. In 1938, Hammond's 240 in the Lord's Test was the innings of the summer, although Len Hutton's 364 at the Oval will have been heavier in the scales, and with three hundreds Bradman's aggregate was bigger than Hammond's.

Hammond foolishly could not resist the chance to have one more go at Bradman after the war and agreed to captain England again in 1946/47. In the Test Matches he found he was no longer up to it, while Bradman went remorselessly on, but only after one highly dramatic and significant incident. In the First Test in Brisbane, when he had made 28, Bradman appeared to be so clearly caught by Jack Ikin at second slip that there was no appeal. He stayed at the crease. When the appeal came it was turned down and he went on to make

DON BRADMAN

187. At the end of the over, Hammond said as he passed Bradman, 'That's a bloody fine way to start a series.' It was thought at the time that if he had been given out, he would have packed it in there and then. As it was, Bradman went on to amass almost 700 runs while in four Tests Hammond never passed 50 once and returned home defeated and demoralised. Alan Gibson wrote in *The Cricket Captains of England:* 'Hammond gave to cricket, and cricket gave to Hammond, everything – except the things he wanted most.'

Robertson-Glasgow worshipped at the shrine. 'It is something to have seen Hammond walk out to the Australians from the pavilion at Lord's; a ship in full sail. There is pride in possessing such a player.' And elsewhere: 'To field to him at cover point was a sort of ordeal by fire.' Yet Hammond was an enigma. He had the world at his feet and a talent which is given to so few, but there were also these human weaknesses, which he gave more licence to than he might. On his first tour, to the West Indies in 1926/27, he picked up a contagious social disease which all but killed him and kept him out of the game throughout 1927. In those days before penicillin, activities of the kind in which Hammond must have indulged in the Caribbean were high-risk adventures which could have the worst of consequences. The establishment closed ranks when Hammond returned and there was a discreet silence about the whole thing as he fought for his life in hospital.

Hammond had supported Jardine through the Bodyline tour and the following summer in England he was cut by a lifting ball when the West Indies fast bowlers attempted Bodyline at Old Trafford. 'Well, we began it, you know,' he said that evening, 'and now you can see just a bit what it was like. Just the luck of the game.' He was a romantic figure too, with that light blue silk handkerchief always just peeping out of his trouser pocket. In the slips he caught swallows and perhaps only Percy Chapman was his equal there, while he drove the ball through the covers with a glory which has never quite been equalled. His career leaves the one unanswerable question: if Bradman had never existed would Hammond have remained the batsman who took Australia by storm in 1928/29 or would those human imperfections have always taken over? He must have been a deeply troubled and unhappy soul and it may have been that only when he was at the crease was he able to find the peace of mind he desperately needed. Then Bradman came along and spoiled even that.

Australia's most formidable pair of opening batsmen, the two Bills, Woodfull and Ponsford, spent most of their careers being overshadowed by Bradman. Neither was a giggle a minute, although Fingleton tells us that Ponsford had a good sense of humour, if so, too few of his *obiter dicta* remain for us to share. Whatever else, they were both solid citizens of the first order. Woodfull became the only man to win back the Ashes twice in England, in 1930 and 1934, in spite of Verity's fifteen wickets on a drying pitch at Lord's which took England to an innings victory. As his pictures suggest, Woodfull was quiet and extremely likeable. Ponsford, too, was not a man given to excesses, except with a bat in his hand. He was a supreme player of slow bowling with amazingly fast, shuffling footwork which seemed to have been borrowed from a boxer. Their first-class records were almost indentical with more than 13,000 runs and an average of around 65. Ponsford, who was colour-blind, had the mentality to go on and on and twice topped 400 in state matches which was once more even than Bradman, and he did not score his runs a great deal more slowly. They fitted surely, purposefully and effectively into the canon of Australian cricket and their lives were as well regulated as their strokeplay. Cricket will always need players and characters like Woodfull and Ponsford and they will perhaps never receive quite the headlines or the publicity they deserve. Will anyone who played with Bradman?

In dramatic contrast to these two and at about the same

time, came the first of the famous West Indians who was to be the forerunner of so many other wonderfully exciting cricketers from the Caribbean as the twentieth century unfolded. Learie Constantine was another of the game's great originals who strongly influenced the development of West Indies cricket and therefore the history of the game. He was born into cricket in Maraval, just outside Port of Spain. His father, who was also Learie, had gone to England with the West Indies side in 1900 as a wicket keeper batsman. Six years later he had four children and, although he was again selected to go to England, he could not afford it. He went in to Port of Spain to have a few drinks with the players and to see them off. He arrived too early and was standing in Frederick Street when he was spotted by a great cricket supporter, Mr Maillard, outside his merchant premises. He thought Constantine had come to say goodbye to him and was horrified to find he was not going to England. In spite of his protestations, Mr Maillard said, 'Never mind that, you have to go.'

He sent Constantine back to Maraval in one of his carriages pulled by his fastest horse, while Mr Maillard went shopping and by the time Constantine returned, he had a packed trunk ready for him. He also produced enough money to look after the family while he was away. When they got to the jetty, they found the boat which took the passengers to the sailing ship a couple of miles offshore had left and that the ship itself had slipped anchor. Mr Maillard chartered a fast launch and they caught up with it before it reached the open sea. A rope ladder was lowered and Constantine joined the party. I wonder what Jardine would have thought if, some time before the ship which took him to Australia had reached Plymouth, a couple of reinforcements had scrambled up a rope ladder. I suppose as long as they had been fast bowlers he might not have minded. By the time of the 1906 tour Constantine had become a bowler/batsmen who could keep wicket if need be. A useful chap to have about. Old Cons, as he was known, was a Roman Catholic and a stickler for tradition and fair play. He brought up his son to walk if he was caught behind and knew he had hit the ball.

Young Learie went to England with the West Indies side in 1923 where he made his mark as a brilliant cover point but nothing much else, although Jack Hobbs gave him some useful advice. Not a great deal happened back in the West Indies but on the tour to England in 1928 which saw the West Indies play their first Test Matches, Constantine made a thousand runs, took a hundred wickets and showed that he was the finest fielder anyone had ever seen. His enjoyment of what he was doing was self-evident and infectious. It was all a great big adventure for him. He never scored a boring run in his life and the expectation surrounding him was enormous. He grabbed the country's attention when he scored 86 and 103 against Middlesex at Lord's and picked up 7/57 in their second innings, six of them coming for only 11. His figures in Test cricket were disappointing, but his name and his memory remain strong because he was the first one to walk the road the West Indies have trodden with increasing success ever since. In 1928, Learie Constantine seized the moment to show Englishmen that the West Indians could indeed play cricket. It was he more than any other individual who put West Indies cricket on the map and gave them their reputation.

League cricket in the north of England suffered badly from the slump because the money was no longer there to pay the professionals. Nelson in the Lancashire League decided to buy their way out of trouble and in 1929 employed Learie Constantine for £750 a year. It underlines the impact that Constantine had made the year before that a League club in Lancashire, in dire financial straits, was prepared to take such a gamble on him. Black men were a rarity in those parts of the world and Constantine had a great novelty value. In those days racialism was not a factor. Constantine stayed with Nelson

for nine years in which they won the League title on seven occasions and refilled their coffers many times over thanks to his mercurial displays. He became a folk hero and all the world in the north knew him as 'Connie'. Nelson's last professional had been Ted MacDonald the Australian fast bowler. This produced a good story. A school mistress in Lancashire asked a pupil when Ramsay MacDonald had last been Prime Minister. 'Don't know, Miss,' came the answer, 'but I know 'e were t'pro for Nelson before Connie.'

I count myself extremely lucky to have met Learie Constantine on a number of occasions when he was in the press box in the 1960s on behalf of the *Daily Sketch*. He was unfailingly kind to and interested in young whippersnappers and he was always ready for a laugh. I also remember meeting him once or twice at the house in South Kensington of the author, Denzil Batchelor, for they were the closest of friends. Learie was always a man of the great good cheer and he went on to become a considerable political figure. He was Trinidad's High Commissioner in London which earned him a knighthood. He was later awarded a Life Peerage as Lord Constantine of Maraval, and from the House of Lord's he was in the vanguard of the fight against racial discrimination.

When Bosanquet unleashed that first googly at Lord's in 1900 which bounced four times before having Sam Coe stumped 2 runs short of his hundred, even he was unlikely to have realised what he had started. Four South Africans, Schwarz, Faulkner, Vogler and White tormented all visitors to the Cape before shovelling their art sideways across the seas to Australia where the tradition has thrived. The first serious exponent there was a dentist called Doctor Hordern who took thirty-two wickets when Australia lost 4–1 to England in 1911/12. This was appropriate for dentists are artful creatures whose drills instil the same feelings of apprehension in their patients as a googly bowler creates in uncertain batsmen. Hordern was then succeeded by Arthur Mailey who joked, spun and drew his way into the fabric of the game before being pushed to one side by a dry, wizened and almost middle-aged little New Zealander called Clarrie Grimmett. The two of them played together for a couple of series, making a bizarre contrast. While Mailey cheerfully spun the ball miles and bowled like a profligate millionaire, Grimmett looked like an ascetic miser on a diet with a Groucho Marx walk. Small, bald – he always bowled in a cap – and bright-eyed, he bowled with hunched shoulders and his arm was so low as to give a good idea of what round-arm bowling must have looked like. He was as crafty as they come and would have been a natural for a walk-on part in *David Copperfield*. When he bowled his flipper which hurried off the pitch he could not prevent his fingers from clicking. He quickly taught himself to click the fingers of his left hand which he did when bowling leg-breaks or googlies so that the batsman should not be able to read him by ear.

Grimmett had been born in Dunedin and went to school in Wellington. He had begun life as a fast bowler before a Mr Hempelman – another Dickensian name – persuaded him to turn, rather reluctantly, to leg spin. In New Zealand he found it impossible to convince anyone that he was a serious bowler. As a result he moved first to Sydney, where the New South Welshmen were not convinced either, and so he packed his bags and went on to Melbourne. He had a few outings for Victoria and in one, against South Australia, he took eight wickets and, grateful for their generosity, hopped on a bus and made his home in Adelaide. It still took time for him to gain the recognition he was after. Then in 1925, at the age of thirty-three, he found the ultimate reward when he was picked for the Fifth Test against England and took 11/82 in a match Australia won by 307 runs.

In eleven years Grimmett took 216 wickets for Australia, including forty-four in the series in South Africa in 1935/36 which was to be his last. He was an amazingly accurate

bowler, especially for a wrist spinner. There can have been few who have ever had such command of length and direction – perhaps only Shane Warne. Grimmett was not a big spinner of the ball but on a pitch with some bite his leg break would turn sharply. His googly was not the best in the business and his most dangerous ball of all was the top spinner which was quicker and dipped late in its flight. It brought him many of his wickets, usually with batsmen lbw trying to play him off the back foot. He loved to give the ball plenty of air to tease batsmen who were afraid to use their feet. On the other hand, those who were keen to get after him would invariably find it dropping short and wide and it would be difficult to attack. When Grimmett first appeared in Australian cricket, he cross-examined Mailey who happily told him everything he knew. Years later at a reception Crusoe Robertson-Glasgow, in his customary good form, takes it up: 'Grimmett, probably elated by unaccustomed good cheer, for he was a man of abstinence, came up to Mailey and said in that voice like a ventriloquist speaking through a watering-can: "Arthur, you told me wrong about the Bowzie." Rather as if Virgil had been accused by Horace of giving misleading information on the number of feet in the hexameter!'

In 1930 in England Grimmett had no leg spinning assistant and his only help came from the variable left-arm spin of Percy Hornibrook. Eighteen months later he was joined by Bill O'Reilly, tall, balding, irascible, and of Irish origin, who was the next in the leg spinning line. In 1930, Don Bradman wrote off O'Reilly as a failure 'who could turn the ball both ways, but never achieved outstanding success on turf wickets'. In later years Bradman was to say that O'Reilly was the greatest bowler he had ever batted against. O'Reilly will have known all about Bradman who was two years younger. In 1925/26 he played for Wingello against Bowral and on the first Saturday of the match, Bradman, who was seventeen, was twice dropped in the slips off O'Reilly and was 234 not out at the end of the day, having hit four sixes and six fours in his last 50. When the game was resumed the following Saturday, O'Reilly bowled Bradman with his first ball. Perhaps O'Reilly never forgave Bradman for that innings, for he always had plenty to say against him as a man, although not as a cricketer. When the Great Man was bowled for nought by Eric Hollies at the Oval in 1948 in his last innings in Test cricket, the press box rang with the laughter of O'Reilly and Jack Fingleton as he walked back to the pavilion. O'Reilly will have been especially pleased it was a googly that did the deed.

He lived up to his nickname of 'Tiger'. He hated all batsmen and reckoned that bowlers were the underprivileged lackeys of the game. His first inclinations had been to become a fast bowler before he realised he had a real talent for spinning the ball. He was self-taught, learning by the process of watching others, and the end-product was a most unorthodox but highly effective bowler. He and Grimmett were perhaps an even bigger contrast than Mailey and Grimmett. O'Reilly was tall, robust and a bundle of impulsive energy, while Grimmett was short, slight and measured in everything he did. If Grimmett was stirred to anger he found it affected his concentration, but when O'Reilly was worked up he was at his most dangerous. An over from O'Reilly would contain six (in England) or eight (in Australia) different but potentially lethal deliveries, while Grimmett was more intent on wearing a batsman down. O'Reilly's leg break was 'rolled' rather than spun, although it gave him plenty of turn on a helpful surface and on hard Australian pitches he found a disturbingly inconsistent bounce. He spun his top spinner more and gave his googly a real flip. His fiercely independent nature was revealed soon after he first came north to Sydney. In the nets at the Sydney Cricket Ground, Arthur Mailey was one who suggested he would be better off if he got rid of the stoop in his delivery stride and altered his grip on the ball, for he would never be a bowler unless he spun his leg break. In typical fashion,

O'Reilly replied, 'Then I won't be a bloody bowler,' and there will have been plenty of spin on that one.

O'Reilly's run up to the wicket was a work of art on its own. He would walk back a dozen paces, turn to face the batsman, put his head down and give it everything. His feet pounded the ground and his arms twirled around before he collected himself right at the end, although there was still a pronounced stoop in his final stride. His right arm came over in a lovely smooth slinging action which cleverly hid changes of pace at the same time as prompting a remarkable accuracy. The frenetic activity which went into it all hardly suggested consistency, but it showed off the fiery, Irish-Australian temperament. I have an idea that if Sir Toby Belch had taken up leg spin bowling his approach to the stumps would have been similar to O'Reilly's.

O'Reilly and Grimmett came together for the last two Test matches against South Africa in Australia in 1931/32 when Bradman scored 806 runs in five innings. They stayed together for five years, although Grimmett only played in three Tests in the Bodyline series. The Australians then decided that Grimmett was too old. He missed the series against England in 1936/37, which Australia won 3–2 after being two matches down, and in 1938 they also refused to take him to England where the softer pitches had always suited him. O'Reilly won the Fourth Test of that series for Australia at Headingley when he took five wickets in each innings, but was to suffer indignities at the Oval which were to remain for ever engraved upon his Irish soul. Walter Hammond, whose rivalry with Bradman continued undimmed, won the toss in what was a timeless Test, and batted on without mercy until England had made 903/7. It was pay-back time for Hammond. By then the young Len Hutton had made 364, beating the 334 Bradman had made at Headingley eight years earlier, and Bradman and Fingleton were both out of the match with injuries. O'Reilly bowled eighty-five overs and took 3/178 and had not enjoyed

the experience, neither had 'Chuck' Fleetwood-Smith whose eighty-seven overs had gone for 298 runs, a tall price to pay, even for Hammond's wicket which he took yet again. Australia lost by an innings and 579 runs which remains the largest ever margin of victory. O'Reilly would not have made a good dinner companion that evening or for some time afterwards.

This was Australia's last Test Match before the Second War and O'Reilly was only to play one more, against New Zealand in March 1946 when he took 8/33 all told in a match at Wellington which was over in two days. His Test career brought him 144 wickets in twenty-seven matches. There were many who not only thought he was a better bowler than Grimmett but also said he was the best spin bowler between the wars. Ian Peebles, himself a leg spinner who bowled for England and took Bradman's wicket, told Wally Hammond that he had heard an England cricketer say that he thought Grimmett was the better of the two. 'Maybe,' said Hammond, 'he was never there long enough to see.' O'Reilly would have enjoyed that reply. Nonetheless, those three wickets at the Oval took his tally past twenty for the fourth time in four series against England.

In the many seasons I spent in Australia, I was lucky enough to come to know both Bill O'Reilly and Jack Fingleton and what excellent company they were. They missed nothing, on the field or off. O'Reilly's articles in the *Sydney Morning Herald* made compulsive reading, especially when Kerry Packer became involved with cricket. O'Reilly never missed a chance to have a go at Packer's World Series Cricket and none of his punches were pulled. Fingleton's writing was also a joy, with a heavily sardonic twist when it came to dealing with the game's administrators. I had been lucky enough to play one or two games of cricket against him when he had turned out for the Duke of Norfolk's XI at Arundel. He was a good conversationalist in the field and I am not altogether sure what he made of some of His Grace's field placings.

When I first went to Australia in 1968/69 to watch a West Indies tour, I ran into Fingleton who was writing about one of the early games in Perth. He climbed the stairs into the old press box, looked round, saw me and said, 'Blofeld, take those plums out of your mouth,' followed by the poker face which soon turned into a suppressed smile. He was a great help on that tour and no one was quicker to ask how it was all going. I was in the press box at the Adelaide Oval one morning just before the start of play in late January. The day before, Charlie Griffith had run out Ian Redpath for backing up too far without first giving him a warning, in the time-honoured way. Griffith was roundly condemned, except by O'Reilly and Keith Miller who both said he was right to do what he did. Enter Fingleton wearing his I Zingari tie.

'Tiger, you would never have run a man out for backing up too far in a million years.'

'When I was bowling, Fingo,' O'Reilly came back as quick as a flash, 'I never met a batsman that keen to get up the other end.'

Until the Second World War Test cricket may seem to have been all about England playing Australia which is unfair on South Africa. Their leg spinners, especially Ernie Vogler and Aubrey Faulkner, soon turned South Africa into formidable opponents. Faulkner also scored four Test hundreds, including 204 against Australia at Melbourne, and averaged more than 40 in his Test career, in addition to taking eighty-two wickets. South Africa's googly bowlers had wagged their fingers at England's batting in 1905/06 when they beat the first official MCC side to visit the country, under Warner's captaincy. While it was extremely encouraging for the South Africans, it was far from a full strength England side. South Africa won again in 1909/10 against another side which was a bit of a mixture, thanks to Faulkner and Vogler who took sixty-five wickets between them. This was the one series which George Simpson-Hayward, the last of the old fashioned lob bowlers, played for England. If the South Africans had thought this was a joke, it was Simpson-Hayward who had the last laugh, taking twenty-three wickets at just over 18 apiece. The South Africans found the Australians, who fielded their best sides, a tougher proposition and they had to wait until 1966/67 before they won a series against them, although they won their first Test against Australia at Adelaide in 1910/11.

They beat England again before the Second World War, in 1930/31, and then they won their first series in England in 1935. The First Test in 1930/31, which South Africa won by 28 runs, brought together two unusual players. South Africa's captain was Buster Nupen who was born a Norwegian and had been blind in one eye since, at the age of four, he had banged two hammers together and a splinter had flown into an eye. He first played for South Africa in 1921 and he was the last of the great matting bowlers. His stock-in-trade were sharp medium paced off breaks, interspersed with leg cutters. In this match at Johannesburg on a matting wicket, he took eleven wickets and was the decisive difference between the two sides. It was inexplicable that he should then have been dropped as captain and 'Nummy' Deane recalled from retirement to take over for the next two matches before Jock Cameron got the job for the last two, all of which were drawn. Cricket has never known what to make of its selectors.

In that First Test Match South Africa brought in Xenophon Balaskas who bowled leg breaks and googlies and was of Greek origin. He was a small man with heavy dark Grecian looks who only played in nine Test Matches but helped South Africa to their first Test win in England, at Lord's in 1935, when he took five wickets in the first innings and four in the second for a total of 103 runs. That performance was inspired by an extraordinary piece of superstition. The night before the game began, Balaskas was walking along Shaftesbury Avenue with the South African writer, Louis Duffus. They came upon Greek Street in Soho and, seeing it as an omen,

turned into it. The little leg spinner suddenly spotted, in Duffus's words 'a loiterer conspicuously destined to become a mother in the near future "Now here's luck," Balaskas exclaimed. "If I pat her I can't go wrong." With light banter he patted her and within the next few days his strange super-stition brought him the best performance of his career.' If cricketers went about with that sort of superstition these days, they would be more likely to be up in front of the beak the following day than taking wickets in a Test Match at Lord's. The catch question is to name the Greek, the Chinaman and the one-eyed Norwegian who played Test cricket. Ellis Achong who played in the 1930s for the West Indies, was the Chinaman.

The scars which had been left behind by the Bodyline series healed more quickly than they might have done thanks to an excellent series in Australia in 1936/37. England won the first two Test Matches and, with Bradman scoring heavily, Australia took the last three. England were captained by Gubby Allen who had taken twenty-one wickets opening the bowling with Larwood four years earlier, but had refused to bowl short and at the batsmen. It was an excellent decision to put the reputation of England's cricket in his hands for this tour. Diplomacy was going to be an extremely important quality. In the event, it all went off better than anyone can have expected, although Allen himself will have been fed up at throwing away such a splendid position in the series. The critical moment came during the Fourth Test in Adelaide. When Australia's first wicket fell in their second innings, Bradman appeared, although he had gone in fourth in the first innings. He found himself facing Hedley Verity for whom Walter Robins had been fielding on the square leg boundary. Bradman had a careful look at the legside field but when Verity's arm came over, Robins had crept up to square leg by the umpire. The first ball was a long hop which Bradman would normally have pulled for four, but being his first ball and knowing there was an easy single behind square, he paddled it round the corner and it went in the air straight to Robins. It would be hard to imagine a much easier catch and for some reason he dropped it. Robins could not avoid Allen at the end of the over and apologised profusely. Allen, who was a kind man and a great friend of Robins's, smiled cheerfully and said as he passed, 'Not to worry, but the gaffe has probably cost us the Ashes.' He was right, for Bradman went on to make 212 and Australia won that match by 148 runs and the one after by an innings.

After England's mammoth total against Australia at the Oval in 1938 they went on a visit to South Africa where they won the only Test to be decided. The last match was played as a timeless Test in Durban and South Africa set England to make 696 to win. At the end of the tenth day, England were 654/5 when the match had to be abandoned to give the Englishmen time to make the two-day train journey to Cape Town to catch their boat back to England. A young man called Bill Edrich made 219. There was then just time for three Tests in England against the West Indies who were beginning to show the flair that was to serve them so well in the years to come. This was Learie Constantine's last series and his final innings of 79 in the Third Test at the Oval came at a furious pace with the help of a six and eleven fours. He went out as he had come in. The West Indians caught an early boat home towards the end of August and the following month Hitler moved into Poland.

CHAPTER 9

LIFTING THE POST-WAR GLOOM

CRICKET was kept going through the war whenever possible, and it must have done a great deal for morale. Pelham Warner, President of Middlesex Cricket Club from 1937 to 1946, who was largely responsible, put it neatly when he said: 'I had the feeling that if Goebbels had been able to broadcast that the war had stopped cricket at Lord's it would have been valuable propaganda for the Germans.'

Great names took on unusual guises as well known players homed in on Lord's where the ubiquitous Warner presided and would no doubt have resided if bed-and-breakfast had been available. Lieutenant-Colonel Gubby Allen and Flight-Lieutenant Walter Robins will have been bowling at Sergeants Len Hutton and Denis Compton when the opportunity arose and wartime garb could be safely shed for a few hours. One of the most famous photographs to come from Lord's was the sight of the players lying flat on the ground in the middle of an over that Bob Wyatt was bowling at Jack Robertson in a match between the RAF and the Australian Airforce. A doodlebug, whose engine cut out over Lord's, had a close look at proceedings before crashing and exploding just beyond the Nursery End in St John's Wood. As the war progressed and the Allies' fortunes improved, more and more cricket was played. When the hostilities were eventually over, the game celebrated with the Victory Tests against Australia which created enormous interest. The impetus of cricket in England was given a helping hand by the Australian Prime Minister, John Curtin, who loved the game with a passion. When he had been in England in 1944, the powers-that-be at Lord's had asked him for any help he could give in the resuscitation of cricket. He wasted no time in seeing to it that a number cricketers who were serving in the Australian armed forces were immediately posted to England for 'special duties'. The Victory Tests spelled out the message that life was beginning to return to normal. Sadly, too many players had been killed in the six years of fighting and, as in the Great War, a large chunk of cricket had been taken out of the lives of so many others.

The understandable urge was to get things going again as soon as possible. The Indians agreed to come to England in 1946, which in the immediate post-war period was bleak and uncomfortable. The country was bankrupt, almost nothing in the way of luxury was available and ration books were the order of the day. Added to which, 1946 was one of the wettest summers on record and the Indians, under the Nawab of Pataudi whom we last heard of as a conscientious objector in Sydney late in 1932, did not have an easy time of it. Walter Hammond, another surviver although no longer the man he was, continued to captain England who had already received an invitation to tour Australia the following winter. In purely cricketing terms this invitation should probably have been resisted and MCC thought long and hard before accepting. The Australians were keen that a series for the Ashes should be played as soon as possible for they felt it would be a big help to the general process of recovery. Also it would raise important money for the game. So the England players had to buckle down first to the job of beating India and then to the hardest job of all, a tour to Australia. South Africa had

accepted an invitation to tour England in 1947, New Zealand played one Test, their first ever, against Australia in 1945/46 and another against England a year later. The West Indies then played host to England in 1947/48. Cricket had been hurt by the war, but as soon as peace returned it was quick to cast aside its crutches.

The British Raj had brought the game to India and it had been flourishing there for a long time. The Parsees had toured England before the turn of the century and the Indians had shown a natural aptitude for it. Of course, the three princes, Ranji, Duleep and Pataudi, who had all been to Oxford or Cambridge, had played for England. India did not play their first official Test Match until 1932, in England – it was the only Test of that summer. In the absence of their official captain, the Maharajah of Porbandar, a stately name which unfairly implied an ample girth and a marked lack of mobility, they were led by C.K. Nayudu and, although they lost by 158 runs, three of the players, including the acting captain, were injured. Douglas Jardine's side won two of the three Tests in India in 1933/34 when the Yuvraj of Patiala who, by sleight of hand, was to become Lieutenant-General Yadavendra Singh, Maharajah of Patiala, played in his only Test, at Madras. He made 24 and 60 which was more than either Lala Amarnath or Vijay Merchant who were to become such considerable cricketers. After that the poor chap presumably had to get on with being a Maharajah in between drilling his troops on the North-West Frontier or wherever, and his talents were sadly lost to the game. Apart from hitting the ball past cover like a shot out of a gun, he was a wonderfully colourful figure. He stood 6'4" tall, he wore either a light blue or a pink turban or puggaree, and a pair of sparkling diamond ear-rings.

Nonetheless, it got better and better because when India played three Tests in England in 1936, they were captained by the Maharajkumar of Vizianagram who had many qualities, even if cricket was not foremost among them. Not long before the Second Test he was knighted and became, most impressively, Sir Gajapatairaj Vijaya Ananda, the Maharajkumar of Vizianagram, a name that gave the printers of scorecards who are not best known for their linguistic coherence, the most appalling headaches. He didn't have a very successful series, scoring 33 runs in six innings, although, to be fair, he was twice not out. I came across him much later in India, in 1963/64, when he had become a ball-by-ball commentator on the wireless. He was hysterically funny, even if it was unintentional and he told the listeners very little about the cricket that was remotely comprehensible. When introduced to him his invariable catchphrase was, 'Call me Vizzie.' He was a large man who didn't spare the calories and he moved around in a procession with masses of retainers.

England retaliated against this name-dropping when, in 1937/38 with MCCs blessing, a side went out to India under Lionel Hallam, the third Lord Tennyson, although they did not play any Test Matches. The Indians probably felt that in comparison to some of the noble names they had come up with, Lord Tennyson was pretty small beer, faint but pursuing, almost. During the tour, the Jam Sahib of Nawanagar, who was Ranji's cousin, arranged a panther shoot for Lord Tennyson. In the jungle one evening soon after dark they were waiting in a hide by a clearing watching the tethered goat in front them when the panther burst on the scene and got to work on the goat. Taking careful aim, Lord Tennyson fired and the panther looked up, rather surprised, before bounding back into the jungle. Several of the side were watching from the hide with Lord Tennyson and the silence was broken by Alf Gover with the immortal words, 'Good Lord, my lord, you've shot the goat.'

The aristocratic *motif* was still up and running in 1946 when the conscientious objector, the Nawab of Pataudi, was

in charge. Nawab is Muslim for Maharajah and so, roughly speaking, it was business as usual. India had some good players such as Vijay Merchant, Mushtaq Ali, Vinoo Mankad, Vijay Hazare and Lala Amarnath, but in a wet summer they did not make much impression, especially against a young seam bowler called Alec Bedser who took eleven wickets in each of his first two Test matches. Bedser was as important a figure in England's immediate post-war cricket as Len Hutton and Denis Compton who had begun their Test careers in the years leading up to the war. As always, Australia were the toughest nut to crack. The tour to Australia in 1946/47 was a better PR exercise for the Australians than for England who lost the series 3–0. They had produced a new crop of formidable young players to blend with Lindsay Hassett, Sydney Barnes and of course Don Bradman who had come through the war unscathed. If Bradman had been given out when he was 28, caught by Ikin in the slips in the First Test at Brisbane, who knows what would have happened. A final score of 187 was a powerful inducement for him to push all such thoughts to the back of his mind. After that he did untold damage to the Indian bowling in Australia before winning 4–0 in England in 1948 where he made that famous duck at the Oval in his last Test innings. If he had made four he would have averaged a hundred in Test cricket but, after receiving a rousing reception, Eric Hollies' second ball was the perfect googly and he had to be content with 99.94.

After the war Australia had come up with one of the great fast bowling combinations of all time in Ray Lindwall and Keith Miller. Cricket may never have had a more romantic player than Miller, unless it was Ranji or Compton. Before the war, Miller lived near the Caulfield Racecourse in Melbourne and as a boy he was so small that he was hoping to become a jockey. As it was, the turf was never far from his mind and if he had become a jockey I daresay that a large chunk of the post-war history of racing would have had to have been rewritten. He was to grow almost a foot between the ages of sixteen and seventeen and he was only seventeen when he made 181 for Victoria against Tasmania in his first innings in first-class cricket. In his fourth match he scored 108 for Victoria against South Australia for whom Clarrie Grimmett was still tweaking his leg breaks. At that time Miller was only a batsman, although at the nets he would pick up a ball and start spinning it as if he was some sort of O'Reilly and then he would go on to bowl unpleasantly fast off a short run.

He has always been a man of great personal charm and there was a fierce streak of individuality about him. If the situation in the game was desperate, no one was more likely to come up with a startling performance than Miller, but if the game was boring, his attention would almost certainly wander. This was irritating for his captains who never quite knew which Miller they were taking out on to the field with them. He was a wonderful entertainer and a great favourite with the crowds, for he had the invaluable knack of being able to involve them in everything he did. Against Essex in 1948 when the Australians made 721 in the day at Southend, Miller who was batting down the order, thought more than enough runs had been scored and he allowed himself to be bowled first ball by Trevor Bailey. Ian Johnson, his fellow Victorian and a future Australian captain, wrote that the ball was a fast yorker and in Bailey's version of the story I am sure it moved about all over the place as well. It will not have worried Miller one iota that he was out first ball for nought. If it had been a tight situation in a Test Match, one could be equally certain that ball would not have bowled him. When he was in charge of the New South Wales side, Miller's brand of captaincy was as unusual as it was in character. On one occasion when the side reached the middle someone said with some surprise to Miller, 'There are twelve of us out here.' To

which the reply was, 'Well, you'd better bugger off then, and the rest of you spread out.'

Bowling became a serious option with him in England during the war when he was in the RAAF flying Mosquitoes. Miller, who was as brave as a lion, and Biggles will have had much in common. He soon made himself into one of the great allrounders in the history of the game. It was hardly surprising that he and the single-minded Bradman did not get on, any more than it was a shock to discover that Denis Compton and Len Hutton were never really birds on adjacent twigs. Bradman, who always reckoned that Miller's bowling was his trump card, will not have been amused by his unpredictability. Of course, Miller couldn't have cared less what Bradman thought. There is no doubt that if he had not bowled, he would have made more runs than he did, for he had so much ability. For all that, he still had 2,958 runs in Tests with an average of almost 37 to put alongside his tally of 170 wickets at twenty-three apiece. It is just that the bare figures tell nothing of the man and how he made his runs, took his wickets, held his catches and lived his life. The innings for which Miller is perhaps still remembered longest is the 185 he made for the Dominions against an England XI at Lord's in 1945. In the second innings he was 61 not out overnight and in ninety minutes the next morning he hit another 124 and won the match. He hit seven sixes and came within a few inches of equalling the feat of another robust Australian, Albert Trott, who, in 1899, drove a ball over the Lord's pavilion, although it had bounced on and up off a tile right at the top. Trott played Test cricket for both Australia and England.

Miller, always a great conversationalist, would stand in the slips, apparently with little more than half an eye on the game. Then he would suddenly launch himself sideways and hang onto a half chance which would change the course of the match. At other times he would stand still, apparently unconcerned and watch a ball fly past him at a catchable height.

You never knew what you were going to get. When he was bowling and was hit for four, he couldn't wait to get the ball back to have another go at the batsman who was well advised to watch the next one pretty carefully. In Melbourne on the eve of the Third Test against England in 1954/55 when the sides were one-all, Miller told Ian Johnson, his captain, that his knee was still not a hundred per cent fit and that he would rather not bowl. The next morning, just before the start, he told Johnson that he had done some exercises in his bedroom and thought he could try a couple of overs to see how it stood up. He then bowled right through the first session and in a superb spell took three wickets for 5 runs in nine overs. In the next Test, at the Adelaide Oval, England needed 94 to win the match and the Ashes with it. Miller seized the new ball and soon they were 18/3, Miller having taken all three. Not long afterwards he held onto a remarkable diving catch in the covers to get rid of Peter May. It took a fine piece of batting by Denis Compton to make sure that Miller did not win the match, and England got home by five wickets.

I was lucky enough to play against Miller when he turned out for Nottinghamshire as a guest against Cambridge University at Trent Bridge in 1959. He made a hundred against us and what I remember most was the lovely straight clean swing of the bat as he hit through the line of the ball. His cover drive was a gem and he was looking that day to get on to the front foot when he could. To the delight of a good crowd I dropped him at deep mid wicket in front of the ladies' pavilion. He also used the new ball and in the first over of the innings he bowled me a quick leg break with that mane of brown hair flopping all over the place. It was all a thrilling experience. I was to know him later when he frequented the press box on behalf of the *Daily Express* and what a character he was. At every county ground in England he would know one of the gatekeepers or the lady who ran the players dining room or the man behind one of the bars or the chap who

organised the bookstall. His first port of call in the morning would be to go and see whoever it was and have a good old natter. He was an inveterate racegoer and at Royal Ascot in his morning coat and topper you were as likely to find him talking to one of the gatekeepers whom he had fought with in the war as in the smartest champagne bar. There was no side about Keith Miller who was the best possible friend and would do anything to help those he knew who had fallen on hard times. Looking back now from an age of dull conformity, he stands out, above all, as a gloriously free spirit, admittedly at a time when spirits were still allowed to be free.

His partner, Ray Lindwall, bowled fast outswingers as well as any man has ever done. He was a very different bowler from Miller and a perfectionist in his art. After moving effortlessly to the crease, he had a lovely smooth action which would have been classical but for an arm which, in the best of circles, was rather too low. If it had not been for Lindwall, England, who had a more than adequate batting line up, would have scored many more runs in the immediate post-war years. The contrast between Miller and Lindwall was sharp. Miller performed for the music hall audience, while Lindwall was for the Old Vic or Stratford-on-Avon. Miller was made great by nature, while Lindwall worked hard at his art, perfecting each small detail so that nothing was left to chance. Every ball he bowled was premeditated. His accuracy was a byword and this came about as a result of the precise functioning of all the composite parts which made up the mechanism of his bowling. He used his bumper sparingly but it was a devastating weapon and difficult to avoid. He was able to vary his pace without the batsman detecting it and he was especially adept at spotting a weakness in a batsman and then exploiting it.

He took 228 wickets in sixty-one Tests at just over 23 runs each and he was no mean performer with the bat, as his two hundreds suggest. Lindwall played cricket by the book while

Miller's inspiration was the light of nature. Many fast bowlers excel at repartee on the field. Lindwall seemed to feel that actions spoke louder than words. Once in South Africa when, because of injury, he had made a late start to the tour, he bowled his first ball in the country to Eric Rowan who was nothing if not outspoken. This ball was delivered at a cautious pace and it was short. Rowan hooked it for four and advanced down the pitch towards the bowler giving tongue as he went, 'Ya bum, someone said you were a fast bowler.' While some fast bowlers would have been keen to debate the point, Lindwall waited for the ball and walked quietly back to his mark. He and Miller were the closest of friends and on the boat to England in 1948 developed the habit of calling each other 'Jackson' which was to prove disconcerting for strangers. They were the best of company and the most genuine of men.

Lindwall moved from Sydney to Brisbane before the end of his career. When he retired, he and his wife ran a florist's shop – an unlikely profession for a fast bowler – and he liked to come and watch Test Matches at the Gabba. I well remember him enjoying his schooner of beer in the committee room of the Queensland Cricket Association. He was always full of good humour, interspersed with a pithy common sense and rounded off with a cheerful chuckle. Bradman and Lindwall will have accommodated each other, but maybe neither would have been as well suited as Miller to flying a Mosquito.

While Australia's cricket revolved around Bradman, Lindwall and Miller in those first years of peace, England's cricket hinged on Hutton, Compton and Bedser with a touch of Godfrey Evans thrown in. Len Hutton carried on the long single-minded Yorkshire tradition and, like Herbert Sutcliffe, came from Pudsey, although from the other end of the village. Denis Compton who, together with Hutton, had made a hundred in his first Test against Australia in 1938, was for a time bigger box office than any cricketer had been before, except possibly WG. Life in post-war Britain was gloomy as the island went

about the business of paying off its debts and trying to bring back a sense of order to its life. There was a touch of the larrikin in Compton, just as there was in Miller, and they soon became the greatest of friends. Both were unpredictable and Compton was spectacularly absent-minded, and unreliable if you were running with him between the wickets. He played his first match for MCC, against Suffolk, in 1935, three years after joining the Lord's groundstaff. When the train arrived in Felixstowe, he found that he had forgotten his cricket bag. He wired Lord's asking them to send it on. Back came the reply: 'Bag on the way. You'll leave your head behind one day.' Compton was 5'8" tall and for the first day's play he had to borrow kit from the old Hampshire player, George Brown, who stood at 6'3" – with startling results.

Compton was a genius who also played the game by nature. There was nothing contrived, studied or preconceived about his cricket. He was wonderfully instinctive and innovative in his strokeplay, his judgement and his footwork. His batting was best summed up by a story told me by Neil Adcock, the South African fast bowler who formed such a hostile partnership in the fifties and early sixties with Peter Heine. The South Africans came to England in 1955 when Compton was getting on, and the Third Test was played at Old Trafford. Both sides practised there as usual the day before the match, but Compton had not turned up for the England session. Peter May, who was captain, and Gubby Allen, the chairman of the selectors, were fed up with his unreliability and had made up their minds to leave him out of the team. To their amazement, when they arrived at Old Trafford the following morning they found that Compton was the only England player there and he had already changed and was getting ready to have a net. After a couple of moments of the well known Compton charm, they relented.

What they did not know was that he had left his bat behind in London. This was the first time Fred Titmus had been chosen for England, although in the end he was twelfth man. Compton asked Titmus if he would mind lending him his bat. It was an elderly and not particularly impressive instrument but Titmus handed it over to his Middlesex colleague who waved it about a bit and said it felt fine. England, who won the toss, were soon 22/2 when Compton took it out with him and played an innings of 158 which was superb even by his standards. Adcock told me, somewhat ruefully, that his 71 in the second innings was, if anything, even better. At one point, he bowled three almost identical balls to Compton, a fraction short of a length, pitching on or just outside the off stump, at a fierce pace. The first one hit the boundary just behind square on the offside, the second disappeared over mid wicket and the third went first bounce into the crowd at deep extra cover. These three strokes encapsulated the genius of the man and when he was in this sort of mood there was nowhere you could safely bowl to him.

He was one of the great originals. He effectively invented what has become known as the paddle sweep. The full-blooded sweep, when the ball is hit square with the wicket, is a dangerous stroke on a pitch with an uneven bounce. The stroke Compton put his patent on differs from this in that the front foot goes down the pitch well inside the line of the ball which is then paddled round in the direction of fine leg. It is a great deal safer because the ball is being helped on its way rather than being dispatched at right angles to the flight. Compton made it seem a cheeky, rather dashing stroke, in keeping with the man. He also played his own variation of the late cut which was more a steer wide of the slips than a wristy cut. Both of these were given impetus by his wonderful natural sense of timing.

His *annus mirabilis* had been 1947 when South Africa were the visitors to England. That summer Compton made 3,816 runs with eighteen hundreds, both of which remain as records, while his friend and Middlesex colleague who came from the

farming community in east Norfolk, Bill Edrich, had made 3,539. They were known as the Middlesex twins and they not only scored a huge amount of runs but they made them so quickly. The South African bowling was less exacting than the Australian, and Compton soon became a national hero. His easy going good looks and his infectious style brought him film star status and then there were his Brylcreem advertisements plastered all over the hoardings. The glistening swept-back dark hair was in itself a symbol of national well being. His postbag was enormous, but being the man he was, the letters were largely unopened. Compton's excuse was that he was 'not the most methodical of men'. The following year he ran into an Irishman called Bagenal Harvey who was horrified at the huge number of letters chucked into the back of the Compton car. He collected them up, took them home and opened them. Some contained business offers and Harvey suggested that he should become Compton's agent and this was the start of an extremely profitable relationship for them both. It was the forerunner, too, of many similar liaisons which nowadays have become almost compulsory.

Compton also played football on the left wing for Arsenal and early in 1946 was picked for England against Scotland in what was officially known as a wartime international. In 1950 he played for Arsenal in the Cup Final. After a poor first half, the manager, Tom Whittaker, had a word with him. 'Denis, you are giving up football. You have just forty-five minutes of your career left. Now I want you to go out there and give every ounce you've got.' The trainer then produced a stiff glass of whisky for him and he had a cracking second half which saw Arsenal to victory and a cup-winner's medal for Denis. I doubt Sir Alex Ferguson sanctions many half-time tots of whisky at the other Old Trafford. Throughout that season he had been playing with a bandaged right knee and, although it had behaved well enough, it was not long before

Times have changed. Cricket was played in London EC1 at this ground of the Honourable Artillery Company – without the gun powder.

Sussex play Kent at Brighton in 1840. The toffs in the members enclosure sense a photocall - or are they on the lookout for a sudden French invasion?

The West Indies in 1976 positively 'grovel' at the dismissal of Tony Greig.

The man himself – Kerry Packer, the lord of all he surveys, in a benevolent mood and without a cigarette, which is rare.

Bring on the dancing girls – cricket à la mode du King Packer, 1977.

Below Jeff Thomson embodies a glorious contest – primeval pace versus a cheerful smile. He is a highly successful landscape gardener and a hell of a nice chap.

Above Dennis Lillee of the perfect action – brilliant, fast and Machiavellian, and there's the small matter of 375 Test wickets.

Below Professors M.J. Brearley and D.K. Lillee debate the merits of an aluminium bat one sunny afternoon in Perth.

Clive Lloyd, the lugubrius one, does his best to make his presence felt against India at Lord's in the 1983 World Cup.

Has teeth, can smirk but prefers to appeal – Richard Hadlee signalling that another batsman's time has come.

Those two great pals ... well, yes, when playing together for Somerset, but not when on duty for England and the West Indies. Ian Botham and Viv Richards.

or such a modest, retiring guy, Sri Lanka's captain Arjuna Ranatunga can so easily create
he wrong impression. This cosy chat is with match referee Peter van der Merwe in
delaide in January 1999.

ngland manager Ray Illingworth waves the white flag with Michael Atherton at
eadingley, but then maybe he's judging the direction of the wind.

Sachin Tendulkar, arguably the best of the lot, shows the MCC bowlers a thing or two when batting for the Rest of the World at Lord's in 1998.

That wonderful wizard of Australia, Shane Warne, war paint and all, frightens the life out of another England batsman at Old Trafford in 1993.

Inzamam-ul-Haq, looking forward to a decent lunch, celebrates a great knock at Old Trafford in 2001.

Aravinda de Silva, another good trencherman, puts the England bowlers through their paces at The Oval in 1998.

uicksilver on the go – Jonty Rhodes stops another easy one at Lord's in 1998!

dash of old scrumpy touches the spot.
arcus Trescothick, England's find from
unton, gets to work on another half volley.

Darren Gough, 'The Dazzler', doing his best
against Pakistan at Lord's in 2001. No one
gives more, no one enjoys it more.

Montgomery made Rommel feel like this at El Alamein. Matthew Hoggard faces Saqlain Mushtaq without a friend in the world.

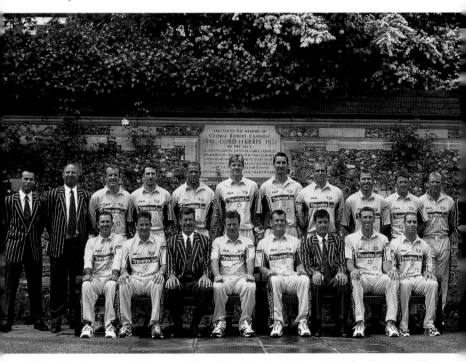

Probably the greatest side ever – Steve Waugh's Australians in England in 2001. Their power and precision is awesome.

this was to become a real problem which bedevilled the rest of his career. His mobility was now restricted and as his fast footwork had been the basis of his batting, he was badly handicapped. It came to a head early in 1956 when he had to have his right knee cap removed.

It looked as if that might be the end of his cricket, but he was determined to get back. His first game after the operation was for Forty Club, captained by his old Middlesex skipper, Walter Robins, against Eton College. Robins's side consisted of eleven former first-class cricketers and one of them, Arthur Morris, had opened the batting for Australia only the previous year. I played in that game for Eton and we won the match, thanks largely to some fine fast bowling by Edward Scott, a lifelong friend who now conducts the affairs of John Swire & Sons with a rather greater precision than he usually showed with his bowling. That day he removed Compton and Morris. Compton, standing virtually on one leg, bowled a few overs, without the help of a run up, and then made 60 remarkable runs. He wanted to move his back leg but was unable to and yet he still played some extraordinary strokes and gave us a glimpse of his astonishing powers. Compton had always been my personal hero and it was unbelievable to have played against him. After that match at Eton, it seemed that his chances of again playing first-class cricket were non-existent and yet in August he was able to play in the Fifth Test Match against Australia at the Oval and made 94. Don Bradman who was watching from the press box, described this innings as the best of the whole series.

Compton and Miller had so much in common. They were both originals and the greatest entertainers of their generation. The age of conformity had not yet arrived but even so they broke the mould. There was a wonderfully touching moment after Compton's splendid memorial service at Westminster Abbey in the summer of 1997. Keith Miller, who was not at all well, had made the journey from Australia to the

Abbey and I saw him after the service shuffling across the forecourt with the help of his metal frame. He was stooped and the hair was grey, but they were the same long and unruly locks which had flown about all over the place when he had run into bowl. He knew a great many people there and enthusiastically greeted them all by name as they passed him. The unquenchable spirit which he had brought to the game of cricket was still there. His voice was as cheerfully enthusiastic as ever. I daresay Denis would have been more pleased that his old adversary had been able to make it than anyone else in the huge congregation – one old trouper honouring another – and how much they both did at opposite ends of the world to lift the post-war gloom and give people something to laugh and cheer about.

While Denis Compton is an important figure in the development of the art of batting, so too was Len Hutton who carried on the tradition of Jack Hobbs. He was a classically correct batsman and Yorkshire through and through. While Denis Compton made his cricket bat laugh at the bowlers, there was determination rather than humour in Len Hutton's. It is seldom that a coaching manual is a laughing matter. One epitomised the north and Pudsey, just as the other could only have been a product of the south where they lived more dangerously. I am sure that Compton will have made Hutton draw in his breath sharpish on occasions and that every now and then his emotion will have sunk to something even lower than downright disapproval. Hutton will not have found Compton's careless laugh and shrug of the shoulders a helpful reply either. They were the Roundhead and the Cavalier.

John Waite, the former South African wicket keeper, tells the story of Hutton and Compton meeting unexpectedly at dinner one evening at the Queen's Hotel in Birmingham. Relations between the two of them had been cool since Compton had written a book in which he was critical of Hutton's captaincy. Wilfred Isaacs, a South African business man who

DENIS COMPTON

was a great cricket lover, was one of Waite's companions and so too was Hutton. They were sitting at a table near the door and Compton dashed in to have a word with Isaacs. It was too late to do anything about it when he noticed Hutton. Compton smiled, they greeted each other and Compton stayed to dinner. Later in the evening, Hutton who had been saying that cricket was the greatest game of all, turned to Compton and said, 'You never loved a hard fight in a Test Match, Denis, did you?'

There was a stunned silence. All those present remembered only too well the rearguard actions Compton had fought successfully for England. Compton himself was puzzled by what Hutton exactly meant and looked round the table hoping someone might enlighten him. Hutton's meaning could sometimes be a trifle misleading as a result of his Yorkshire sense of humour.

After quite a pause, Compton replied, 'No, I suppose I didn't exactly love them, Len,' and the tension eased.

'That's the difference between the southerner and the northerner,' Hutton explained. 'Up north cricketers absolutely revel in a fight. They prefer it to a match that lacks high tension.' He meant that, although Denis could fight as well as the next man, he was at his happiest when he had the freedom to play his strokes and to delight the crowd. For those born up north nothing could beat a real dogfight between Yorkshire and Lancashire. His original question was meant as a compliment to Compton that a man with his happy-go-lucky temperament could buckle down so well to a scrap when he had to.

Hutton aimed at perfection and there were no short cuts, no easy access to that end. He knew he had to work hard and had a worker's natural suspicion of the man who found it all too easy. But being artist as well as artisan he was able, just occasionally, to throw off his own shackles. In the Sydney Test in 1946/47, he played an innings of 37 in which he showed off powers of improvision no one had any idea he possessed. It was an innings which Cardus said was, 'so dazzling in clean diamond-cut strokes that old men present babbled of Victor Trumper'. It was very seldom that he let his hair down like this and when he did, he will have had a quiet word with himself afterwards. There is no doubt that he had more of a sense of humour than his bat. He loved to pull legs and the joy of it was that, like Compton in John Waite's story, no one could be completely sure that he was not being serious. When he captained England in Australia in 1954/55, the twenty-two-year-old Colin Cowdrey had a wonderful series. If the weather had not ruled out play on the first three days of the Fifth Test, Cowdrey, who was ill, would not have been able to play. After the second day had been called off, May, the vice-captain, returned to the team's hotel, visited Cowdrey and later that evening knocked on the captain's door. He had to knock again before receiving a somewhat hesitant invitation to come in. The England captain was sitting in an arm chair, looking up at the ceiling and appeared to be contemplating the infinite. After a moment he looked round at May with a question mark on his face.

'I think Colin may be fit,' May said hurriedly, probably feeling that he was intruding. Hutton looked away for a moment or two and then turned quickly back to May probably beckoning him over at the same time with a curled index finger.

'Colin who?' he asked and without the flicker of a smile.

Apart from his technical skill as a batsman, there are two things which will be remembered longest about Hutton. The first was his innings of 364 against Australia at the Oval in 1938 and the second was that he became the first professional ever to captain England. The first of these achievements was extraordinary enough. A twenty-two-year-old, in only his second season as a Test cricketer, was able to bat for thirteen hours and seventeen minutes in what was a timeless Test match. It was not the best innings he ever played, but the

mere fact that he was able to play it at all told one so much about him. As a fourteen-year-old, he had been at Headingley in 1930 when Bradman scored 309 in the day and went on to make the record Test score of 334. He will not have enjoyed the discomfort of the England bowlers then and there was no chance of him throwing his wicket away eight years later. During the war, as the result of an injury, Hutton was left with a left-arm which was two inches shorter than his right, but you would never have guessed it from his batting.

Of course he was the right man at the right time when the selectors made him the captain against India in 1952 but, although society was slowly shuffling towards change, they will not have made this move without great thought. When they finally made their choice, Lord Hawke will have performed a noisy and extremely censorious revolution in his grave. Hutton was to prove him wrong in that he became one of only two captains who have won successive series against Australia in the twentieth century. Percy Chapman was the other. He also proved his lordship wrong in that the system did not quiver and disintegrate because a professional was in charge. Perhaps the worst mistake Hutton made in the job was one of communication. After the disastrous First Test at Brisbane in 1954/55, he dropped Alec Bedser for the Second, who learned the news with considerable dismay when he saw the team sheet pinned up in the dressing room. This was clumsy and unnecessary. Hutton beat India, Australia twice and New Zealand and drew a difficult series against the West Indies in 1953/54. Shortly before his retirement Hutton wrote a letter to the writer, Alan Ross: 'I refrain from saying too much,' he began. 'I am Yorkshire bred and born, you know. I have bought a drink but not too often.' Again, that slight twinkle at the end. I fancy Len Hutton, wherever he may be, will be enjoying the last laugh of all.

Alec Bedser was one of only four England bowlers to have

taken more than a hundred wickets against Australia. He took 104 in twenty-one Test Matches at a lively fast medium and joined Robert Peel, Sydney Barnes and Wilfred Rhodes – a formidable quartet. Alec, like his almost identical twin brother, Eric, is a huge man who was always determined to give of his best. He is a gentle giant who has never settled for anything less than the old fashioned standards and disciplines which served him so well. He took twenty-two wickets in his first two Tests, against India in 1946. In 1948 he dismissed Bradman four times in successive Test innings and in 1953 against Australia he took thirty-nine wickets in the series. Perhaps the best ball he ever bowled was in Adelaide in 1946/47 when he bowled Bradman for nought. 'It was delivered,' recalled the Don, 'on the off stump, swung very late to hit the pitch on the leg stump, and then came back to hit the middle and off.' The Almighty would have been hard pressed to lay a bat on that one.

Bedser insisted that his wicket keeper always stood up to the stumps and there has been no finer sight in cricket than Godfrey Evans keeping wicket to him. Evans, a real jack-in-the-box, was the most explosive and mercurial of keepers and a great inspiration to his fielders. Some of his stumpings and catches down the legside were amazing and he was one of the game's great characters. Bedser took 236 Test wickets in all and the most remarkable part of it was that he received no real help from the other end. He was always having to do it on his own. With his huge fingers, he spun his principal weapon, the ball that moved from leg to off, as Barnes had done rather than cut it off the seam as most bowlers do. He could bat a bit too and once made 79 going in as nightwatchman against Australia at Leeds. He was then run out by Denis Compton who unwisely chose to run to a misfield in the covers by Sam Loxton. As Bedser vainly tried to make his ground, he said in rhythm with his ever more frantic strides, 'You've – done – me – you – bloody – fool.' And he was well done

too. No more genuine or more friendly man has ever played cricket than Alec Bedser.

With characters like these, cricket was assured of recovering from the war and again becoming a wonderful entertainment.

CHAPTER 10

CARIBBEAN PUNCH

O NCE THE GAME had re-established itself after the war, it
was to be dominated more and more by the West Indies.
Learie Constantine had given the world a taste of what they
could bring to the game and then the baton was picked up
by George Headley, the small Jamaican batsman, who first
played Test cricket against England in 1929/30. He scored 176
in the First Test Match of that series, two separate hundreds in
the Third, and 223 in the Fourth, when the West Indies had
been left to score a mere 836 to win. These runs were admittedly made against something less than a full England side
because England were playing another Test series in New
Zealand at the same time. Just before the war began, Headley
became the first batsman to score two separate hundreds in
a Test match at Lord's. His remarkable career, in which he
scored 2,190 runs in twenty-two matches and at an average
of almost 61, leaves him to stand comparison with anyone.

Headley was known as the 'Black Bradman'. He was said
to be a better bad wicket batsman than Bradman and at the
time he played the West Indies won very few matches, which
created pressures Bradman did not often have to cope with.
Headley was a beautifully balanced player who, when he
began, scored all his runs on the offside. He found that he
was constantly being attacked on the leg stump with the
fielders on the off. His reaction was to teach himself to become
a fine player on that side of the wicket too. He had one most

unusual quirk. Before he was due to bat in a Test Match he lay awake all night with his mind playing every type of ball each one of the opposing bowlers might produce the next day. It was a strange form of preparation and, I would have thought, extremely exhausting but it seemed to provide the answer.

He was a man of few words who fought to gain recognition for the black people of the Caribbean, for the majority of whom life was a considerable struggle. I met Headley in the old pavilion at Sabina Park in the mid-seventies. I had just written my first book, *Cricket in Three Moods*, which was about three series involving the West Indies, and something in it had upset him. I cannot remember what the passage was, but I know he felt that I was being derogatory about his fellow Jamaicans. He told me quietly and severely in an unforgiving tone where I had gone wrong and, having said his piece, moved away in a manner which did not suggest that it would have been wise to try and continue the conversation. He made me feel very small and in that short exchange I could see the strong-willed determination which must have made him such a fearsome opponent on the field. I don't think much leg-pulling will have gone on in his corner of the dressing room.

Like so many, the war robbed him of several more highly productive years. When it ended, West Indies cricket found they had three young men in Barbados who were performing remarkable feats in the inter-colonial competition, as it was then known. By a strange coincidence their names all began with the letter W: Frank Worrell, Clyde Walcott and Everton Weekes. These three, with some help from 'Those two friends of mine, Ramadhin and Valentine', and one or two others like Allan Rae and Jeff Stollmeyer, soon turned the West Indies into a major cricketing power. In 1947/48 another England side, captained by a recycled Gubby Allen in his dotage and without several of the best players, were beaten 2–0. India were conquered in the Subcontinent with Weekes scoring four

consecutive Test hundreds which made a sequence of five in all, a record which still stands. He was run out for 90 in his next innings. England were then demolished 3–1 in England with Ramadhin and Valentine taking fifty-nine wickets between them in the four Test Matches which was all the West Indies were, rather patronisingly, allowed.

The three W's performed what must have been regarded as a miracle in the Caribbean. It was largely thanks to their efforts that within three years the West Indies side was standing shoulder to shoulder with the best in the world. It was Weekes, Worrell and Walcott who laid the trail for Worrell himself, Sobers, Hall, Kanhai, Gibbs and the rest to take them right to the top of the pile where they were to remain for the best part of thirty years. The pivotal figure of the three was Frank Worrell. Like the other two, he was a brilliant cricketer, but he had a greater goal in life than just playing cricket supremely well. He wanted, in so doing, to show that West Indian players were as good as any others in the world. He wanted to raise the status of the game in the Caribbean and he saw it as a vehicle through which West Indians might earn worldwide respect. He was also determined to improve the lot of the coloured West Indian players. Constantine was the first to say that the West Indians were as good as any other players in the world. When he was asked by the writer, C.L.R. James, why they lost so regularly, replied, 'We need a black captain.' This had nothing to do with race. Constantine knew the West Indians did not play as a team and to do so, they needed a captain who respected his players who in turn would respect him. That was the way forward because only then would you bring the best out in the team. Worrell will have understood this all too well.

Worrell moved to Jamaica in 1947 because of a legacy of bitterness from his days at school which is probably code for racially entrenched privilege. Jamaica was a more open society. He began to flex his muscles with the cricket authori-

161

ties when he was picked to tour India in 1948/49. He asked the West Indies Board of Control to pay him a reasonable but modest fee. The Board considered this to be a gross impertinence and refused to negotiate with him. Worrell dug in his heels and did not go to India. By doing this, he had shown the Board that the days when they could exploit black professionals were coming to an end. Everyone, the Board, the players and the public, knew then that there was more to Worrell than just cricket. The following year, 1949/50, he went to India as captain of a hastily put together Commonwealth side, collected from players in the Leagues in England. He batted magnificently and his captaincy showed that he had an outstanding cricket brain, as well as being a natural leader. He had made his point and from then on the West Indies Board offered their players rather better contracts. In his dealings with anyone, be it his next door neighbour, his fellow players or the Board of Control, Worrell was shrewd and humorous and showed unfailing courtesy. These will have been strong weapons against the sort of antagonism he will have faced. Without Worrell, the West Indies would not have developed as quickly or as successfully as they did.

John Goddard, the white patriarch from Barbados and a good enough batsman to have added more than 500 with Worrell against Trinidad, had captained the West Indies in India. He was now to take the side to England in 1950. The batting of the three W's and the unfathomable spin of Ram and Val, gave the West Indies the most important victory in their history so far. At one point of the tour Everton Weekes was in blistering form and Worrell gave him some interesting advice. 'Everton, you must not hit the ball so hard. You give the fielders no chance, so they don't chase the ball. Hit it a little less hard and they will have to run after it. Watch how quickly they will tire.' Weekes, the most cheerful and delightful of men and also an outstanding bridge player, laughed, conceded the point and continued to hit the ball as hard as

ever – he couldn't help himself. The West Indies lost the First Test at Old Trafford, but won the next three. On Australian wickets in 1951/52, the spinners were not so effective, while Lindwall, Miller and left-arm seamer, Bill Johnston, coped with the three W's. Australia won 4–1 after a series which was more exciting and closer than the overall outcome suggests. It was some time before the West Indies were able to get the measure of Australia.

Gary Sobers made a quiet entry into Test cricket at Kingston's Sabina Park as a slow left-arm spinner, in the Fifth Test against England in 1953/54. England won the match by nine wickets and drew the series 2–2, but then, in 1957, the West Indies came to England hoping to repeat their triumph of seven years earlier. They wheeled out the same cast of players and brought back the ageing Goddard, through no fault of his own, as captain. This must rank among the crassest selections made in the history of a game which is overflowing with dubious decisions most of which were in favour either of bringing back the birch or giving new life to the feudal system. Goddard, a decent enough all-round cricketer in his day, now became the last symbol of a dying order.

It all fell apart in the First Test, just when it looked as if Ramadhin had done it again – Valentine was left out of the side on the morning of the match. Ramadhin took seven wickets and England were bowled out at Edgbaston for 186. The West Indies made 474 with Collie Smith, who was tragically to be killed in car crash two years later at the age of twenty-six, making 161. In their second innings, England were poised at 113/3, Ramadhin having taken two wickets, when Peter May and Colin Cowdrey came together. By the time they were separated they had put on 411 and the bubble of Ramadhin had burst. He took only fourteen wickets in the series and Valentine not a single one. When the match finished the West Indies were hanging on desperately at 72/7 in their second innings. It was an astonishing metamorphosis. England went

on to take the series 3–1 and they won all three of their matches by more than an innings. Morale within the West Indies side broke down and discipline with it. In 1950 Goddard had captained a winning side and victory cements players together. Now the West Indies were losing, everything fell apart and Goddard did not then have the credentials either from a cricketing or a social point of view to pull it all together.

But still the old dinosaurs who ran West Indies cricket could not get it right. One of the old school who saw the future was Jeff Stollmeyer who, with Allan Rae, had formed such a fine opening partnership in 1950 and thereabouts. Stollmeyer who briefly succeeded Goddard after his first spell as captain, had been effectively booted into touch, presumably as a left-wing revolutionary – the bring back the birch syndrome again. When Goddard departed the second time, they looked to find salvation in Gerry Alexander, the white Jamaican wicket keeper. He took charge of the side for their series against Pakistan in the Caribbean which saw the brilliant flowering of Gary Sobers. It is extraordinary to think that Sobers played sixteen Test Matches before scoring a century. He had batted well in the first two games against Pakistan. He emerged from the pavilion at Sabina Park for the third match with the scoreboard showing 87/1. When he finally returned, the West Indies had amassed 790/3 and he had scored no less than 365 not out, beating Len Hutton's 364 against Australia at the Oval as the highest ever Test score. Alexander then took the side to India and Pakistan on a tour which saw a young and wonderfully talented fast bowler, Roy Gilchrist, sent home for bowling fast beamers against a beturbaned Sikh, Swranjit Singh, in a Zonal match. Gilchrist, who was genuinely fast, came from the poorest of backgrounds and was full of complexes, and never played for the West Indies again. He had just taken twenty-six wickets in four Tests against India. The establishment were not of a mind to offer a helping hand and

slammed the door behind him. Alexander stayed on to captain the side against England in 1959/60, although he himself had begged the Board to appoint Worrell who was back in Jamaica after finishing his degree at Manchester University. The Board wouldn't hear of it. Surprisingly the West Indies lost that series to England 1–0 and now no one was able to stand in Worrell's way.

The Board, who had behaved for much too long as if they were an assortment of First World War generals, made him captain for the tour to Australia in 1960/61 and I am sure it was done with the greatest reluctance. There would have been those who would have rubbed their hands with glee if it had all gone wrong, but they did not know their man. Worrell's opposite number was Richie Benaud and they could not have been a more perfect combination. Cricket was in the doldrums in Australia and both captains agreed to play attacking cricket and were true to their word. The First Test in Brisbane produced the first tie in the history of Test cricket and the series went on in that vein. The scores were level at Brisbane with Australia'a last pair at the wicket and Wes Hall still had two balls of the last over remaining. Worrell went up to him and said quietly, 'Remember, Wes, if you bowl a no-ball, you'll never be able to go back to Barbados.' Hall said he was so frightened by what his captain had said to him that his foot landed about a yard behind the crease. By putting it humorously as he did, Worrell had ensured that the need not to err stayed at the front of Hall's mind. It was a measure of Worrell's skill as a captain and a man manager. In the end Australia won the series 2–1, but only after Australia's last wicket pair of 'Slasher' Mackay and Lindsay Kline had survived for the last hundred minutes of the Fourth Test in Adelaide. More than half a million people turned out on the streets of Melbourne to say goodbye to Worrell and his team when they left the country. It was the greatest series ever, masterminded in part by the first black man ever to captain the West Indies, a man

who had been inextricably drawn to the post since the day he had left Barbados as a result of the racial elitism.

That series and Worrell's part in it established once and for all that the old order of things in the Caribbean was on the way out, even if its elderly protagonists were to do their best to hang onto it for as long as they could. But, before he finished, Worrell was to do even better than that. He took the West Indies to a comprehensive victory by five matches to nil over India in the Caribbean and then he brought the side to England in 1963. They won that series 3–1 and again Worrell's captaincy was an object lesson, not only from a tactical point of view, but also from the way in which he handled his troops. When England won the Third Test at Edgbaston with Fred Trueman taking twelve wickets, a side under a lesser captain might have found itself at a crisis point and have fallen apart, as the West Indies had done under Goddard in 1957. Worrell, who was thirty-eight, did not allow this to happen and gave point to Constantine's words that the best would not be seen from the West Indians until they had a black captain.

It is in many ways a sombre tale, but one which was so important for West Indies cricket and therefore for the history of the game. Having achieved all that he had set himself to do, Worrell retired from the captaincy after the tour to England in 1963 and was to die of leukaemia four years later at the age of forty-two. Gary Sobers, who was Worrell's choice, took over and the side continued for a few years to play the joyful and successful cricket his predecessor had ordained, until age took a hand at the end of the decade. When Sobers received a letter from the West Indies Board offering him the captaincy, it was some time before he answered it. He was overawed that someone from his poor background should be offered the job and he was not yet sure he wanted to take on the added responsibility. It was Sobers' opinion that 'a captain has to be about half a dozen men, all rolled into one. He has to have

the nerve of a gambler, the poise of a financier, the human understanding of a psychologist, ten years more cricket knowledge than he can ever possess, and the patience of a saint.' No wonder he hesitated. C.L.R. James had no doubt that he fulfilled all these many sided requirements. After Sobers' first Test as captain, James wrote, 'To see in the course of one day Sobers despatch the ball to all parts of the field with his bat, then open the bowling, fielding at slip to Hall or Griffith, change to Gibbs and place himself at short leg, then go on to bowl slows, meanwhile placing his men and changing them with certainty and ease, this is one of the sights of the modern cricket field. I cannot visualise anything in the past that corresponds to it.' He captures the genius of Sobers.

Sobers was the fairest of captains, even if he did not have quite his predecessor's insight into human nature, and he loved nothing more than to take part in a good game of cricket. Worrell was a more cautious captain and understandably so when one considers the importance of the exercise he had undertaken. He could not risk the charge of irresponsibility which those First World War generals would have seized upon at once and equated with the perceived fallability of the black man. Worrell's success had made it possible for Sobers to take over his job. Perhaps only Sobers, and none of his predecessors, would have declared at Port of Spain in March 1968, leaving England to score 215 in 165 minutes with Charlie Griffith unfit to bowl. His thinking, prompted by the West Indian team manager Everton Weekes, was that it would need only ten balls to win the match, but those particular balls were not forthcoming and England won by seven wickets. Sobers was pilloried for his declaration and even accused of being light-hearted about West Indian nationalism.

When he arrived in Guyana the next day for the Fifth Test Match, he was given a police escort. He had no regrets for he will have felt it was a legitimate gamble and in the Second Test in Kingston, he had himself almost enabled the West

Indies to pull off a miracle after they had followed on. The West Indies, 233 runs behind on first innings, were 204/5 when the crowd rioted. Sobers went on to make 113 not out and at the end England were hanging on at 68/8 on an unscheduled sixth morning to make up the time lost because of the riot, Sobers having taken three wickets himself. Being the player he was, he had won back most of his opponents a little over two weeks after losing in Trinidad when he made 152 and 95 not out in the Fifth Test, although in the end he was frustrated by the last England pair of Alan Knott and Jeff Jones. He could not bear nor understand defensive cricket. It was his bad luck that, after winning again in England in 1966, old age began to take its toll of his side, although it was not until the tour to Australia in 1968/69 that it began to disintegrate. There were too many ageing prima donnas. The selectors first decided to leave behind the twenty-nine-year-old Hall. Sobers wanted Hall and said that if he was dropped, they would have to find another captain. Of course, Sobers and Hall were both in the party, so too was a young man called Clive Lloyd who had established himself in the side in the series against England the year before. Enormously tall with a prowl rather than a walk and with glasses seemingly perched well down his nose, he looked, for all the world, more like a biology student than a Test cricketer. It was John Arlott on the BBC's *Test Match Special* who aptly described him as 'looking more like Paddington Bear than Paddington Bear'.

Sobers was now into his thirties and although his own personal performances continued to be remarkable, he did not enjoy captaining a losing side. He began to let things drift just when he should have been doing everything to encourage his players and to stretch them to their limits. By now, he was playing for Nottinghamshire in the English summers and it was in 1968 when they visited Swansea to play Glamorgan that Sobers famously struck the left-arm spin of Malcolm Nash for six consecutive sixes in one over. The following year

GARY SOBERS

his unworldliness took over when he was invited to go to Southern Rhodesia and coach young blacks. He accepted the invitation without talking to anyone who could have given him important advice. Ian Smith's white regime was under attack everywhere and in the Caribbean the idea of Sobers going out there in support caused an immediate and inevitable uproar. It never occurred to Sobers that he was doing anything wrong. When he understood what he had done, he was quick to apologise roundly and profusely and was forgiven by almost everyone. There was an engaging innocence about him which seemed to radiate out of his distinctly boyish figure and was part of his charm.

Sobers was a romantic figure and humour was never too far away either because he was one of those rare people who so obviously loved what he was doing. For him cricket has never been anything other than a game, whether it was played on a beach in Barbados or in a Test Match at Lord's. His introduction to first division cricket in Barbados was unusual, to say the least. He was playing for the Barbados Cricket League which is a sort of second division to the Barbados Cricket Association (BCA). Denis Atkinson, who played for Barbados and the West Indies, introduced him to Captain Wilfred Farmer who was captain of the Police cricket team who played in the BCA. Sobers bowled him out in the nets and Farmer said to him, 'How would you like to play first eleven cricket? I could get you into the Police band and that would qualify you to play for the team.' Although he had never played an instrument in his life, he accepted. The following Monday he joined the band at the St Cecilia Barracks as a bugler. In his first innings for the Police, he tried to hook a short one and was hit in the mouth and forced to retire. This severely impeded his bugle blowing. He shirked the next few practice sessions and was replaced. Captain Farmer now arranged for him to join the Police Boys Club which meant that he could still play for the Police and he stayed with the club throughout his career.

He lost the three-match series in England in 1969 and in 1971/72 he was still captain when New Zealand managed to draw all five of their Tests on their first tour to the Caribbean. Sobers was blamed for this and the captaincy now went to his contemporary, Rohan Kanhai from Guyana who must go down as one of the great batsmen in the history of the game. Kanhai was not such a sympathetic captain as Sobers or Worrell and was too emotional for his own good. But in 1973 he took the West Indies to victory in England and in the last of the three Test Matches, at Lord's, he and Sobers both reached 150 in a valedictory display of dashing and exuberant West Indian strokeplay, taking their side to victory by an innings and 226 runs. Kanhai could only draw the series against England in 1973/74 when Dennis Amiss and Geoff Boycott batted brilliantly. Tony Greig, bowling slow off breaks for almost the first time, took 13/156 in the Fifth Test in Port of Spain, and in what was to be Sobers' and Kanhai's last Test Match, steered England to victory by 26 runs. The West Indies now decided it was time to move on and when they went to India in 1974/75, Clive Lloyd was the captain and a new era in West Indies cricket was about to begin.

CHAPTER 11

TESTING NATIONS

THERE WAS a marked increase in the amount of Test cricket once the game was up and running after the Second World War. Australia ruled the roost for the first few years after hostilities had ended before the West Indies and England had their moments. The West Indies, as we have seen, India and New Zealand who had established not much more than a toehold on the international calendar in the ten years before the war, now began to take a fuller part in international competition. Touring sides came to England every year and in the winter, even if England themselves were not involved, there was one if not two Test series being played somewhere. Partition in India meant that Pakistan came on the scene and played their first Test Matches south of the border in India in 1952/53. The chance of this initial series, which was won by India, being completed without interruption, not to say blood-letting, seemed remote, but the only hold-ups were caused by rain and not riots. These series, which were only ever played intermittently because of the political tensions between the two countries, were to become excruciatingly boring as neither side was prepared to take a chance that might end in defeat and national disgrace.

In England the distinction between amateurs and professionals was abolished in November 1962, bringing an end to one of the showpiece games of the year, Gentlemen v Players. The man on the public address system at Lord's would

never again be asked to announce that the one change in the scorecard was that F.J. Titmus should read Titmus, F.J. The feudal system had decreed that the initials of amateurs should precede their surname, while the initials of the professionals should follow theirs. Now everyone was a cricketer. The first limited overs competition, the Gillette Cup, came into being in England in 1963 and this form of the game was to proliferate. In 1975 the first limited over World Cup competition was played in England and two years later the game was stood on its head by the Packer revolution. By the turn of the century, the body politic of international cricket had increased to ten countries as first Sri Lanka and then Zimbabwe and Bangladesh were given Test Match status. By then the evils of match-fixing, inspired by the illegal gambling community in Bombay and their wealthy backers in the Middle East and Malaysia, were beginning to come to light. Cricket, as Cardus pointed out, has always followed society, but as the game careered helter-skelter through the nineties up to the twenty-first century, there were moments when it seemed anxious to become the leader.

The game was still full of rich and diverse characters. After Bradman, the Australian captaincy had gone to Lindsay Hassett who, although even smaller than the Don, could hardly have been a more different sort of person. He was one of the great leg-pullers and delightfully impish as well as being a fine captain and a brilliant batsman. Rumour has it that after Australia's defeat at the Oval in 1953, when England regained the Ashes for the first time since the Bodyline tour more than twenty years before, the Australian dressing room needed plastic surgery after the game, and that the Australian captain was largely responsible. But after the match he made a handsome speech congratulating the English which, he himself later said in private, he considered to be generous as Tony Lock had chucked out five of his batsmen in the second innings. One of his greatest moments came five years after

he had retired. Jim Swanton, the famous cricket writer, had been married in 1958 and he came out with his wife, Ann, to cover England's 1958/59 tour of Australia on an extended honeymoon. The general billet for the First Test was the old Lennon's Hotel in Brisbane and one night, a fair while after the Swantons had gone to bed, Hassett knocked furiously on their door and, when Jim opened it, an impressively saturated Hassett, who was dwarflike in comparison to Swanton, ducked under his arm and, fully dressed, jumped into bed with his wife. Swanton drew himself up to his full height and was heard to say in those unmistakeable booming tones which rang down the corridors, 'Really, Hassett, this time you've gone too far.'

On his first tour of England in 1938, the Australians were staying at Grindleford in Derbyshire. Bill O'Reilly was sharing a room with Stan McCabe and they were both woken up in the middle of the night by the heavy breathing of a muddy goat as it walked about the room. No one owned up, but when Hassett sent a suit to the cleaners the next morning, it was considered to be strong circumstantial evidence. At the time of the Second World War, the laws of the game allowed the bowling side to take a new ball after 200 runs had been scored. Hassett was in an Egyptian port during the war when they came across a hugely rich Arab attended by a vast retinue. They were told that this sheik had 198 wives. Hassett thought for a moment before saying, 'Hm, two more and he'd be entitled to a new ball.' He loved to have a go at pomposity and pretension. At a civic reception in Nottingham he asked the mayor, 'If I pull your chain will it flush?' It was all done in a way no one could object to. He was a batsman with an unusually delicate touch and he made the late cut his own. He scored one century every five times he went to the wicket which put him as close to Bradman as anyone. As captain, he won fourteen of his twenty-four Test Matches, only one fewer than Bradman. When he finished playing, he graced

the press and commentary boxes and was a constant source of merriment, once saying as he looked out of the Lord's press box, 'I'm glad I wasn't up here when I was down there.'

In 1954/55, the England selectors took a plunge and picked Frank Tyson, an extremely fast but undisciplined bowler for the tour of Australia. Fred Trueman had gone to the West Indies the winter before but had not had a good tour, either on or off the field, even if his alleged 'Pass salt, Gunga Din' request to the governor of a small island was malicious fabrication. Nonetheless, it is fair to say that he kicked over the traces enough to have few supporters when the selectors picked the side for Australia the following winter. Another greenhorn chosen for Australia was the twenty-two-year-old Colin Cowdrey. Len Hutton won the toss in the First Test at Brisbane, put Australia in to bat and watched while they amassed 601/8 declared. England lost by an innings and Tyson took 1/160.

In the sixteen days before the Second Test, Tyson was persuaded to shorten his run by half and this was also the point at which Hutton made the decision to drop Alec Bedser without apparently having the guts to tell him.

Tyson's short run was the answer and he took twenty-five wickets in the next three Tests, bowling as fast as anyone has ever done. Don Bradman said that he was the fastest he had ever seen although, of course, he never faced him. Tyson was a very strong man and the short run enabled him to harness his energy better and achieve a rhythm which had been missing in the first match.

England won the next three Tests, but not without a number of anxious moments. Brian Statham was the perfect partner for the 'Typhoon', an inevitable and well-earned nickname. Godfrey Evans's wicket keeping was superb and his catching off Neil Harvey, far down the legside early on the last morning of the Third Test in Melbourne, was remarkable even by his standards, as well as being a decisive blow. Hutton's captaincy

was sound and shrewd, while not being given to flights of fancy. It was a series I followed at school with my ear glued to an illegal wireless which I hid under the bedclothes. I don't think I have ever experienced anything so deeply exciting as hearing the Australian accents of Alan MacGilvray, Johnny Moyes and the others through the snap, crackle and pop of the atmospherics at about half past five or six o'clock in the morning in December and January's chilling pitch dark.

By the time the Australians had arrived in England in 1956, I had graduated to television by the kind permission of the man who ran the School Office at Eton. When Jim Laker took those nineteen wickets in the Fourth Test at Old Trafford, I was perched for as long as I could in a medievally dark room on the edge of a hard and uncomfortable armchair which had been extensively embroidered. The pitch may have been a disgrace, but for a chauvinistic boy that couldn't have mattered less. I shall take the bewildered looks of all those Australian batsmen to the grave with me. I have never understood why the controller of the England dressing room doesn't carry with him a tape of all nineteen wickets and play it whenever morale is looking a trifle shaky. David Lloyd when he was the coach, apparently played Winston Churchill's wartime speeches. Laker would have had my vote every time.

An ageing England side returned to Australia in 1958/59 full of confidence but they found that Richie Benaud's shrewd captaincy and an assortment of bowlers, who chucked or dragged and sometimes both, an insuperable obstacle and lost 4–0. Ian Meckiff was thought to have a kink in his arm at the wrong time, and Keith Slater and Jim Burke were, to say the least, questionable. Then there was Gordon Rorke who dragged his back foot so far that he eventually released the ball from about eighteen yards which made him a nasty proposition. Suspect bowling actions have aroused strong feelings since John Willes was no-balled for bowling round-arm at

Lord's in 1822. Don Bradman summed up the problem when he said soon after this series: 'It is the most complex question I have known in cricket, because it is not a matter of fact, but of opinion and interpretation. It is so involved that two men of equal goodwill and sincerity could take opposite views.' Don Bradman, still very much the man in charge in Australia, got together with Gubby Allen, his counterpart at Lord's, and they agreed that those with suspicious actions should not be chosen. This meant that the immediate crisis was alleviated and the Australians did not choose Ian Meckiff to tour England in 1961. It did not do much to help the problem in the long term as the hooha over the Sri Lankan, Muttiah Muralitheran's action, at the turn of the century was to show. The philosophy may be that a slow chucker is not so bad as a fast chucker but, in truth, this is another problem the game's establishment has made a business of ducking whenever it thinks it can get away with it.

Before the war, South Africa had never been a consistent threat to England or Australia. The pattern continued afterwards and in 1947 they had the bad luck to run into the full blast of Denis Compton and Bill Edrich. Things were not much better in 1951 when they were beaten 3-1. This was a tour which produced one absurd incident which caused a great amount of wailing and a good deal of gnashing of teeth besides. In their match against Lancashire, Eric Rowan, who, as we have already seen, could be an awkward chap, and John Waite, their eternally cheerful and charming wicket keeper, opened the batting and put on 81 in two hours before lunch. They were roundly barracked for their slow scoring by 15,000 spectators which was hypocrisy taken to new levels because they had been brought up on a diet of hard fought battles between Lancashire and Yorkshire when 81 runs before lunch can only mean batting without due care and attention. The two batsmen sat down on the pitch in protest. Rowan was out after lunch and had plenty to say when he went through

the members' stand on the way back. His version was that someone has said to him, 'Go back where you come from, you South African bastard.' Rowan's reply had been spectacularly unprintable and the result was an uproar. That evening the manager decided to send Rowan home, but in the end after Dudley Nourse, the captain, had intervened, Rowan made a written apology which was given to the press. It caused a furore in South Africa and almost certainly led to the dropping of Rowan for the tour to Australia in 1952/53. It had even been suggested that the tour to Australia should be called off to allow South African cricket to get a grip of itself. Even in those days cricket deserved its well-earned reputation for getting its knickers into a twist.

In the First Test of that tour, Nourse, arguably South Africa's best batsman to that point in their history, won the game with an extraordinarily brave innings of 208. In their match against Gloucestershire he had broken his left thumb and by the time the side came to Trent Bridge for the First Test, a steel pin had been inserted. He was given a local anaesthetic to numb the pain and during his innings the pin moved out of place. He batted for nine and a quarter hours and received considerable barracking from a big crowd which did not know about his handicap. Every time he hit the ball he took his hand off the bat in pain and to make things worse he pulled a muscle in his thigh towards the end of his innings. It was in the Fifth Test of that series that Hutton became only the fourth man ever to be given out in first-class cricket for obstructing the field. A ball from Athol Rowan, the left-arm spinner, ballooned up from the top edge of his bat and, in trying to stop it coming down onto his stumps, Hutton prevented Endean, the wicket keeper, from making the catch. It was not until the second half of the sixties that South Africa produced a side able to beat all comers, but within a year or two of that, Prime Minister Vorster decided he would not allow England to take Basil D'Oliveira on a tour of South

Africa and, because of their apartheid policies, they were ostracised for more than twenty years.

It took New Zealand a long time to make their presence felt at the top level. They had played their first Test Match, against England at Lancaster Park in Christchurch in January 1930, at the same time as the Honourable F.S.G. Calthorpe's side was engaged in a Test Match against the West Indies in Barbados. The match against New Zealand was made memorable by Maurice Allom, an amateur fast bowler from Surrey, who went on to become President of MCC, when he took four wickets in five balls in New Zealand's first innings in only his eighth over in Test cricket. When New Zealand came to England for three Test Matches in 1937, they picked a twenty-year-old, Martin Donnelly, who was to go on, all too briefly after the war, to become one of the greatest left-handed batsmen of all time. He played in only seven Tests and all of them were in England, three in 1937 and four in 1949 when New Zealand were allowed nothing more than three-day Test matches by the imperial hierarchy at Lord's. When peace returned, Donnelly went up to Oxford and played an innings of 142 in the 1946 University match which was considered probably the greatest innings ever played in those matches. A year later, this short and rather stocky left-hander made 162 not out for the Gentlemen against the Players and then, in 1949, he scored 206 for New Zealand against England in the Lord's Test Match. This completed a sequence which has only ever been achieved by Percy Chapman who, as we have seen, made hundreds at Lord's for Cambridge, the Gentlemen and England. Donnelly was a remarkable athlete and played one rugger international, for England against Ireland where, a stand-off half by trade, he played out of position in the centre.

Donnelly was terrific fun in his whimsical way and the most charming and modest of men with a great sense of humour. No fairer sportsman can ever have existed. Captaining Oxford

against Sussex in 1947, Donnelly recalled Peter Doggart, the brother of Hubert who played twice for England, against the West Indies in 1950, when he had been given out leg before. Donnelly's own account of the incident shows how much times have changed since those days. 'There was a bit of moisture in the wicket and I was fielding at silly mid off . . . I was crouching there, watching the batsman closely as Mallett bowled, and there was no doubt in my mind that he hit the ball. I followed its flight as it flew to Travers at first slip, where he dropped the bloody thing . . . Mallett appealed and the umpire gave Doggart out, leg before. I thought the dismissal was unfair and Doggart had to stay . . . I told the umpire I was certain the ball deflected from the bat. The umpire realised I was entitled to take this course.' The umpire, who was at the time on trial as a candidate for the first-class list, may not have been quite as understanding as Donnelly thought.

Another delightful story about Donnelly at Oxford is told by Tony Sutton who also won Blues for cricket and rugger at the same time as Donnelly. They were both up at Worcester and again, it is a story of the time.

One evening Martin and I went to a ball at Pembroke. The porter saw us going out in our white ties and tails. As he didn't see us come back before midnight, which we were obliged to do according to the College rules, [Donnelly had been a major during the war and Sutton a captain, but College rules were College rules] he reported the fact to the Dean, one Colonel Wilkinson, who summoned us to his rooms. He asked us at what time, and by which method, we had returned to College the previous night. We had to admit that on our 3 a.m. return, we had climbed over the wall. He then gave us a quotation from a poem and told us that we must let him know the correct source of the poem by 6 p.m. that evening. If we failed to meet the deadline we would each pay him a fine of five pounds, a

lot of money in those days. We sought out a chap who was doing English and he referred us to the *Oxford Dictionary of Quotations*. We found the quotation, wrote a note to the Dean giving the name of the poet and the poem, and then rushed off to the Parks to play for the university, play starting at 11.30 a.m. During the afternoon, the Dean arrived in the pavilion and happily sat, smoking his pipe and watching the cricket. At the tea interval he beckoned Martin, who was in the middle of an innings, and myself, and produced a book containing the poem we had named. He proved to us that the quotation was not contained in that poem. Consternation! Martin and I discussed what should be done. Martin got himself out (immediately after tea) so that he could rush back to College to consult the English scholar and his dictionary. They discovered that in our haste we had mistakenly taken the source from above where it was printed, instead of below it. Martin was able to provide the Dean with a copy of the original poem and its source just before the 6 p.m. deadline. The Dean thoroughly enjoyed the whole incident.

When the New Zealanders came to England in 1949, they also had the young Bert Sutcliffe in the party who was another truly formidable left-hander. It was Sutcliffe and Donnelly who enabled the New Zealanders to beat Lancashire at Aigburth when they had been left to score 153 to win on a dusty pitch in an hour and a quarter. They put on 120 in fifty minutes and they won by nine wickets with seven minutes to spare. It was a sign of the sporting way the game was played in those days that 25.5 overs were bowled in sixty-eight minutes. There was a lovely easy fluency about Sutcliffe's stroke play, while Donnelly took more risks, played more creative strokes and his footwork made the bowlers appear to be bowling exactly the length he wanted. Donnelly was paid the ultimate tribute by C.B. Fry. When he was asked if he had ever seen a left-hander better than Donnelly, he answered, emphatically,

'No, not one.' According to Denys Rowbotham who watched the game against Lancashire for the *Manchester Guardian*, Donnelly remained poker-faced throughout, although there was an abundance of humour, if not outright laughter, in his batting. He and Sutcliffe repeated their performance against Hampshire when the target was 109 in thirty-five minutes. They won with five minutes to spare and 11.5 overs had been bowled in half an hour. John Reid, who was to be such a central figure in New Zealand's cricket for so many years, was another young man on that tour and the side was captained by Walter Hadlee who became surely the most remarkable cricketing progenitor of them all.

Sutcliffe's most extraordinary innings was played at Ellis Park in Johannesburg in 1953/54. He went in when New Zealand were 9/2 and his third ball, from Neil Adcock, hit him a nasty blow on the head, forcing him to retire. He was taken to hospital and fainted while his head was being X-rayed. He returned to the crease at 81/6 and, scoring 80 out of 106 in 112 minutes, hit seven sixes and four fours while the other four wickets fell. His head was bandaged all the way round and, when it came loose, medical staff came from the pavilion to help. The occasion was made even more poignant because on the first day of the match, Christmas Eve, an appalling rail crash in New Zealand on the Auckland to Dunedin line had killed 151 people. The fiancée of Bob Blair, the last man in, had been one of them and the New Zealanders had left Blair at their hotel that morning. When the ninth wicket fell at 154 the players made as if to leave the field. But, to complete silence, Blair emerged from the pavilion and helped Sutcliffe add 33 for the last wicket in what may have been Test cricket's bravest ever stand. One Johannesburg writer described Sutcliffe's innings as 'The greatest 80 ever made in Test cricket'. That would be difficult to deny. Blair's six, which came in one stroke off Hugh Tayfield, deserves a defining label. Sutcliffe scored 2,727 runs for

New Zealand in forty-two Tests and was never once on the winning side. It was not until the 1970s that New Zealand became a consistently stronger side. Sutcliffe never threw off the effects of that blow on the head and was not the same cricketer afterwards.

Pakistan's first Test match was played in Delhi in October, 1952 which, in view of recent events on the Subcontinent, hardly seemed an inspired setting. Pakistan lost the match by an innings and the series 2–1 and, again mercifully, the only interruptions came from the weather. Pakistan were captained by Abdul Hafeez Kardar who had played three Tests for India in England in 1946. A difficult man, who had played for both Oxford and Warwickshire, Kardar took charge of Pakistan cricket both on and off the field and was a man determined to have his own way. Michael Melford, the gentlest of men, once described him in the *Daily Telegraph* when covering a tour in Pakistan as a man 'who had never been known to blur an issue with goodwill'. While Kardar was the mastermind behind Pakistan cricket, he had under him a genius called Hanif Mohammad who was only seventeen at the time of that first Test in Delhi. He was 5'3" tall and, wearing a pith helmet, there was something about Hanif's appearance which suggested he might have been an invention of Lewis Carroll's. Three of Hanif's four brothers, Wazir, Mushtaq and Sadiq also played for Pakistan and so Mr Mohammad, their father, was a serious rival to Walter Hadlee in the procreational stakes.

England did not play a Test Match in Pakistan until 1961/ 62 when Ted Dexter's side won the only Test of the three to be decided. An MCC 'A' team had visited Pakistan in 1955/ 56 and will be best remembered by some for an incident off the field. Frustrated by some questionable decisions made by a local umpire, Idris Begh, the MCC players trapped him into visiting their hotel, where they chucked a bucket of water over him. Idris Begh took it all extremely well, but the pot was stirred by Abdul Hafeez Kardar, and the President of the

MCC, Field Marshal Lord Alexander of Tunis, even offered to call off the tour – the side became known as Alexander's Ragtime Band –; he gave a severe dressing down to Donald Carr, the player's ringleader in this prank. The incident was later immortalized in some verses written by Alan Ross, the last of which was as follows:

> If we cannot make a run, chaps,
> At least let's have some fun, chaps,
> If we fail to take a wicket
> We can say that it's not cricket.
> When you're badly out of luck, boys,
> Give the umpire a duck, boys,
> And even up the score
> With a bucket at Peshawar.

Pakistan's overriding problem has been their unerring ability to beat themselves. Politics have always raged in cricket in Pakistan and often half the side seem to be more interested in the failure of the other half than in winning the match. The captains have, more often than not, been the main reason for splitting the dressing room into two camps and Imran Khan, the most important figure Pakistan cricket has yet thrown up, may well have been the only exception to this. His purpose was always to see his country win and he was never afraid to bang heads together. Imran was one of the greatest allrounders the game has known. He was an exceptional fast bowler and, when he put his mind to it, was a most able batsman too. He also went round the social circuit in London and elsewhere in about seven under par. The beautiful girls who have been seen on his arm are legion and this argues an exceptional line in chat and perhaps even more than that. His eventual marriage to Jemima Goldsmith was a great personal coup and his performance in the witness box when questioned by his counsel, George Carman Q.C., when defening a libel case brought against him by Ian Botham and Allan

Lamb, was formidable. There was not a dry eye in the house and, more particularly, in the jury box. It was during this trial that Geoffrey Boycott gave evidence in his shirt sleeves, wearing a shirt with *Air India* emblazoned across the front. And, what is more, he was allowed to get away with it by Mr Justice French on what was for him an especially bad day.

Pakistan cricket politics came into focus once again in the early months of 2001. It was said that Pakistan lost a Test Match by an innings to New Zealand because the players saw overwhelming defeat as the best way to get rid of an unwanted manager, Javed Miandad. Starting with Hanif, the Little Master, they have produced any number of brilliant individuals over the years. Both Hanif and Imran's families have produced minor dynasties. Hanif had three brothers who played for Pakistan, while Imran's two cousins, Javed Burki and Majid Khan, both went on to captain their country which meant that three sisters each produced a future captain of Pakistan which seems a record of Bradmanesque proportions. Another cousin, Arif Abbasi, was on at least two occasions an outstanding chief executive of the Pakistan Cricket Board. Asif Iqbal, Zaheer Abbas and Javed Miandad were all brilliant batsmen, Abdul Qadir and Mushtaq Ahmed have both bowled leg breaks and googlies with unusual skill, even if they have been accompanied by oriental histrionics which sadly seem to be obligatory, and Wasim Akram and Waqar Younis were for several years the best pair of new-ball bowlers in the world. The hinterland of Pakistan remains a huge untapped reservoir of sporting talent.

Pakistan cricket has had its characters too, and none more so than Sarfraz Narwaz, a wonderful seam bowler, but not perhaps the most reliable of men, although he was a Member of Parliament for some years, which he was well fitted to be. More latterly, Inzamam-ul-Haq has been an unusual batsman while Saqlain Mushtaq has been that rare object, an off spinner who can also turn the ball from the leg. Nonetheless, the

IMRAN KHAN

truth is that politics and intrigue have seen to it that Pakistan have not, over the years, won the matches they should have done. They have felt that they have been victimised by the rest of the world, even if, for them, the root of all evil lies over the border in India. Fuelled by daily events in Kashmir, matches between the two produce open warfare in the stands, even if the players themselves are good friends. While Hindu fights Muslim, this state of affairs is always likely to continue.

CHAPTER 12

SUSPECT ACTIONS

AFTER THAT FIRST unnecessary post-war adventure under Walter Hammond in Australia, the game in England settled back to relish the months of blue skies, the excellent batting pitches and the cavalier strokeplay of Denis Compton and Bill Edrich against a weak South African attack in 1947. The dinosaurs in the committee rooms up and down the country sat back in their chairs, crossed their legs and decided whether to have a whisky and soda or a gin and tonic. Everything was set fair and through the windows they could see the serfs doing their stuff and, by and large, what they were told. They did not find it easy to see the writing on the wall, let alone to understand what it was saying. The relief that hostilities had ended and that people were at last free to do what they wanted, if they could afford it, was overwhelming. But, in 1945, the electorate installed a Labour Government under Attlee which was hardly the vote of thanks Churchill will have anticipated. This should have set a few alarm bells ringing. A good deal of belt-tightening went on as the country did its best to cope with the penurious aftermath of victory over Hitler. The feudal system was being forced more and more onto the back foot and already there were a few bouncers pinging their way past its ears.

In 1948 Don Bradman's Australians made sure that English cricket did not get ideas above its station. The old guard will have been raising their eyebrows on an almost daily basis.

There was even a photograph of the Don walking through the grounds at Balmoral, talking to the King with his hands in his pockets, although no one made an attempt to ship him off to the Tower of London. A year or two later the supply of eligible amateurs from whom England captains had been chosen, dried up and the unthinkable happened. In 1952 Len Hutton became the first professional captain of England and it was not made especially easy for him. Of course it was a sign of the times, besides being a huge honour for Hutton, but he did not find it easy or enjoyable to stroll through the corridors of power and privilege to which he was now reluctantly admitted. It was bad enough having a chap with a Yorkshire accent leading England out onto the field, and Lord Hawke had had plenty to say about that some years before. It was really insufferable to have to have the blighter loitering around in the committee rooms. Those who ran the show had never entirely forgiven Hutton for kicking the ball over the boundary at the Oval in 1938 when Australia were doing none too well in reply to England's score of 903/7 declared. Hutton had been trying to make sure that Bill Brown did not pinch the bowling at the end of the over. The umpires were one move ahead of Hutton though, because they gave Brown four runs in addition to the single he had already run, and so he was able to face the next over just the same.

To his eternal credit, Hutton made a pretty good fist of the job on the field in a professional, safety first way. He did not take risks any more than he did when he was batting, but he still beat Australia in 1953 and in 1954/55. Although few England captains have beaten Australia once, let alone twice, Alan Gibson, in his book about the captains of England, perhaps allowed his judgement to be clouded by his own Yorkshire origins when he described Hutton as the best England captain of them all. When Hutton returned to Yorkshire after leading England in a Test Match, he found the doctrine of Lord Hawke still applied. Norman Yardley remained in charge

in the Ridings, and Hutton found himself back in the ranks. It was ready made for Gilbert and Sullivan. However, another brick in the walls of the committee room crumbled when Cyril Washbrook, who had the presence if not quite the figures to be immortalised as Hutton's other half, wrote in his autobiography that playing county cricket six days a week was too much of a good thing. The Holy Grail itself was being questioned.

The atmosphere in the England dressing room was changing too. When Hutton took charge, he found that he had to cope with his fellow Yorkshireman, the young Fred Trueman, who exploded on the scene against India in 1952 when, at Headingley, India lost their first four second innings wickets before a run had been scored. 'Fiery Fred', as he had been nicknamed by Norman Yardley, took three of them. The miner's son had brought a brilliant fast bowling talent to the game with an action which was made in heaven and a late outswinger with similar origins. As a young man he was considerably less than reticent. Of course, he captured the public imagination, but he will not have been easy to handle and Hutton was not the man to do it. In the West Indies in 1953/54 under Hutton, we have seen how Trueman overstepped the mark and maybe it would have needed an amateur captain to bring him into line. As it was, Trueman's alleged innermost thoughts cost him his good conduct money and a place in the party to tour Australia the following winter. Although England drew a remarkable series in the Caribbean after being two Tests Matches down, it was not a happy or a popular trip. In the West Indies it was felt that the England cricketers saw it as their job to bolster the waning influence of the white West Indian minority. It was a tour, too, which saw the Test Match in Guyana interrupted by rioting spectators when a local hero, Clifford McWatt, was run out in a match England won.

The previous summer in England, Trevor Bailey had bowled

consistently down the legside at the Australians at Headingley with six fielders on that side of the wicket. They were unable, as a result, to score the 177 they had needed in 115 minutes. Bailey relished this type of situation. In this same Test Match he was batting with about a minute to go before lunch when he met his partner in mid-pitch. 'It's a lovely day,' he began, 'and we haven't a chance of an appeal against the light. But I can't say I feel like another over before lunch.' He immediately appealed and by the time the umpires had met and spoken about it, the clocked had ticked past half past one and off they all came. It was increasingly as much about stopping the other side winning as about winning yourself. By now, almost all of the so-called amateurs were earning good money from the game in one way or another and even England's two young public school and Oxbridge men in Australia in 1954/55, Peter May and Colin Cowdrey, knew they had to play the game the professional way if they were to succeed – and they did so with knobs on. It was no longer form to wear the dreaded Harlequin cap made famous by Pelham Warner and Douglas Jardine, or aspire to the independence which came with that colourful product of Oxford University.

Cricketers were on the move, too. Willie Watson, who should by rights, as the senior professional, have succeeded to the Yorkshire captaincy, fled to Leicestershire who offered him a lucrative contract to succeed Charlie Palmer as captain. Yorkshire had appointed a thirty-nine-year-old amateur, Jock Burnett, something of a martinet, who within a couple of years had won them the Championship, which will have caused much glee in the committee room. By then, Johnny Wardle, who had never taken kindly to authority, had published some petulantly critical articles in the *Daily Mail* and had been sacked by Yorkshire. The philanderings and machinations of well known players off the field had begun to make headlines and sell newspapers. Jim Laker, the hero of Old Trafford in 1956, had a book ghosted for him by a *Manchester*

Guardian cricket writer, Christopher Ford, which spilled the beans in capital letters and, as a result, was banned from both Lord's and the Oval. The status of the amateur was being increasingly questioned, although in 1959 a committee under the Duke of Norfolk insisted, predictably enough, that they were 'of great value to the game'. But in November, 1962, the MCC bowed to the inevitable and the distinction between amateurs and professionals was abolished.

As far as the traditionalists were concerned, things went from bad to worse during the sixties. John, Paul, George and Ringo echoed round the country; Christine Keeler had effectively forced the Secretary of State for War, John Profumo, to obstruct the field; at hunt-balls, tail coats and white ties were being watered down by the odd dinner jacket. In the City of London there were those who ventured to wear soft rather than stiff collars and, worse still, collars that were permanently attached to the shirt, to say nothing of ready-made suits. The old order was crumbling and even bowler hats were in retreat. The walls of the Lord's pavilion shook and almost crumbled in 1963 when the first limited overs competition was held. It was sponsored by Gillette who had been asked to underwrite possible losses to the fearsome amount of £6,500. What a precedent that was to be. The gates at county matches had been shrinking consistently since the early post-war enthusiasm had worn off. One-day cricket was invented as a daring way to try and reverse the trend and thereby help the game's finances. The old farts, at Lord's and elsewhere, didn't know where to look. If Lord Harris and Pelham Warner, to say nothing of Lord Frederick Beauclerk, had been buried in the same cemetery, passers-by would have thought there was an earthquake going on. The very foundations of civilisation were falling apart. It was worse still for the *ancien regime* when this new experiment proved to be a success and the appeal of a game which produced a result in one day was clear for all to see. The punters loved it.

In 1958/59 in Australia, the bowling actions of a few of the locals had been highly suspect, but Don Bradman and Gubby Allen appeared to have knocked that problem on the head when they had agreed that no one with a suspect action would be picked. But it did not end there. In 1960, on South Africa's tour of England, Geoff Griffin, a fast bowler who took the first ever hat-trick in a Test Match at Lord's, was no-balled eleven times for throwing during the same innings. England won in just over three days and in an exhibition game on the Saturday afternoon, Griffin was effectively no-balled out of the tour and Test cricket by Sid Buller. His final over had to be completed underarm. English cricket was left with the thorny problem of Tony Lock whom Lindsay Hassett had identified as a thrower back in 1953. Lock received a stern warning from Gubby Allen himself which must have been not unlike bumping into Jack the Ripper in the bathroom. Presumably he was shaking so much that he only took 3/250 in three matches against Australia in 1961. Lock went on to remodel his action and became, late in life, a most capable left-arm spinner with the purest of deliveries. Until then, his quicker ball had been an outrageous explosion. The next bowler whose action was to come under close scrutiny was the West Indian, Charlie Griffith. In England in 1963, there were those who had faced him who claimed that he threw his yorker which was a significantly quicker ball. Frank Worrell had had his own doubts about Griffith's action and had urged his fellow selectors not to pick him in the first place.

It had been Sid Buller, England's most fearless umpire, who had ended Griffin's career, but three years later he had remained uncannily silent at square leg when Griffith produced his controversial yorker. Perhaps Gubby had had a word in his ear too. The following year Griffith played in some exhibition matches in England and one of the umpires there reported him to Lord's who, with old fashioned courtesy, thanked the umpire for being so discreet and then sat on the

report, saying that they would consider it in the fullness of time. Eventually Lord's moved down that familiar and well rehearsed path but not before keeping the world poised in agonised suspense. To the accompaniment of much shaking of heads, drawing in of breath between the teeth, intermingled with the knowing looks they considered to be the prerogative of those who had over the years accumulated a huge supply of wisdom, they set up a sub-committee. With a stroke of genius and the air of producing a rabbit out of a hat, the sub-committee said, 'Hey presto' in unison and ordained the formation of an adjudication committee. There was much rolling of drums in St John's Wood. The adjudication committee rolled up its sleeves and marked out its long run and, with the help of film, considered the action of Harold Rhodes which had been under suspicion since 1960. In June 1965 he had been no-balled by the fearless Buller in Derbyshire's match against South Africa. The adjudication committee put Buller in his place when, in 1969, they decided to clear Rhodes's action. They must now have taken a sabbatical for it was the only decision they got round to. By then Rhodes had virtually hung up his boots, so this one decision could hardly be termed a brave riposte, although it will have been well-meaning to a point.

Griffith festered on. The brave, mercurial and mildly enigmatic Ted Dexter, who had taken over the captaincy from Peter May when he retired somewhat faint-heartedly at the age of thirty-two had, to start with, kept his doubts about Griffith's action to himself. He had thrashed Griffith into submission when he made that incredible 73 against the West Indies in poor light at Lord's in 1963. Then, the following year, he went public in his column in the *Observer*. When, early in 1965, the Australians toured the West Indies, Richie Benaud had by now taken his seat in the press box and was adamant that Griffith threw. He wrote accordingly in Australian, West Indian and English newspapers and produced

photographic evidence to support his opinion. Jim Swanton, of the *Daily Telegraph*, a great friend of West Indies cricket and a diplomat, if not a fence-sitter, did his best to dissuade Benaud from going public. Benaud, who has never shirked an issue in his life, said, to his credit, 'I'm sorry, but after Brisbane [when umpire Egar no-balled Ian Meckiff out of cricket] if I could prove my own brother threw I'd expose him.' After the tour was over, Norman O'Neill, one of the Australian batsmen, also accused Griffith of throwing in a series of articles which persuaded the West Indies Board to complain to their Australian counterparts. The Griffith saga was never brought to a satisfactory conclusion.

Cricket was no longer the comfortable imperial stroll it had been when it was controlled by all those hirsute peers of the realm and their friends who ruled all that they surveyed out of the committee room window at Lord's. The game was now not unlike a Victorian matron who had been compelled to cope with a low-cut dress which had a particularly draughty mini-skirt and wasn't much enjoying the process. No sooner had she managed to circumvent the problem of her knees and thighs than her cleavage was all over the place. In 1967 Brian Close, who had succeeded to the England captaincy the year before and won an impressive victory against Gary Sobers' all-conquering West Indies side in the Fifth Test at the Oval, was the favourite to captain England in the West Indies in 1967/68. In a crucial County Championship match for Yorkshire against Warwickshire at Edgbaston towards the end of the season, Close orchestrated such appalling time-wasting by his bowlers that Warwickshire were unable to win. Far from offering a fulsome apology, which would almost certainly have been accepted, Close refused to see the folly of his ways and, being the chap he is, went so far as to say that he would do the same again in a similar situation. Although the selectors still chose him as captain for the tour, the MCC committee did not agree and Colin Cowdrey was chosen

instead. When Cowdrey heard of his appointment he said he felt as if he had just come in third in an egg-and-spoon race.

England won that series thanks to Gary Sobers' sporting declaration at Port of Spain and Cowdrey returned from the Caribbean with the captaincy his as of right for the first time. If the spectators during the Second Test at Kingston's Sabina Park had not indulged in a most unpleasant orgy of bottle-throwing when a plentiful supply of teargas was needed to quell the outburst, England's margin of victory would have been larger. In 1968, Australia were again the opposition. England managed to draw the series after the spectators at the Oval in the Final Test had helped the groundstaff dry the ground after a deluge at lunchtime on the last day. The sun came out and when the effects of the roller had worn off, Derek Underwood finished the Australians off with about time for two more overs remaining, and we all felt much better. But what additional dramas that match contained. Roger Prideaux, who had batted well in the Fourth Test at Headingley, was selected for the Oval Test but had to withdraw because of a slight injury, feeling, no doubt, that he had done enough to ensure his selection for that winter's tour to South Africa. His replacement for the Oval was Basil D'Oliveira who, after a poor tour of the West Indies, had been out of favour. D'Oliveira was a Cape-coloured by birth and prevented from playing Test cricket by the odious apartheid policies in South Africa. He had settled in England and, after a spell playing for Middleton in the Lancashire League, was taken on by Worcestershire from where he played himself into his adopted country's Test side. It was a story which was as inspiring as it was romantic and, of course reflected nothing but dishonour on the prevailing South African political system.

He grabbed his chance at the Oval with both hands, scoring 158 which was a not insignificant contribution towards England's victory over Australia. The selectors who were choosing the side to tour South Africa that winter, met at Lord's on the

evening that match ended and, mysteriously, mistakenly and mystifyingly, decided that D'Oliveira did not merit a place in the party. At this distance of time, it is impossible not to argue that the selectors knew exactly what they were doing. Sir Alec Douglas-Home and Lord Cobham both former Presidents of MCC had both recently met the South African Prime Minister, Mr Vorster, who had obviously told them that in view of his Government's racial policies, D'Oliveira would not be acceptable as a member of the MCC touring party. They had passed on the information to Lord's.

This was bad enough, but events now showed what a pusillanimous lot those in charge of England's cricket were. It was so awful that it is difficult to believe that responsible men could have behaved as they had. If it hadn't been so serious, it would have been hysterically funny. Tom Cartwright had been chosen for the tour as a seam bowler, but soon after selection had to cry off because of injury. The selectors got together again and this time they picked the batsman, D'Oliveira, as a replacement for Cartwight, the bowler. No wonder Vorster and all the rest in South Africa cried foul and said they would not accept a team forced upon them by the anti-apartheid movement. It is hard to think of a more inglorious moment for English cricket and all it stands for. A hastily arranged tour took England to Pakistan. Two years later, in 1970, South Africa were to due to come to England and it was not until Jim Callaghan, the Home Secretary, had called the chairman and secretary of the Cricket Council to his office, and formally asked them to cancel the tour, that this was done, even though a Springbok rugger tour the winter before had been badly disrupted.

By the time of Callaghan's intervention a dozen county grounds had been damaged by demonstrators and MCC had bought three hundred rolls of barbed wire which would have given the Campaigners for Nuclear Disarmament something to think about. It was a painful but important part of the

game's history that it should have impaled itself so conclusively on the stake of racialism. South Africa's apologists were an unblushing lot and they were fortunate indeed that the game did not suffer greater retribution after their astonishingly blinkered approach to a regime which most deafeningly did not stand for the one thing which has always been synonymous with the game of cricket: fair play. It was ironical that South Africa should have had at the time their best ever side with players like Graeme and Peter Pollock, Barry Richards and Mike Procter, Eddie Barlow and Denis Lindsay. In the sixties they gave both Bobby Simpson and Bill Lawry's Australian sides a good hiding and, given the chance, would have doled out the same medicine for some years to come, but that was most emphatically not the point. They had been captained first by Peter van der Merwe and then by the inscrutable Dr Ali Bacher.

It was at this time that one of the great modern characters the game has known was buckling on his pads for England. Colin Milburn, a Geordie who played for Northamptonshire and cheerfully weighed more than most bathroom scales will have registered, opened the batting and hit the ball like a kicking horse. He was a dear man and hugely entertaining, if a trifle ill-disciplined in much that he did. He was technically a highly accomplished batsman who brought his own distinctive and pleasing flair to the game which was underlined by the ever increasing bureaucratic approach of so many of the game's best players at that time and since. He scored two hundreds for England in nine Tests and the second was on this improvised tour of Pakistan when he joined the side as a reinforcement for the Third Test Match. Back in England the following season, 1969, he was the passenger in a car crash and was blinded in his left eye which effectively finished his cricket. He later worked as an expert on BBC's *Test Match Special*. There was one famous occasion during a Test Match in Leeds when he forgot to go to Headingley for the early

morning *Today* programme. The Sports Room rang him at his hotel and they began the interview pretending he was in position in the commentary box. Halfway through, the interviewer asked him what the weather was like and, forgetting himself, he said, 'I haven't opened the curtains yet.' Ollie, as he was affectionately known, liked his pint and was to die at the ridiculously young age of forty-eight in his car in a pub's car park. He was another of those gloriously free spirits which the game has always needed. He was a Billy Bunter of a batsman and the best of men.

We have seen Willie Watson move to Leicestershire and he had been followed by Ray Illingworth, lured by an entrepeneurial, *avant garde* and highly persuasive secretary, Mike Turner, who was also extremely successful. It was Turner who had persuaded Tony Lock to come back to captain Leicestershire from Western Australia, where he had gone after finishing with Surrey. Lock's influence began a run of spectacular success for the hunting county which continued under the shrewd captaincy of Illingworth who had by now become a considerable all-round cricketer. When, in 1969, Colin Cowdrey ruptured an Achilles tendon, the selectors turned to Illingworth to captain the country. Although the distinction between Gents and Players had been done away with in 1962, Illingworth was effectively the third professional, after Hutton and Close, all of whom were Yorkshiremen, to captain England. He was as uncompromising as a captain as he was as a player and a man. Although Cowdrey's Achilles tendon mended and he came back into the reckoning for the captain's job, the selectors decided to stay with Illingworth for the Australian tour in 1970/ 71. Reluctantly and after much hesitation, Cowdrey agreed to go as vice-captain to Australia for the fourth time and, although England regained the Ashes, it was a watershed tour. It indelibly underlined the way the game was continuing to change and how it was to be played from then on. Illingworth's brand of leadership will have caused apoplexy not only in the committee

room at Lord's, but in all places where tradition and its trappings are considered to be important. It caused apoplexy in the columns of the national broadsheets too, but the tabloids embraced Illingworth as a hero and vigorously applauded all that he stood for. The old school tie had received a sharp one in the *solar plexus.*

Illingworth's relations with his manager, David Clark of Kent, were strained throughout. Clark had been chosen with Cowdrey and not Illingworth in mind as captain which goes to show that the left hand at Lord's did not have a clue what the right was about. The captain did everything his way and was not in the least concerned with formality or effect. He was anxious to get the best out of his players and to beat the Australians and no one can reasonably deny that he did both. The tour came to its unpleasant climax in the Seventh Test of the series, and the second held at Sydney when umpire Lou Rowan, a detective in the Queensland drug squad, warned John Snow for intimidatory bowling at Terry Jenner, the Australian leg spinner. In answer to Rowan's intervention, England's captain who was becoming much too big for his boots, protested and gesticulated vigorously at the umpire. At the end of the over, Snow sloped off to field at fine leg where he was molested by members of the crowd in the Paddington corner of the ground, and a bottle or two were thrown. Whereupon Illingworth, without conferring with the umpires, led his players off the field in protest. The game should have been awarded to Australia then and there because of default by England. As it was, the umpires who were not ungenerous, in the circumstances, themselves went to the pavilion and told Illingworth that the game must continue at once. If not, England would presumably have forfeited the match. It was a messy and unpleasant incident which might have been handled better by a captain too intent, as ever, on making the point that the old ways had disappeared and that things were now going to be done his way or not at all. This was

the tour which produced the first ever one-day international after the Test Match in Melbourne had been abandoned without a ball being bowled. What a precedent that was to prove.

Life in the Ridings of Yorkshire was having a bumpy ride. When Brian Close departed for Somerset after 1970, the committee appointed as his successor Geoffrey Boycott who as a batsman was the epitome of selfishness. He was a most capable and largely self-taught player without any real natural flair who had decided early in his life that the way to get on was not to get out. Occupation of the crease was everything and the devil take the hindmost. It is hard to think of a more spectacularly unsuitable characteristic for a captain. Richard Hutton, who played for Yorkshire with Boycott, put his finger on it when he wrote, 'As long as he scores runs, in whatever fashion is irrelevant, even if detrimental to the team effort, nothing else seems to matter.' Boycott's first year as captain, in 1971, had been a disaster but, as he was to do throughout his career in cricket and afterwards when controversy was still relentless in its pursuit of him, he spoke forcibly in his own defence and got away with it. He remained as captain for six more dismal years. Boycott's tentacles stretched far and wide and he engendered a passionate and irrational support which almost led to civil war within the county club. How his opponents must have longed for Lord Hawke to have been reincarnated. The nearest they got to this was some years later when Lord Mountgarret was appointed to the presidency. He was an enthusiastic but humble cricketer who made his name in a unique manner. On a day's shooting on his Yorkshire estate, an anti-blood sports contingent arrived overhead by hot-air balloon and his lordship became so angry that he loosed off his gun at the balloon. While causing no dramatic damage or injury, the protesters did not enjoy being peppered by shot from below and took him to court. His lordship could be peppery too.

Boycott is the strangest of men. In 1974, after playing in

the First Test against a weak Indian side at Old Trafford, where he was dismissed by the gentle pace of Abid Ali and Eknath Solkar for very few, he announced that he was withdrawing from Test cricket. He retired to his tent muttering about its 'pressures and tensions' and was able to concentrate on his benefit, which produced the considerable sum in those days of £20,639. After skulking in his tent for thirty Test Matches, Boycott saw that the Australian attack in 1977 was pretty agreeable and once more put himself forward for selection in time for the Third Test. He made a hundred in that match at Trent Bridge and in the next, at Headingly, he made 191 which was his hundredth first-class hundred. It all left a funny old taste in the mouth. The following year, he was kicked out of the captaincy which was taken on by none other than the redoubtable Raymond Illingworth at the age of forty-eight. Not that that was an especially happy return. He had now returned to his native heath from Leicestershire and moved around the cricket world like a latter day north country despot, certain he knew all the answers. But his track record, first as an elderly captain of Yorkshire and then as their manager before taking over the role for England, is against him.

Cricket was becoming a more violent game. Leaving Bodyline apart, fast bowling had become more unpleasant. In 1956/57 in South Africa, Peter Heine with Neil Adcock had formed a most hostile pair of opening bowlers. Wes Hall was fast and ferocious but fair, while Charlie Griffith's elbow occasionally got up to its tricks. Fred Trueman, Brian Statham and Frank Tyson took some playing but all three were scrupulously fair bowlers. But generally tailenders were liable to receive a few more bouncers than they had done in the old days. Although it was not a pleasant spectacle to see bowlers ducking and weaving for their lives, it was sometimes good value to see fast bowlers receive a dose of their own medicine. This was especially so much later on when Dennis Lillee came to the wicket because he simply couldn't handle the short-pitched

ball and went through a cringe-making performance whenever he received a bouncer at anything much above medium
pace. In 1974/75 when Lillee and Jeff Thomson joined forces
against England they were as fearsome a pair of fast bowlers
as any there have been and, until Packer arrived in 1977, kept
Australia at the top of the pile. Thomson's slinging action
generated great pace and in that series England's batsmen
found the ball constantly flying past their noses with the
crowd baying for blood and some of the bowlers belittling
the batsmen with their gestures. Fast bowling was becoming
a more antagonistic pursuit and the batsman was now the
perennial Aunt Sally.

Under Ian Chappell's robust captaincy, Lillee and Thomson
destroyed England on their own pitches and beat them again
in 1975 when the Australians stayed on to play four Tests
after the first World Cup. England's selectors now realised
what they were up against and chose tougher, more appropriate, sides and three of the four matches were drawn. Mike
Denness who had been captain in Australia, had got into a
muddle with the weather forecast for the First Test at Edgbaston and lost by an innings after putting Australia in to
bat. Tony Greig, that mercurial lamp post of a man, was given
the job for the rest of the series and the selectors now made
a dash into the unknown when they picked the grey-haired
bespectacled figure of Northamptonshire's David Steele for
the next game. He was a doughty county middle order batsman with buckets of resolve which the Test side had been so
notably lacking.

Quietly determined, Steele was seldom the first into the bar
to buy drinks when a game was over and thereby acquired
his nickname of 'Crime'. Notice boards outside the police
stations of the country proclaimed that 'Crime doesn't pay.'
The score at Lord's was only ten when Lillee removed opener,
Barry Wood, and Steele, looking more than ever like a myopic
academic who was late for his next lecture, picked up his

trusty blade and set off. He went down one flight of stairs to the Long Room level in the Lord's pavilion, but instead of pushing through the glass door into the Long Room, he went down the next flight of stairs as well and to his mystification found himself in the basement with nowhere to go. It took him a moment to realise his mistake and his initial entry into Test cricket was noticeably delayed. When he had retraced his tracks and eventually arrived in the middle his studious, not to say academic, appearance, surprised some of the Australians. Steele himself takes up the story: 'People were looking at me. I could hear them muttering, "Who's this grey old bugger?" as I walked past. Thommo stood with his hands on his hips. I said, "Good morning, Thommo." He said, "Bloody hell, who've we got here, Groucho Marx?"' Steele gave them an excellent answer when he made 365 runs against them in six innings in the remaining three Tests. The following year he made over 300 against the West Indies fast bowlers. Steele was one of Test cricket's more unlikely characters and he was an inspired choice.

Old fashioned standards of behaviour which had traditionally surrounded cricket at all levels of the game, were cracking fast. We have seen Snow and Illingworth in Australia in 1970/71. Ian Chappell was another who worried only about results and getting the best out of his players. Ends will have justified means and sledging had by now become a part of the game. If opposing players allowed themselves to be upset by comments made to them by the close fielders, that was their look out. It was a man's game and this was now an accepted part of it.

'Walking', whereby batsmen who knew they were out, caught behind the wicket for example, went without waiting to see how the umpire was going to answer the appeal, was no longer the done thing. Batsmen stood their ground and left it to the umpire for it was his job. It had been the devil's own job to get Bill Lawry, an earlier Australian captain than

Chappell, to leave the crease and even if the bail came off, it was by no means certain that he would go. Chappell's view was that it was the umpire's job to answer appeals and it was up to him. If he was given out, rightly or wrongly, Chappell left quickly and always uncomplainingly for the pavilion, but there is no doubt that his Australian side helped enlarge and improve the close-to-the-wicket repartee. I am sure he will have had some choice epithets for that 'grey old bugger', David Steele, but it was water off a duck's back. The West Indies were quick to learn the language of sledging and I daresay the Indians had a bit to say early in the seventies when those four spinners, Bedi, Prasanna, Venkataraghavan and Chandrasekhar were weaving their spells. The morality of the Pakistanis will not always have been beyond blemish either. The more money that came into the game, the more the winners pocketed. It was not worth coming second if it could possibly be avoided. Slowly the laws were pushed to the limit, the umpires were tested and it became a rougher and more violent game. It was not surprising because the social *mores* of the time had descended to the point where Mary Whitehouse, that self-appointed keeper of the nation's conscience, was beginning to make St Vitus look an advocate of statuesque immobility.

Lillee and Thomson were soon to be shaded by the West Indians. Clive Lloyd had now taken on the captaincy of the West Indies and he had a humbling experience in Australia in 1975/76 when Lillee and Thomson were the main reason for their heavy defeat. But they still managed to win an extraordinary match on a typically fast wicket in Perth. This game saw Andy Roberts and Michael Holding bowl together for the West Indies for just the second time and give an idea of what was soon to follow. With Roy Fredericks, a mercurial left-hander from Guyana, playing a prodigious innings of 169, his hundred coming off only seventy-one balls, they went on to win by an innings and 87 runs. Soon, and for a

long time to come, Lloyd presided over an attack which invariably consisted of four fast bowlers who used the slow over rate as a tactical consideration every bit as much as the bouncer. It became extremely difficult for batsmen to score enough runs against the West Indies and almost impossible to score them at a fast enough rate to give their own bowlers the time to win the match.

The West Indians were wonderful cricketers and their fast attack was made doubly decisive by batsmen with the ability of Lloyd himself, Viv Richards, Gordon Greenidge and Desmond Haynes and the rest to score runs at a such a phenomenal rate. It was a brilliantly successful strategy in terms of results and was well orchestrated by Lloyd, although it was not always the most edifying of spectacles. Perm any four from Roberts, Holding, Garner, Marshall, Daniel, Croft, Ambrose and Walsh, and then duck. Every time a batsman went to the wicket it was as if he found Hannibal Lecter bowling at one end, only for Attila the Hun to be marking out his run at the other. If lip service ever needed to be paid to spin, there was Richards and Larry Gomes to purvey a few gentle off breaks. The relief factor alone brought them a number of wickets.

In 1976 in England, the West Indies fast bowlers reached a peak of nastiness which may have been their response to what they had been on the receiving end of against Lillee and Thomson in Australia the winter before. The opportunistic Tony Greig may also have been responsible. Before the series began, and with quite a bang on the drum, he announced it as his intention to make the West Indies 'grovel'. It was not perhaps quite the wisest verb for someone who was in origin a white South African to use when referring to the West Indies. I have no doubt that the fast bowlers will have had him in their sights from the moment they read that word. Greig hardly reached double figures in the series, except at Headingley where he made 116 and 76 not out with typical flamboyant

bravery. The West Indies bowling was at its most mephisto-
phelian at Old Trafford where England opened the batting
with Brian Close and John Edrich who were forty-five and
thirty-nine respectively. The ball whistled round their ears
and the umpires, Bill Alley and Lloyd Budd, said and did
nothing. Greig, the captain, at last found himself on the winning side on the tour of India that winter. England won the
first three Tests and the series and it was during that tour that
John Lever was accused of using Vaseline to help make the
ball swing. No one talked a better game than Greig and his
gunboat diplomacy at a press conference on the rest day of
the Test in Madras saved the day. He ticked off the Indian
press for being sidetracked by such an absurd issue when they
should be writing to give their side encouragement and hope.
Amazingly, the assembled company of Indian scribes did just
that in the next day's papers.

In its early days the game had been kept afloat by the
patronage of the gentry and the aristocracy who were quick
to make up any financial shortfall and to give their services
whole-heartedly to the game. When the Reverend George William Gillingham was honorary secretary to Worcestershire, he
turned up at his office one day to find that the River Severn
had burst its banks and flooded the ground. He promptly dived
into the water, swam across to the pavilion, collected the
account books and swam back across the ground carrying the
sacred documents in his teeth. This was the selfless spirit of
the pioneers who looked after the game in England and spread
it to the far corners of the old British Empire. Of course, these
benefactors extracted their pound of flesh in return. Benny
Green speculates, in his introduction to his *Wisden Anthology
1963–1982*, whether it would be more unfortunate to be
marooned on a desert island with Lord Harris or to be rescued
from it by Lord Hawke. Our old friend, the Reverend Lord
Frederick Beauclerk, can consider himself distinctly unlucky
not to get a mention in this context.

Two world wars and the ravages of death duties effectively scuppered the avuncular system of patronage. After the golden year of 1947, attendances at county cricket had steadily fallen. Once, 2,000,000 had come to watch a season's play; now it was under 700,000. Something had to be done, and quickly, if survival was to be guaranteed. The collective establishment pinched their noses and shut their eyes or looked the other way and on Sunday 1st May, 1963, Lancashire and Leicestershire stepped onto the field at Old Trafford to do battle in the first ever limited overs one-day match played between two counties. The competition was sponsored by Gillette and commercialism had stepped up to take the place of patronage. The governing body of the Lord's Day Observance Society will have spluttered over their toast and coffee that morning.

Alas, it did not all go off quite according to plan because the weather took a hand, as it can do at Old Trafford, and the first ever limited overs one-day match became the first ever limited overs two-day match. But the cricket authorities are a conservative lot and they were not taking the leap in the dark it may at first have appeared. The precedent had been set by the International Cavaliers, a team sponsored by Rothman's, who had for a few years been playing county sides on Sundays in front of television cameras on behalf of the local county beneficiary. These jaunts had been planned by Bagenal Harvey of whom we last heard when he was clearing up all those letters in the back of Denis Compton's car. These games had appealed both to spectators and the viewers on the box and Bagenal Harvey and Rothman's had every right to feel a bit miffed that their idea was pinched like this.

The Gillette company had undertaken to promote cricket as well as razor blades and its success was such that within a few years it had spawned other similar sorties into the vulgar world of commerce. In 1969 the Lord's Day Observance Society had to weather an even greater shock when John Player agreed to sponsor a one-day competition of forty overs

a side on Sundays. Cyril Washbrook had had his say about cricket six days a week, but the authorities had clenched their fists and decided to have no truck whatever with insubordination like this. As a result, they rubbed the players' noses in it on the seventh day as well, no matter what the Bible may say. The forty over slog about on Sundays was the ultimate corruption or debasement of the coinage. Cricketers, if they were unlucky, now had to pack up their bags after the first day of a County Championship match on the Saturday and drive to whatever the destination was for their one-day game on the Sabbath, and back that night. Taunton to Scarborough and back would have been one to relish. If they were lucky, they stayed where they were and took on whoever turned up on the Sunday in a game which had an entirely different set of rules. The players gritted their teeth because they were glad of the extra money and the public loved it. In that first year, 280,000 spectators came to watch the John Player League, while less than 330,000 paid to watch the County Championship. Limited over one-day cricket was indeed becoming the financial palliative it had been hoped.

In 1973, tobacco got into the act again when the Benson & Hedges company embraced another limited over one-day competition played with a different format in the first part of the season. The purists squirmed and not without reason for standards were being corrupted by so much instant cricket. Bad habits were creeping in which could be justified by victory in a limited overs game but were highly damaging when it came to playing two innings cricket. The Benson & Hedges competition produced one memorable example of the cynical ways of modern cricketers who were beginning to spend as much time trying to find ways round the rules as they did in trying to outwit their opponents. For the early matches the counties were split up into four geographical groups and two sides from each went into the quarter-finals at which point it became a knock-out competition.

In May 1979 Somerset visited New Road, Worcester for their last zonal match. Somerset were three points ahead of both Worcestershire and Glamorgan and with a vastly superior wicket-taking rate which decided which side would go through if they were equal on points. Brian Rose, the Somerset captain, declared his innings after only one over which had produced one no-ball. It then took Worcestershire ten balls to score the two they needed to win and, although they had drawn level on points with Somerset, they were unable to improve their wicket-taking rate and guaranteed Somerset's place in the quarter-finals. Quite rightly, there was an uproar and the Test and County Cricket Board held an emergency meeting and banned Somerset from the competition for their indefensible declaration. Although Rose took the blame, the decision was taken by a committee within the team. I can see Ian Botham chuckling in the Somerset dressing room.

The limited overs game took such a hold that in 1975 the first World Cup was held, in England, which in the early days seemed the only possible place for it. It was a great success and the West Indies won a thrilling final against Australia at Lord's by 17 runs and the game did not end until 8.43 in the evening. The first Gillette Cup match had been held in England in 1963 and the first one-day international had not been played until England's tour to Australia in 1970/71. This form of the game had come a long way in a short time and by now even the most confirmed cynics must have realised that it was here to stay. It remained a game which disturbed the purists and it undoubtedly corrupted standards. Nonetheless, it was the game's answer to the needs of a fast changing society with its increasing urge for instant gratification. The advent of blatant commercialism produced more money for a game which has always been strapped for cash. Cricket has remained the poor relation among the major sports as much as anything because it did not hold the attention of the Americans, in spite of a most promising start in the nineteenth

century. England's first overseas tour had been to Philadelphia in 1859 and in John Barton King the Americans produced one of the great fast bowlers in the history of the game. But the trans-Atlantic upstarts had had the nerve to invent a rival attraction called baseball.

CHAPTER 13

CRICKET ISN'T CRICKET

B Y THE TIME Rose and his Somerset cabal had got up to their tricks on the banks of the Severn, the game had had to weather the greatest threat it had ever faced. In March 1977, with Tony Greig at the helm, England had gone to Melbourne for the Centenary Test Match. This was played exactly one hundred years after the first Test Match between the two countries, although it was not until some years later that this first game had been officially called a Test Match. It was a wonderful occasion and by a miraculous and surely divinely inspired coincidence, produced an identical result to the one in that first ever Test Match, with Australia winning by 45 runs. It later came to light that Mr Kerry Packer and his cohorts had been lurking in the corridors of the Melbourne pavilion and that England's captain had been actively involved as his recruiting agent, which took away some of the glitter. Greig was as opportunistic in life as he was on the cricket field.

The Packer revolution holed the game amidships and below water. Packer, a mega-rich media magnate in Australia, had tried to buy the exclusive rights to televise international cricket in Australia for his Channel Nine television network. He had offered the Australian Cricket Board (ACB) a great deal more money than the Australian Broadcasting Corporation (ABC) was currently paying for the rights, but the ACB obstinately and obtusely dug in its heels and refused to do

business with Packer, a man used to having his own way and with the money to make sure that he did. He was, too, a most confrontational character. This infuriated him and he decided to lay on his own matches. As a result, he bought up the leading players from around the world and put on five-day Super Tests between his Australian, West Indian and Rest of the World sides. There were also a great many one-day internationals played under floodlights and these were the signature tune of Packer cricket, with the players wearing coloured pyjama-like outfits. The ACB found that they were left to run series against India, England and the West Indies with what effectively amounted to not much more than a third XI which was unlikely to hold its own for long in the popularity stakes. They first brought back former Australian captain, Bobby Simpson, another opportunist, to lead the rag-tail XI the ACB were now able to muster.

Battle lines were drawn up and both sides were memorably intransigent and inflexible. Packer's World Series Cricket (WSC) won a decisive victory in the High Court in London. The establishment at Lord's had tried to prevent those who had signed for Packer from playing in any cricket they ran. In wanting to protect his players, Packer backed three of them, Tony Greig, John Snow, and Mike Procter, and encouraged them to bring a case against the English authorities arguing Restraint of Trade. It was heard by Mr Justice Slade who found overwhelmingly for World Series Cricket and Packer. The establishment did not appeal, which may have been ironical for rumour had it that Lord Denning, a great cricket lover who was then Master of the Rolls, had decided to keep that one for himself. The second time around WSC might have been batting on a distinctly sticky wicket.

The English establishment had been particularly bitter because Tony Greig had been one of the first players outside Australia to join Packer while actively engaged as England's captain. One of the joys at the time was to listen to Greig's

oft repeated attempts to justify his decision which one could have been forgiven for thinking had more to do with money than altruism. The ACB had gone around the cricket-playing world mobilising support from all the other Boards of Control. It was difficult in the third world countries, because the players were paid so little that Packer's dollar was irresistible to them. The ACB then operated for two seasons in direct opposition to WSC and, finding it increasingly difficult and more and more expensive to hold their own, suddenly decided to surrender in a manner which did no credit to the leading protagonists. A 'peace' treaty, which included a shameful fianancial agreement, was signed and the ACB handed over its birthright to Packer who conducted himself throughout as a curious mixture of King Kong and Ben Hur, with more than a touch of Oddjob thrown in.

The rest of the cricket world were understandably horrified at this pusillanimous reaction by the ACB and they felt they had been badly let down. The deed was done and cricket in Australia was now controlled by the Packer Organisation. Channel Nine must have made a killing which was Packer's prime objective. The case in London's High Court had cost the establishment a quarter of a million pounds which was a lot more money in 1977 than it is today, and there was general disgust at the way in which the ACB had waved the white flag. They had been foolish, first in not listening to Packer with a more conciliatory approach in the early stages of the argument, and then they panicked, after cajoling the rest of the world to lend its support, and surrendered. The way in which Bob Parish, who was by then in charge of the ACB, flew round the world explaining his Board's decision, would have made Neville Chamberlain green with envy. The Packer revolution predictably produced more money for the top players – the speed with which they were prepared to turn their backs on their erstwhile employers showed that the establishment had taken their eye of this particular ball.

Floodlit cricket was an immediate success, coloured clothes helped the new sexy image, and the one-day cricket, in particular, packed in the crowds in Australia and drew people to their television sets.

At the same time, the split caused enmities which have not altogether been healed, the game was divided irrevocably into two, a lot of money, which it could ill afford, was wasted – all to further the business interests of a hugely competitive television entrepreneur whose often professed love for cricket did nothing to prevent him from splitting the international game. It left the game enveloped by a dark cloud of suspicion and maybe it was from the moment that WSC was set up that the phrase 'It isn't cricket' ceased to have any meaning. Cricket had at last been dragged kicking and screaming into the modern world. The walls of tradition had finally collapsed. One advantage to England was that Cornhill Insurance were persuaded to come up with a sponsorship worth £1,000,000 for the Test Matches involving England. It was a sponsorship which was to continue until 2000. As a result, players fees now rose from £3,000 to £5,000 for tours and from £200 to £1,000 for home Test Matches which, it was hoped, would prevent more defections to WSC.

Packer had gone into bat on the well worn precept that every man has his price and was not disappointed. Packer himself, referred to with admirable precision by Ian Wooldridge who had broken the original story in the *Daily Mail*, as 'the man in the stocking mask', was a huge man with a face carved out of unmallable blancmange. He made one feel that the Almighty had got into something of a muddle when assembling the original parts and might have liked another crack at it. Packer had been rather too over-emphasised. He was not always the easiest of men either. If he liked you, he was apparently lavish in his hospitality and generous to a fault. If you had the temerity not to agree with everything he said, he was a dab hand at being gratuitously rude. He was,

and still is, colossally rich and does not give a thought to losing ten million in whatever currency suits him in one session at a casino in Las Vegas or the Ritz Casino in London's West End. This, on its own, tells a story. He is a brilliantly successful business man and larger than life in everything that he does, although there is something a shade too deliberate about his eccentricities which are legitimised by his enormous bank balance. He is bound, one day, to be the subject of a penetrating and revealing biography. It will then be interesting to see how the final balance sheet works out. It is to his credit that he inspires such feelings of almost fanatical loyalty among his supporters, although super-rich men often seem to have a following which borders on the sycophantic.

It is in keeping with the man that when he had a heart attack playing polo, a game he took up when he was getting on, he died for a few minutes before the medics managed to resuscitate him. When he was up and about again, he wasted no time in consigning Jesus Christ, Christianity and any other religion or belief that embraced the hereafter, to the wastepaper basket. 'I've seen the other side, son, and there's nothing there' was his theological conclusion. The more likely scenario is that, having had a quick look, the Almighty may have decided to let his unfaithful servant, Kerry Francis Bullmore Packer, go through to the wicket keeper. But then again he might have been in transit to another place. With any luck the Almighty has decided against a heavenly casino with croupier Packer in charge.

World Series Cricket's leading protagonists tried to steal the moral high ground by swearing that they and Packer had acted for the good of the game and those who played it. How silly of us to think it had anything to do with their own bank accounts. One huge surprise was that Geoffrey Boycott, who is not normally known for hanging back when confronted by a financial lure, had apparently refused to join WSC. But perhaps an unusual show of altruism for once clouded his

judgement. Nevertheless, it was unlike Geoffrey to throw up good cash for a mere point of principle. There are many important questions to which we may never know the answer.

Over the years England had more than held its own on the Test grounds round the world, even if Australia always seemed to have their noses in front when it came to comparing the tally of victories. Now, there was more money in the game and, by buying up players from all over the cricketing world, Packer had ensured that the gospel of commercialism was spread far and wide and in time this produced massive change. In the coming years all the other countries went professional and in so doing, left England far behind. The English authorities, sticklers for tradition, could not conceive that there could be anything wrong with the system which had served them so well for the first hundred years of Test cricket. India with their spinners, had already won a series in England under Ajit Wadekhar in 1971 and in the early eighties Pakistan and New Zealand were to follow. At the Oval shortly before the end of the century Sri Lanka were to hand out one the most comprehensive and humiliating defeats England have ever suffered. England were paying the penalty for their inflexibility. The old farts unanimously rejected change and it was only when, through the eighties and nineties, the results became worse and worse that they reluctantly began to face up to the reality of the situation. Even when, it required a certain legerdemain to bring in a newly retired grocer, Lord MacLaurin, to run the English Cricket Board which took over in 1977 from the old Test & County Cricket Board. The old farts then did all that they could to make sure that any new system he tried to devise was strangled to death before it was properly born.

By the time of the Packer revolution, change was on its way and he now kicked the game into the modern age. All of his innovations have come to stay. Every Test-playing country now puts on day/night cricket under floodlights,

although those in England are self-deprecatory in the extreme and produce the most modest of glows; coloured clothes, white balls and black sightscreens have become the accepted norm for one-day cricket; and crash helmets are part of everyone's standard equipment. The thirty-yard circles around each wicket and the fielding restrictions were all a part of it too.

Perhaps the best illustration of the way things had changed on the cricket field came from the strained relationship between Denis Compton and Ian Botham. With cricket bats in their hands they were both brilliantly free spirits, yet Compton was the product of the 1930s where emotions were carefully guarded and it was not form to let your hair down. By contrast, Botham was one of the first to let it all hang out, in what he did and in what he said, and in the excesses in which he frequently indulged. In the straitened circumstances after the war, life was much harder than it was thirty years later, and Compton was a product of that earlier regime. In those years, with his Brylcream advertisements plastered on the advertising hoardings, Compton was a super-hero, maybe even bigger than Botham was to be thirty years later, and with a clean cut image which may have hinted at mild naughtiness but nothing worse. Compton now questioned Botham's bowling and as a result had been libelled by Botham in the *Sun*. In answer to Botham's outburst Compton wrote, 'Botham's not a nice chap . . . I suppose this is a new generation. His example to the young is awful.'

Yet it was Compton who was out of touch. Botham was the hero, badly needed by the young who were living in entirely different social circumstances from those Compton had been accustomed to. Botham was the one who was brave enough to do all the things they did not dare to do themselves. It was said that he broke beds in steamy all night sessions with a former Miss Barbados, he got into a well publicised fight in an aeroplane in Australia, he admitted to smoking pot and yet he largely got away with it. He was also the man

who scored 149 not out against Australia at Headingley in 1981 when England had followed on, and made it possible for Bob Willis to bowl England to victory. Later, Willis was to claim that Botham had been 'as drunk as a skunk' on every night of that match. Botham's superhuman feats on the field of play were many and it was uncharitable, if understandable, of Compton who did not then like the life he saw around him to say, 'Don't associate me with him! He was overrated. Botham only did well because all the best players had joined Packer.' For all that, Compton was an honourable man who was appalled to see behaviour which would have caused immediate excommunication in his day. This was how much the times had changed. Had these two played in the same era, they would surely have been the greatest of pals and would have indulged together in whatever excesses were the going rate at the time. Comparing the thirties and post-war forties to the late seventies and eighties is like comparing horses to cows. Yet surely Denis Compton will have had more than a sneaking admiration for the man who twice walked from John o' Groat's to Land's End and once across the Alps to raise money for leukaemia research.

Compton, too, was a great supporter of South Africa. He had married a South African and he had sons there. When it was thought that MCC as a private club might be able to send a touring side to South Africa in spite of the Gleneagles Agreement of 1977, in which the members of the Commonwealth agreed 'to discourage contact by their nationals with sporting organisations, teams or sportsmen from South Africa', Compton and Edrich pulled on their old England sweaters and marched on Lord's to report for nets. Everyone knew where they stood. By all accounts, Botham was twice asked to go on a rebel tour of South Africa and refused both times.

The first of these tours was largely organised by Geoffrey Boycott. When England toured India in 1981/82, the Indian

IAN BOTHAM

Government had refused to accept Boycott as he was on the disapproved list because of his connections with South Africa. It looked as if the tour would be cancelled until Boycott publicly denounced apartheid and made a great point of saying how he had played cricket with black children in the West Indies. This was enough to satisfy the Indians. In the Third Test Match he broke Gary Sobers' record for the total number of runs scored in Test cricket, but after the Fourth Test he claimed he was unfit and did not play in the Fifth.

Bad behaviour was by no means only the prerogative of England and its cricketers. England had toured Australia in 1979/80, immediately after the Australian Board's so-called peace treaty with Packer had been signed, and played three Tests against the full Australian side, but as it was only a three-match series, the Ashes were not at stake. The old farts at Lord's had stamped their feet. The First Test was played in Perth when Dennis Lillee, whose ego had flourished as if grown under glass, came out to the wicket with an aluminium bat. When he made contact with the ball it made a deathless and tuneless clang and soon Michael Brearley, the England captain, was carefully examining the ball. Where the ball made contact with the metal bat it was flattened and damaged. After discussions with the umpires, Lillee was told to go and get an ordinary bat. He stood his ground and argued the toss volubly and with much waving of arms. Eventually he realised there was nothing he could do about it and set off to the old pavilion in the corner of the ground. He had only gone a few paces when he opened his arms like a javelin thrower and heaved the bat some distance towards the pavilion. It was not the most graceful of scenes, but as the whole thing was an advertising stunt he will have wanted to attract as much publicity as he could for his new weapon. Of course the television cameras, who had doubtless been warned in advance, were on hand to gobble up each move he made. Metal bats were subsequently banned.

You couldn't keep a good man down and Lillee was at it again in Perth a couple of years later when Pakistan were the visitors. On the fourth afternoon the dreaded Lillee who claimed that he had been upset by abuse from Javed Miandad, which was a bit like Alphonse Capone fainting at the sight of blood, ostentatiously blocked him when he was trying to complete a run. Miandad tried to barge his way past, where-upon Lillee aimed to kick him rather in the way that Bobby Charlton would have admired. At this point Lillee seemed to slip and Miandad stood over him and raised his bat like an executioner who had got more than a good glimpse of an extended neck. It was now that Tony Crafter, the fearless umpire, having no doubt checked mentally on his life insurance policies, stepped between the two combatants while commending his soul to God. It was an appalling incident for which the disciplinary committee of the Australian Board suspended Lillee merely for two one-day internationals.

At that time South Africa was still on everyone's mind because the previous winter, 1980/81, there had been the Jackman fiasco in the West Indies. Robin Jackman, the Surrey seam bowler, had been picked for the tour in spite of his strong connections with South Africa which included a South African wife. When the party arrived in Guyana for the second Test, the Government revoked Jackman's entry permit, declared him *persona non grata* and insisted on his deportation. The party had returned to Barbados and awaited its fate as the foreign ministers of Barbados, Antigua and Jamaica, where the last three Tests were to be played, decided what should be done. In the end the tour continued with Jackman in the party. I would like to think that one of the reasons may have been that Antigua's foreign minister, Lester Bird, was about to become a Test Match commentator for the Fourth Test which was to be the first ever to be played at the Recreation Ground in Antigua. He had been commen-tating for some years on Shell Shield matches and if this

chance went begging, who knows when it might have come again.

It was late in the evening after the second day's play of the Third Test in Barbados that England's much loved and respected coach, Ken Barrington, died of a heart attack. This was the tragic epilogue to a miserable sequence of events.

The authorities at Lord's had, meanwhile, been stirring up trouble over their relations with Pakistan with some typically ham-fisted behaviour. Both countries had been highly suspicious of each other's umpires for a long time. When Pakistan came to England under Imran Khan for a short tour of three Test Matches in the second half of 1982, they were to object to umpire David Constant standing in a Test Match. By now, all Test sides were showing dissent when they disagreed with umpiring decisions and the Anglo-Pakistan pot boiled over further when, in the First Test in Pakistan in 1987/88, Chris Broad refused to leave the crease when given out and his partner, Graham Gooch, had to shoo him away. Cricket was no longer cricket.

Broad's behaviour had been bad enough, but it was compounded by the manager, Peter Lush, who merely ticked the batsman off and spoke in doubting terms of the quality of the umpiring. Small wonder if after all this the Pakistanis were flexing their muscles. Mike Gatting, the captain, emphatically endorsed his manager's views when he went on record as saying, 'When we come to Pakistan the umpiring is always the same. I've never seen it as blatant as this. I warned the young players beforehand what they could expect, but until you've experienced it you can't comprehend how the game is played out here.' According to Gatting, the umpire most to blame was Shakoor Rana who had never been hero-worshipped by any side visiting Pakistan. Yet in his own country he was put on a pedestal for setting standards at which others should aim. Of course, he was selected to stand in the Second Test, in Faisalabad. There will have been a

strident feeling of armed neutrality all round when the players took the field.

When Gatting was fielding at backward short leg to Eddie Hemmings, the off spinner, he appeared surreptitiously to move a fielder behind him on the legside as the bowler was on his way in. Gatting had told the batsman what he was doing, but Shakoor Rana at once accused Gatting of unfair play. The father and mother of all rows ensued with television recording Gatting pointing a furious finger at the umpire, and the pitch-microphone picking up every word. At the end of the day Shakoor Rana announced that he would not continue umpiring unless he received an apology from Gatting for using 'foul and abusive' language. After a two-day stand-off Gatting scribbled the following on a piece of paper, 'I apologise for the bad language used during the second day of the Test Match at Fisalabad [sic].' Although history has seen more fulsome and graceful apologies, it did the trick and the game meandered on to a boring draw. But that wasn't quite the end of it. The chairman of the TCCB, Raman Subba Row, flew out from London with the chief executive, Alan Smith, and the England players were all given a special hardship bonus of £1,000. If that wasn't rewarding dissent, I don't know what was. The Pakistanis had every right to feel bitterly aggrieved and the game of cricket had been badly let down. But having survived Shakoor Rana, Gatting was to be totally impaled by a tabloid-inspired waitress during the First Test against the West Indies the following June.

South Africa was readmitted to the Test arena when Nelson Mandela was released from prison, the hateful policy of apartheid had been outlawed and free elections held. They had a useful side, were in much demand, and they were captained by Kepler Wessels who had already played Test cricket for Australia. Wessels was one of the game's more boring batsmen and a frighteningly unimaginative captain whose dead hand did not help his country's re-emergence onto the international

stage. For some reason the authorities in South Africa, for whom one must read Ali Bacher who had masterminded their cricket ever since they had been ostracised twenty years before, decided against Clive Rice. This must have been a mistake, even though he was getting on. He had been a most successful captain of Nottinghamshire and was still a highly competitive cricketer. South Africa came to England in 1994 for three Test Matches which saw some splendid cricket with each side winning one Test match, but the short series will most likely be remembered longest for one of the most surprising acts to have taken place in international cricket. Michael Atherton, the young Cambridge graduate, had taken over the England captaincy from Graham Gooch and was to remain in the job for longer than any of his predecessors.

At Lord's in the First Test against South Africa he was caught by the television cameras putting his hand in his trouser pocket while he held the ball in the other and appearing to produce a substance from the pocket which he used to rub on the ball. It was discovered that he kept some earth in his pocket and was using it to rough up the ball for reverse swing in flagrant disregard for the Laws of the game. When asked to explain himself by Peter Burge, the Australian match referee, he skirted round the truth. Burge, a marvellous character and a most forthright referee, could not bring himself to believe that an England captain would tell a lie, and accepted his version of events and his reason for carrying earth in his pocket. The ubiquitous Ray Illingworth, who had succeeded Ted Dexter as England's manager, now stepped in and forced the truth from Atherton and immediately fined him £1,000 for having dirt in his pockets and £1,000 more for having failed to tell Burge the truth. This action by Illingworth had the effect of pre-empting both the England Board and the match referee who took no further action. Atherton had been incredibly lucky for he had been doing something which he must have known was not only strictly illegal but also directly

against the spirit of the game. It is extraordinary that he should have been so stupid as not to realise that the cameras would almost certainly spot what he was doing.

CHAPTER 14

SNICKOMETERS AND BOMBAY BOOKIES

As CRICKET approached the turn of the twenty-first century it had acquired many unpalatable ingredients. It had become a game which required serious policing from beyond the boundary. It also needed strong-armed adjudicators whose job now was to watch over the discipline of the participants and to curb skulduggery. It might have been sensible to sign up retired wrestlers. Electronic technology was taking decision-making away from the umpires. It was useful to have umpires of the considerable stature of Australia's Darrell Hair, a man who knows his own mind and who would make you think twice before getting embroiled in a heated argument with him. These days, umpires need Oddjob-like qualities.

In Adelaide early in 1999, England played a one-day match against Sri Lanka during the course of which the Sri Lankan off spinner, Muttiah Muralitheran, was no-balled for throwing. The scenes that followed between umpire Emerson and Sri Lankan captain Arjuna Ranatunga made Gatting's little dust up with Shakoor Rana seem a cosy chat. Boards of Control and the ICC itself were sucked into the controversy, after Ranatunga had attempted to tell the umpire as where to stand and stated, 'I am in charge of the game,' which must have come as a bit of a surprise to Mr Emerson.

Cricket's crying need is for a sin bin where incandescent performers can be sent to cool off. But bad behaviour is not the only problem which affects the gentlemen in white coats. The umpires have inevitably become diminished figures because of the arrival of electronic technology. This has given birth to the third umpire who sits in his own little eerie surrounded by television monitors and all the latest technology has to offer, with the comforting support of the match referee at his elbow. It is the third umpire's main job to watch television replays and to decide whether batsmen are in or out or whether the ball has gone to the boundary or not, but his role is still far from being as precisely defined as it should be. When the third umpire has made up his mind he relays his decision to the two in the middle who are rapidly becoming little more than white-coated rubber stamps.

In the old days the umpire, although a most public figure, was able to conduct his business in relative peace and quiet without prying electronic eyes. As a result, his word was not questioned anything like as much as it is today. With the huge advance in technology the farcical situation has now been reached that if a batsman is given out and a wrong decision has been made, the huge television audience know that he has been the victim of bad umpiring, maybe before he has even reached the pavilion. Even more extraordinarily, the bad decision is allowed to stand. If the game cannot get its decisions right, it deserves to become a laughing stock. With much more money now at stake and players' careers in the balance, it must be fundamentally wrong not to grasp any method which may guarantee a precise answer to questions which the naked human eye often has difficulty in answering. This is part of the mystique of cricket which it is surely not worth perpetuating.

When Channel Four took over the televising of English cricket from BBC Television, they produced a much slicker product. Among their inventions which inevitably have put the umpires under even closer examination, are the Snicko-meter and Hawkeye. The first registers the sound of ball on bat by seismic lines on a screen. This can obviously help with lbw decisions and catches close to the wicket off bat and pad. The Hawkeye shows with the help of a diagram whether the ball would have hit the stumps if the batsman's pads had not been in the way. Gary Franses, the channel's Director of Cricket, is sure that both are infallible. The umpires are unlikely to believe this for, if these latest gadgets were to be adopted, their jobs would be diminished still further. The ICC appears to be sitting on the fence, an exercise in which it is indisputably a world class performer. If there was a gold medal for fence sitting, the ICC would have been allowed to take it home years ago. Of course, more replays than we get at the moment would slow the game down even further, which would be a pity, but not half such a pity as seeing players suffer from wrong decisions. The ICC must try awfully hard not to do what it does best which is to set up a working party. This will ensure that no decision will be taken for at least another year. They must get together immediately with the technicians and instruct them to prove that these aids are infallible. At least it is now being led by a realist, Malcolm Gray, from Australia, who is determined to clean up the game. He has a job and a half in front of him and he'll need eyes all round his head if he is to prevent himself being scuppered from within and from behind. If Gray tries to play fast and loose by introducing the concept of fair play and a level playing field, all hell will break loose. He deserves the support of everyone. Whether he gets it or not is another matter.

Gray has also to tackle the greatest evil the game has ever faced and which seems to have descended on international cricket like a modern plague. The illegal Indian bookmakers clearly decided some time ago that cricket is a game which would pull in the punters and how much more profitable for

them it would be if they knew the result of the match before-hand. Suspicions have been growing for some time that this is what these chaps in Bombay were up to. Then, out of the blue on April 7, 2000, the Indian police picked up no less a person than South Africa's saintly captain, Hansie Cronje, in full spate with the bookies on his mobile telephone.

The cricket authorities everywhere were brimming with moral indignation. But there can only have been a distinct unease that what had been thought to be a Subcontinental disease was now found to have no geographical boundaries and was highly toxic and contagious.

There is nothing more enjoyable in sport than when Australia vigorously claims the moral high ground. They make such a meal of it. After returning from a tour of Pakistan in 1994, three Australians, Shane Warne, Mark Waugh and Tim May had claimed they had been offered considerable bribes by the then captain of Pakistan, Salim Malik, to play badly so that Pakistan would not lose. These accusations, together with the refutations which followed from Pakistan, flew back-wards and forwards across the Indian Ocean with ever increasing velocity and did nothing for diplomatic relations between the two countries.

Eventually, in 1998, a distinguished member of the bench in Pakistan, a Mr Justice Qayyum set up a Commission in Lahore to look into the whole business – the setting up of commissions is another of cricket's more seriously contagious diseases. The learned judge did not have an easy job for some of the important figures in cricket from whom he wanted to hear, like Wasim Akram, refused to set foot in the place. It was never entirely clear to me whether the judge's remit was to salvage the honour of his country or to home in unerringly on the truth, the whole truth and nothing but the truth. Mark Waugh was in Pakistan at the time with another Australian side, but May had retired and Warne was unfit for the tour. As a result Waugh and his captain, Mark Taylor, appeared before the Commission and gave evidence. I can only imagine with their tongues bursting through the sides of their cheeks.

Then towards the end of 1998, as the result of a splendid piece of investigative journalism in Australia, it came to light that, while touring Sri Lanka before going on to Pakistan in 1994, Mark Waugh and Warne had been approached at different times by someone who had actually paid them money for providing information about the weather and the state of the pitch. Waugh had received $6,000 and Warne $5,000. The chairman of the Australian Board and his chief executive took an instant decision back in 1994 to fine the two players an amount in excess of what they had each received and, most damningly, to hush it up. By an unhappy coincidence, the President of the ICC, Sir Clyde Walcott, and his Chief Executive, David Richards who is an Australian, were passing through Sydney. They were told what had happened but were sworn to secrecy which made it seem so dreadfully underhand. What is hardest to credit is the fact that Waugh and Warne, having done what they had, had been prepared to stand up on their return to Australia and point a finger at Salim Malik. They must have felt that attack was the best form of defence. It also strains belief that, while Mark Waugh and Mark Taylor gave evidence to the Qayyum Commission in Lahore, the Australian Board still did not go public about Waugh and Warne. It is even more mind-boggling that the ICC did not say a dickie bird either. This is the mess that Malcolm Gray has inherited and one can only hope that he is given the support he will need as he fights to come to grips with the game's more contagious afflictions.

The Indians then discovered that Mohammed Azharuddin, their one-time captain, had been up to his eyes in match-fixing and, like Cronje and Salim Malik, he received a lifetime ban. Azharuddin is appealing against the ban. As far as one can gather they are still sitting on the dubloons and pieces-of-eight they stored away while conducting their skulduggery.

The South Africans were so appalled by what Cronje had done that they also set up a commission. Cronje fingered various people, including opening batsman Herschelle Gibbs, who was suspended for six months, but is now back in the South African side and also protesting his innocence. So much for life bans, the awful majesty of the law and pragmatic self-interest.

The chief witness for the prosecution was one M.K. Gupta, an Indian bookmaker who reminded one more than anything of a P.G. Wodehouse character who could hide at will behind a circular staircase. Gupta gave Cronje the chance to show that his life was ruled by greed. Gupta pointed a finger at a number of people, including England's Alec Stewart whom he said he paid £5,000 for information about pitches and the weather on England's tour of India in 1992/93. There must be a good chance that Gupta is producing disinformation to muddy still further waters which already seem to be impenetrable.

The ICC's answer to all this has been to appoint Sir Paul, later to become Lord Condon, the former Metropolitan Commissioner of Police in London, to head their anti-corruption squad. He and his colleagues have travelled far and wide in pursuit of the truth and in the search for culprits. They have spent a fair whack of their £2.8 million budget so far. Condon's first report to his bosses at the ICC had been as keenly awaited as the first translation of the Dead Sea Scrolls. In it he underlined the seriousness of the situation, something terribly few people had doubted. He spoke of the likelihood of match-fixing still going on, a view most shared, and he underlined the unwillingness of people concerned to come forward and talk which was hardly a mind-stopping revelation. The Mr Bigs who apparently are based in the Middle East are rich and powerful men. Those who have been sucked into their slipstream fear for their future, if not their lives, should they grass. Lord Condon produced no new names and is presumably terrified of the legal implications if he does so. He has made noises about the involvement of certain administrators, with particular reference to the sale of television rights. Infallible proof has apparently been well nigh impossible to come by. It would be no surprise if countries are trying to block Lord Condon in order to preserve their honour. Whether all this is good value for a budget of £2.8 million is for the game's rulers to decide. They might also find it bizarre that six months after the original damaging accusation was made, the noble lord and his sidekicks had not had a meaningful interview with Alec Stewart. Condon complained that Stewart's lawyers had been dragging their feet in setting up a meeting. As a result it was hastily arranged in the middle of the 2001 season.

Condon has said in his report which makes a damp squib seem like an Exocet, that match-fixing had its origins in English county cricket in the seventies. This is what comes of having a Lord High Executioner who doesn't know his subject. In those days, not surprisingly, a little bit of you-scratch-my-back-and-I'll-scratch-yours went on. Towards the end of the summer two sides playing a County Championship match and a Sunday League over four days may have agreed to let the Championship contenders win the three-day game and the others, better placed to win the Sunday League game, would be allowed to win the Sunday slog-about. Money was not changing hands, the bookies were not involved and this comes under the heading of horse-trading. It would not happen in the best of worlds, but it is still short of being a hanging offence.

Of course, it would be lovely to rattle the cages of all those who have made squillions from selling cricket short. I am sure lots of players are guilty for having accepted the dollar, but the guys I would like to get level with are the barons who had the money to go to the players in the first place. One hears that administrators and television moguls may not be too far away from all this. It would be lovely to see the whites of their eyes and to bring them to book. To be realistic though,

I am afraid it is not likely to happen. The hue and cry and, I suppose, the *obiter dicta* of Lord Condon may deter a few potential miscreants in the future, but I am afraid the big boys won't need any Mogadon to help them get through the night.

I have no doubt the game will go on as always, reflecting the times in which we live, producing enjoyment and artistry and bringing people through the gates or into their armchairs in front of television sets to forget for a moment the tawdriness of life outside. Test Match grounds in England are full to the brim and if the sun shines and England manage to win a few matches, we will all show our contempt for the poisonous few and go along and show we love the game as much as ever.

Meanwhile the frenetic whirligig of modern international cricket gets fiercer and faster. Sri Lanka, Zimbabwe and now Bangladesh have brought the number of Test-playing countries up to ten. The new World Championship of Test cricket, pioneered so successfully by *Wisden* and its distinguished editor, Matthew Engel, will mean more Test cricket. This competition will be decided over a five-year period in which all the countries have to compete against each other. With any luck it may mean a decrease in the amount of one-day internationals which are played almost anywhere that will have them. I have a feeling Lord Condon might say that it was harder to police these off shore one-day competitions. In any case, it is much easier to throw a one-day match than a Test Match. I don't think we, or anyone else, will ever live to see the day when a Test series for the Ashes is decided by the unscrupulous in Dubai, Bombay or wherever. They will find easier pickings.

After the long years of West Indies success, the mantle has been handed on to Australia, where Allan Border and the coach, Bobby Simpson, took up the cudgels. Border's longevity was rare for Australians, who usually retire young, but an indication that the going rates these days are more enticing. Australia have been good to watch for all but the most

THE WAUGH TWINS

chauvinistic Englishmen. There has been an efficiency and a slickness about so much of their cricket and soon after the new century arrived they clocked up a record sixteen successive Test victories before they were smartly brought down to earth by the Indian spinners on their own terrain. The Waugh twins, as different in style and temperament as they are in appearance, have been the engine room of the batting. Mark, flamboyant with his strokes and dashing in all that he does, while Steve is a more considered personality whose name is unlikely ever to have been associated with illegal Indian bookies. If I had to employ someone to bat for my life, Steve would get the nod.

The joker in the pack has been Shane Warne. In 1993 at Old Trafford, he bowled Mike Gatting with a ball from heaven or hell, depending which side you were on. It pitched wide of the leg stump and just flicked the outside of the off and must have caused Gatting recurring nightmares. Injuries have taken their toll of Warne who became the quickest to reach 300 Test wickets. He only has to twirl his fingers to give the batsmen palpitations. Glenn McGrath carries on the Australian fast bowling tradition of quick-tempered murderous intent. Jason Gillespie and Brett Lee won't forgive lax techniques either. Mark Taylor, the best and most charming of men, declared when he had made 334 not out against Pakistan because he refused to go on and beat Bradman's 334 at Headingley as the highest Test score by an Australian. He fought off enemies from within and without who were trying to kick him out of the captaincy when he lost form with the bat. Few will forget his hundred in the second innings at Edgbaston in 1997 which bore impressive testimony to his character. Then, after winning Australia's sixth Ashes series victory in a row and his own third as captain, he called it a day. Steve Waugh is now in charge and after sixteen successive victories has had to survive the shock of those two defeats in India before coming to England as captain for the first time. He has a brilliant side under him, perhaps the best there has ever been. After the problems in India, he himself has become even more focused as the captain and has turned himself into cricket's equivalent of Michael Schumacher. Waugh is as ruthless, single-minded and obsessed with the relentless pursuit of his own chequered flag. He dealt with England in 2001 as if he was using his heel to crush a beetle.

England, meanwhile, have lurched from crisis to crisis since Mike Gatting's side won in Australia in 1986/87. Captains like, Gower, Gooch, Atherton and Stewart have come and gone and coaches have been two a penny. The county system, the old fashioned bedrock in the days when England was the only country to play the game professionally, no longer delivers players of a high enough quality and was riddled with failings and inadequacies. It was defended by the establishment with their blunderbusses at the ready. Eventually all eighteen counties took the deepest of deep breaths and installed a newly retired grocer who had been a considerable captain of industry. Ian McLaurin had taken Tesco to the top of the supermarkets Premier League, but was to find cricket an altogether different and harder nut to crack. Valiantly, he made a start, in spite of opposition from within by those who had given him the job in the first place. He divided the counties into two divisions in a process whose logical conclusion will be the concentration of excellence in the top division.

It was under McLaurin's stewardship that Nasser Hussain became the captain and Duncan Fletcher, who hails from Zimbabwe, was given the coach's role. They have proved much the best combination in recent years and after first weathering an embarrassing obliteration by New Zealand in England in 1999, a course was set and slowly the boat was pulled back onto an even keel and then began to push forward. The habit of a lifetime was jettisoned and one or two young players like Michael Vaughan and Marcus Trescothick were brought into the side. At times of crisis though the instinct was still to

stagger backwards and clutch at well tried and trusted failures. Graeme Hick's run of Test Matches was extended to sixty-five before it finally dawned that at the age of thirty-four he was at best a veteran promising lad and the time had come.

There were still too many of the over-thirties in the Test team on trial which is the business equivalent of taking on sixty-year-old trainees. Whenever Hussain's increasingly brittle hands were broken, the captaincy instantly reverted to Alec Stewart, a magnificent cricketer, but a captain who made Ethelred the Unready look hot stuff. As the twentieth century turned into the twenty-first century, Zimbabwe and the West Indies were beaten in England and then Pakistan and Sri Lanka were put in their places in front of their own raucous crowds. These last three victories showed great character, something England's cricket had missed for far too long. The England dressing room was beginning to serve up something which, if not quite chateau-bottled, was a good deal better than the plonk of old. The ensuing cry of 'Bring on the Australians' was premature and Steve Waugh, stung by his Subcontinental indignities, put England's recovery into a truer perspective in 2001. In that series England were unlucky to be laid low as they were by injuries to key players. Yet, if they had been at full strength and at their very best, they would have had the dickens of a job to prevent themselves being lapped by Michael Schumacher – and there is no disgrace in that.

In their dogged, determined way, the South Africans will always be amongst the front runners, even if Allan Donald's day will soon be up. The mercurial Jonty Rhodes will soon no longer be there to delight, stagger and amuse in the covers. It is almost a contradiction that the greatest and best loved character in modern Test cricket should be a South African for as a side they have always been known for their ruthless application rather than for their highjinks. But Sean Pollock will run a tight ship, Lance Klusener will continue to hit the

NASSER HUSSAIN

sixes and, behind the scenes, Ali Bacher will be pulling the strings as only he knows how.

Sachin Tendulkar will fill the pews wherever India plays and even if he misses out, Rahul Dravid and Sourav Ganguly also have their names up in lights. Then there is Anil Kumble who took all ten wickets in an innings with his wrist spin against Pakistan in Delhi in 1998/1999. Early in 2001, off spinner Hart Singh who bowled the Australians to defeat, has taken up the story along with V.V.S. Laxman who made a telling double century.

Pakistan are still the greatest enigma of them all. They always have eleven brilliantly talented individuals and yet they so seldom do themselves justice. Age is taking its toll of Wasim Akram and Waqar Younis. Shoaib Akhtar is the fastest of all, but his action has got him into all sorts of trouble and may be he is paying the penalty of thinking it was all too easy much too soon. Sleepy old Inzamam-ul-Haq shuffles from slip at one end to slip at the other and seldom breaks sweat. He maintains his avid aversion to fielding practice and any other unnecessary exercise. Saqlain Mushtaq beguiles with his off breaks and those which he miraculously spins the other way while Mushtaq Ahmed twirls away with his leg breaks and googlies. Saeed Anwar still dazzles with his exciting left-handed and often footless strokeplay. While they are performing these deeds, there is no side more worthwhile watching, but too often they concentrate their thoughts and their activities on disposing of some hated figure in the dressing room, be it a coach, a captain or just a player. Then, they are anybody's.

The West Indies are having a lean time of it. The old warhorse, Courtney Walsh, has at last hung up his boots after taking his tally of Test wickets past 500. Brian Lara's bad days considerably outnumber his good ones and cricket will be under increasing pressure in the West Indies if they do not soon get back on the winning trail. None the less, they play the game in their own distinctive way and you can never be sure that a few of their endeavours won't come off. They are now being led by Carl Hooper whose brief retirement has ended and whose scholarly strokeplay is as worth watching as ever it was.

New Zealand don't have a Martin Crowe or a Richard Hadlee at the moment but if anyone should take them lightly they do so at their peril. Sri Lanka, while not the best behaved side on earth, have the trickery of Muttiah Muralitharan, the off spinner with the deformed arm and the double-joined wrist. There will always be those who swear that he throws, but he now has more than three hundred Test wickets to his name, and even the most abrasive and doubting of umpires, including our old friend Ross Emerson, will now surely leave him alone to bowl his way to a comfortable and prosperous old age without let or hindrance. Sanath Jayasuriya, his captain, will continue to rattle up the runs and also to provoke opposing sides into losing their peace of mind. Aravindra de Silva will continue to remind spectators of what he once was and the supply of wonderfully talented cricketers will never dry up on that lovely island.

Zimbabwe are no pushover, although age is gradually taking its toll of a goodish side. One can only pray that cricket does not become too overtly political for only harm can come to it if Robert Mugabe should get the game firmly into his sights. The Flower brothers continue to be productive, although things are nearing the end Heath Streak is still revving up the old engine and there are youngsters coming through. Finally, Bangladesh have hardly had time to cut their teeth at the top level and they will find the learning process painful before victories start to come, in one-day cricket at first and then, with a Test Match or two under their belts, things will look up.

Cricket's history has come to 2001. In a hundred years' time there will many more chapters to write and none of us

now can have any idea of what the game will be like then. But I have no doubt that there will be a game called cricket, that people will watch it and play it all round the world, as they do now, and they did when the great WG was having his way and Lord Frederick Beauclerk before him. The Earl of Winchilsea, the Duke of Dorset and Charles Lennox, not to mention good old Lumpy Stevens, Silver Billy and all the others at Hambledon, all brought in the crowds and, don't forget, there were a few bookies about in those days too. Cricket is a game that will never lose its appeal.